ISBN 978-1-5280-6013-4
PIBN 10238570

FB &c Ltd, Dalton House, 60 Windsor Avenue, London, SW19 2RR.
Company number 08720141. Registered in England and Wales.

For support please visit www.forgottenbooks.com

The Saints and Servants of God.

THE LIFE

OF THE

VENERABLE SERVANT OF GOD,

BENEDICT JOSEPH LABRÈ.

"Gaude Maria Virgo, cunctas hæreses sola interemisti in universo mundo."—*Antiph. Ecclesiæ.*

LONDON:
THOMAS RICHARDSON AND SON,
172, FLEET ST.; 9, CAPEL ST. DUBLIN; AND DERBY.
M.DCCC.L.

We hereby approve and sanction the Series of Lives of the Canonized and Beatified Saints, the Servants of God declared Venerable, and others commonly reputed to have died in the odour of sanctity, now in course of publication by the Congregation of the Oratory of St. Philip Neri, and we cordially recommend it to the Faithful, as calculated to promote the glory of God and of His Saints, the increase of devotion, and the spread of our holy Religion.

Given at London, the Feast of the Purification of our B. Lady, A. D. 1850.

Nicholas

Bishop of Melipotamus

LOYALLY AND MEEKLY BORNE

FOR THE NAME OF JESUS AND THE LOVE OF MARY,

THIS VOLUME IS INSCRIBED,

WITH THE PRAYER

THAT THE ABUNDANT BLESSINGS

OF BETTER AND BRIGHTER DAYS

MAY NOW BE THEIRS,

WHO IN PERSECUTION AND ADVERSITY

PRESERVED INVIOLATE

THE FAITH OF THEIR FATHERS

WITH THE CONSTANCY OF HOPE

AND THE GENTLENESS

OF CHARITY.

St Wilfrid's,
Feast of St Theresa,
M DCCC XLVII.

PROTESTATIO.

CUM SS. D. N. Urbanus Papa VIII. die 13 Martii 1625 in Sacra Congregatione S. R. et Universalis Inquisitionis Decretum ediderit, idemque confirmaverit die 5 Junii 1634 quo inhibuit imprimi libros Hominum, qui Sanctitate, seu Martyrii fama celebres e vita migraverunt, gesta, miracula, vel revelationes, seu quæcumque beneficia, tanquam eorum intercessionibus a Deo accepta continentes, sine recognitione, atque approbatione Ordinarii, et quæ hactenus sine ea impressa sunt, nullo modo vult censeri approbata. Idem autem Sanctissimus die 5 Junii 1631 ita explicaverit, ut nimirum non admittantur Elogia Sancti, vel Beati absolute, et quæ cadunt super Personam, bene tamen ea, quæ cadunt super mores, et opinionem; cum protestatione in principio, quod iis nulla adsit auctoritas ab Ecclesia Romana, sed fides tantum sit penes Auctorem. Huic Decreto, ejusque confirmationi, et declarationi, observantia, et reverentia, qua pars est, insistendo; profiteor me haud alio sensu, quidquid in hoc libro refero, accipere, aut accipi ab ullo velle, quam quo ea solent, quæ humana dumtaxat

PREFACE.

The following Life of the Venerable Servant of God, Benedict Joseph Labrè, is from the Italian of Don Antonio Maria Coltraro, a Roman priest. The original was published at Rome by Salomoni in 1807. It is taken almost exclusively from the Processes, even down to the minutest details; and, as the reader will observe, they are referred to in nearly every page. The Master of the Sacred Apostolical Palace appointed F. Tommaso Maria Mancini, a Dominican, and consultor of the Sacred Congregation of Rites, to examine the work, as censor. His imprimatur is not in the usual merely permissive form, but pronounces a warm eulogium on Coltraro's work: "Non solamente nulla contiene, che opponga si alla Fede, o al buon costume; ma ho anzi osservato la diligenza del pio e dotto autore, il quale *dagli autentici Processi* ha ben raccolto tutto ciò, che *sicuramente* conduce all' edificazione de' Fedeli, proponendogli un nuovo Esemplare di singolar perfezione."

The Oratory,
Feast of St. Romuald, 1850.

CONTENTS.

PART I.

PART II.

NEW AND CONSTANT STATE OF LIFE UNDERTAKEN BY BENEDICT IN ACCORDANCE WITH THE SPECIAL WILL OF GOD.

PART III.

OF BENEDICT'S HEROIC VIRTUES, PRACTISED PARTICULARLY DURING THE YEARS WHICH HE LIVED IN ROME, TILL HIS DEATH.

IN NOMINE DOMINI, AND MARIÆ VIRGINIS IMMACULATÆ.

AD MAJOREM DEI GLORIAM.

THE LIFE

OF THE

VENERABLE SERVANT OF GOD,

BENEDICT JOSEPH LABRÈ.

PART I.

CHAPTER I.

BIRTH AND CHILDHOOD OF BENEDICT TILL THE AGE OF FIVE YEARS.

BENEDICT JOSEPH LABRÈ was born on the 26th of March, 1748, at Amettes, in the parish of St. Sulpice, in the diocese of Boulogne, in France. He was the eldest of fifteen children. His father was named John Baptist Labrè, and was brother to the parish priest of Erin. His mother, Anna Barbara Grandsir, was sister to the parish priest of Pesse; they were both persons of known piety, and, as true Catholics, held in abhorrence the false maxims of Jansenism. They lived decently by the trade of merchant, having more than sufficient for the maintenance of their numerous family. From this circumstance, we may perceive at once, that the state of extreme poverty, which Benedict Joseph adopted, and constantly followed till his death, was not a state of necessity, but of pure choice; it was the effect of the love of God, who by a particular inspiration, which He gave to His servant in this matter, willed to form a copy of His Divine Son; "Being rich, He became poor for our sakes," (2 Cor. viii. 9.) He was a perfect executor, not only of the precepts, but of the evangelical counsels; he had a generous contempt of the three things which form the whole world, "The concupiscence of the flesh, the concupiscence of the eyes, and the pride of life," (2 John, ii. 16,) and which cause the miserable perdition of their unhappy followers.

He was baptised in the parish church of Amettes, on the 27th of March, the day after his birth, and received the names of Benedict Joseph.

His parents had not much difficulty in bringing him up well, for scarcely was he weaned, than they discovered in him dispositions so happy, that they continually poured forth praises for them to God, the Giver of every good gift. A lively, but tractable disposition, a very clear intellect, a retentive memory, a great inclination for virtue, a perfect docility, and so strong a love for piety, that he seemed even then prevented by God with singular blessings so far and in such a manner, that piety seemed to have preceded the age of reason. Thus from his infancy it was held as a common opinion, that he was a child prevented by the graces of God.

Whatever his pious parents taught him, he easily learned; their instructions on the holy

acies now throughout the world. When he attained the age of five years, he earnestly longed to learn quickly to read and write, that he might imprint more deeply in his mind the elements of our holy religion, and the obligations of a Catholic, to which he listened with pleasure when they were proposed to him.

CHAPTER II.

AT FIVE YEARS OF AGE HE IS SENT TO SCHOOL; HIS VERY VIRTUOUS CONDUCT AT SCHOOL AND AT HOME.

As his pious parents seconded the wishes of their amiable son, they sent him at five years of age to the school of an excellent priest named Don Francis Joseph Forgeois, who was then charged with the curacy of Amettes, and after two years and a half, to that of Signor Bartholomew Francis de le Rue. Under such guidance he soon made great progress, no less in literature than in piety.

After having with great facility learned to read and write well, he had some other lessons suited to his age, and one of them was arithmetic. He showed himself so desirous to improve, and so jealous of time, that his master was astonished and sometimes in joke detained him by both hands, but the innocent child tried with all his power to disengage himself, and return to his place, saying pleasantly, "Pray let me go, otherwise I shall not be able to learn my lesson soon."

It sometimes happened in school, that some impertinent boy gave him a blow secretly. Any other child would have resented it, and given way to tears, complaints, and accusations. Benedict concealed it, and was silent. When asked by the master who was the offender, and whether he had been hurt, he answered with a tranquil countenance, that the blow had been given inadvertently, seeking thus to excuse the offender, to spare him the punishment. The master, admiring his patience and mildness, wished to make trial of it himself. He blamed him one day, for some light fault, of which he knew him for certain not to be guilty. He replied with candour, and a serene countenance, a mark of innocence, that he had not committed it. Being then taxed with being culpable, and a liar also, "You merit punishment," was said to him roughly, "go and receive it." He went immediately, presented himself for punishment, without exculpating himself, or without saying a word, but he met with an affectionate reception in its stead.

Having made some mistake in beginning to learn to read, the master rebuking him in a grave manner, said, "You deserve punishment," and putting into his hand a very large corona, added, "Go and recite this immediately." The boy without delay, or saying a word, retired in a corner, and recited it so devoutly, that he gained admiration, and an increase of esteem and affection.

It was Benedict's custom to go out the last when school was over. His master reflecting upon it, asked him the reason of it; "I like to wait," he answered, "till the others are gone out, for though I remain till the last, I shall reach home before the others." His master, not understanding this, watched him attentively, and found that in truth he did arrive the first, though his home was more distant, for he did not stop in the street to play or divert himself like the others, but went straight on gravely quite alone, though he was only between six and seven years old, an age which loves play and amusements, particularly after the tediousness of remaining in school.

The esteem with which the distinguished qualities of this boy inspired his master, made him so dear to him that he could never forget him, and he attested in the Processes, that out of the number of about two thousand children, whom he had taught during many years, he had never known one in whom he found qualities so amiable. He was at this tender age of a serene countenance, sweet and affable, mixed with a gravity which usually belongs to mature age. When circumstances caused him to laugh, he laughed as the Holy Ghost enjoins it, without noise, with no disorderly gesture, and without raising his voice to a loud tone. "A fool lifteth up his voice in laughter, but a wise man will scarce laugh low to himself." (Ecclus. xxi. 23.) He spoke rarely, and when necessity obliged him to speak, his words were few, but weighed, and to the purpose, a proof of great prudence in a man, much more in a little boy. Never was a useless word heard from his mouth; he preferred to listen and treat with persons of piety rather than to speak, according to the advice of the Apostle St. James, "Let every man be swift to hear, but slow to speak." (James, i. 19.)

He gained an increase of esteem by the proofs of great piety which he gavo at so tender an age. Having learned with great eagerness the rudiments of our holy faith, he showed himself to be, as it were, penetrated with Catholic truths, and enlightened by that God, who "sapientiam dat parvulis," and who had chosen him for Himself from his infancy. He had a great distaste for those puerile amusements, in which children usually occupy themselves with great pleasure; he held in horror those small sins of falsehoods, thefts, little quarrels, and disobediences, which are so common, and, as it were, natural to that age. The servants and those who had him under their eyes, and conversed familiarly with him, all attest in the Processes his constant innocence, candour, modesty, and wisdom superior to his age. What causes the greatest wonder, is, that his cempanions even, whatever pains they took to watch his proceedings, could never discover anything reprehensible in him, on the contrary, they proposed him to themselves as a model in their little exercises of devotion, and sought to conform their behaviour to that of Benedict, saying, "This is not the proper way to proceed; Benedict did not do so." His presence acted as a restraint on the passions of the others.

He was a great lover of penances and mortifications, and though he endeavoured to perform them secretly, he could not manage to prevent some from being discovered. His food was very scanty, his sleep uncomfortable; stretching himself sometimes on bare tables, sometimes on the floor, he rested his head on pieces of hard wood, leaving the soft bed prepared for him by his mother; a lover of retreat and solitude, he made it his pleasure to remain at home when he was at liberty from school, employing himself in reading devout books, as if preparing for that retreat and solitude, which were so dear to him during the whole course of his life. In his behaviour and in his words his parents discovered a great inclination for an austere and solitary life, and they tried to moderate it. "My dear son," his mother sometimes said to him, "if you were to live at a distance from home in some solitude, at which you often hint, you would have great difficulty in finding wherewith to support yourself." "The herbs and the roots of the fields would suffice," answered he with holy intrepidity, "as they sufficed to the ancient hermits." "But they," answered his mother, "were at those times of a much stronger constitution than persons now are." "But," answered he, full of confidence, "Almighty God is not less powerful now than He was then, and if then He worked miracles to support them, as you believe, can He not work them now? Ah, mother, everything is possible to a sincere will."

He had erected at home an oratory with a little altar; here, when he was only eight years old, he imitated the mass in his own way, using one of his little brothers as server, he being first well instructed; he sung psalms, made processions, and represented the ceremonies which he had observed in the church, not in a childish manner, but with gravity and exactness superior to his years.

Whenever he could, whether in the morning or during the day, he went to the church. In the morning he employed himself in serving masses, with so much modesty and devotion, that all who observed him were moved. They saw Benedict serve at the altar with his little hands devoutly joined before his breast, his eyes cast down, his head quiet, without ever turning it in another direction. In the ecclesiastical functions he paid attention to the sacred rites, and fixed them in his mind; he went to confession often at five years of age or a little more; during the day he assisted at catechisms, and at the divine offices he never failed to be present; he was, on the contrary, beforehand with every other in his great eagerness. He remained in church with a devotion and recollection greater than can be imagined, so much the more wonderful, as his age was more tender.

Such was the behaviour of Benedict Joseph from the fifth to the twelfth year of his age.

CHAPTER III.

AT TWELVE YEARS OF AGE HE GOES TO ERIN UNDER THE GUIDANCE OF HIS PATERNAL UNCLE THE PARISH PRIEST.

His parents knowing him to be already well instructed in reading and writing, judged proper to send him to Erin under the care of his uncle the parish priest, D. Francis Joseph Labrè, being very sure, that through his affection and the holy zeal by which he edified his whole parish, he would undertake the employment of instructing his nephew in Latin, in the higher sciences, and in the duties of a Catholic. Nor were they deceived. Don Francis found his nephew to be like a beautiful plant, disposed to produce copious and solid fruits, through the talents which God had given him, and the wise cultivation which he had received at home from the time when reason first began to dawn. He sent him to learn Latin at the school of a priest who was an excellent master, and who esteemed him more than any other pupil. With regard to the duties of a Catholic, besides the instructions which he received at school, his uncle undertook himself the charge of explaining them clearly to him at home. Benedict Joseph corresponded wonderfully in his practice to these instructions during the course of little more than six years, which he spent in Erin. Study and exercises of

learning, and how God guided him in that system of life which he constantly followed till his death. In other chapters I will relate the very exemplary manner in which he began to practise his exercises of piety.

CHAPTER IV.

IN WHAT MANNER HE PROSECUTED THE STUDY OF LATIN. WHAT HE HAD TO SUFFER. HIS FIRST DECLARATION OF HIS DESIRE TO RETIRE TO THE VERY AUSTERE CONVENT OF LA TRAPPE.

In beginning to study Latin, he applied himself to it with great pleasure, to obey his parents, who had sent him to Erin for this purpose, and his uncle, who carefully watched over his improvement. On this account he gave to study at home all the time prescribed, showing however a greater esteem for the science of the saints than for human knowledge. In school he was most attentive to the instructions of the master; he always manifested that attention and gravity which belong to advanced age; he was so far from playing, chattering, or acting in a childish manner, that he never gave the master occasion to reprimand him; and his master being obliged sometimes to interrupt his employment for a few days through sickness or some

in his place. It is a wonderful thing, that though boys usually have no fear of similar substitutes of their own age, and taken from their fellow students, and grow bolder than ever, yet they greatly respected Benedict; his presence alone sufficed to impose a restraint on their lively and unquiet dispositions, more effectually even than the presence of the master himself would have done. With some of them who were more impertinent, he never used any remonstrance, except when he foresaw it would be well received, an argument of his great prudence.

He prosecuted this study with diligence for four years. When he had attained to sixteen years of age, he entirely lost the pleasure which he had till then felt in learning Latin well; it became on the contrary so distasteful to him, that he applied to it with less diligence, turning all his fervour towards the science of the saints. Having given himself almost entirely to the reading of ascetic books, he found in them great pleasure and a help to his spirit of devotion; and he felt the holy flames rekindled so strongly in his heart, that he seemed to have quite left off his employment of learning Latin. To open a devout book and feel himself immediately raised up towards God, was one and the same thing. Above every other, the Holy Scriptures were the most dear to him, and he well understood them; he found in them the best nourishment for his devotion, and for this reason, during the remainder of his years, he always carried them with him in his little bundle; he cited passages of them seasonably, corrected any one who altered a word in them, and showed himself ready to draw the Holy Scripture from his bundle, to demonstrate the truth of the text he had cited, to any one who was in doubt about it, and further also, to deny frankly, that there existed in the Holy Writings any text cited through the mistake of others.

His uncle having perceived the relaxation of his diligence in learning Latin, judged it his duty to find fault with him, and inculcated a more profound application. Benedict listened to the reproof with a modest blush and with humility, without saying a word. In order to obey him, he tried to apply seriously. But what followed? He could not succeed, whatever pains he took; scarcely had he opened the book of Cicero, or Quintus Curtius, than he felt, as it were, a great weight and disgust in his heart, and an interior impulse which carried him sweetly in a moment to the reading of his devout books; whichever of these he opened, it was for him like a spark which sets fire to powder, so strongly did his heart burn with the holy flames of devout affections.

His excellent uncle did not know how to reconcile in his nephew this dislike, which had the appearance of disobedience, with the prompt obedience which he always, and in all things, showed him, preventing his signs sometimes; with his care to preserve himself from any sin, however small, with the sincerity of his behaviour, and with his edifying devotion, which was praised by all. He once made a friendly complaint about it to a parish priest who was in his confidence, and who, taking advantage of a good opportunity, insisted on the advice of the uncle, and encouraging him, incited him to study, saying to him, that he must apply well, in order that when he became a priest, he might assist his uncle in his labours, when in old age he would stand in need of help. Benedict frankly answered, "I shall not remain in the world; my wish is to retire into a wilderness."

His uncle hearing this, reprimanded him one day more strongly. Benedict now judged it a proper time to declare to him openly, but with modest respect, that he felt himself moved by God to other designs than to remain in the world, that the study of Latin had become exceedingly wearisome to him, and so would any other human science in comparison with the divine, which teaches us to know God and the best manner of securing the great affair of eternal salvation, which is common to all; he manifested to him the sweet violence by which he felt himself drawn by Almighty God to a total abandonment of the world, in order to attend to God alone, and to eternal salvation in a cloister, which should be the most austere of any, and this he thought was that of La Trappe. His uncle was astonished at so unexpected an answer. It is true that the rigorous system of life which Benedict had undertaken made him suspect his interior designs of quitting the world, but he could never make himself believe that he thought of La Trappe; turning towards him, "Ah my dear nephew," he said, "your design is not prudent. Do you know what it is to live among the solitary monks of La Trappe? If you knew how rigid is the system of life which they there follow, you would change your mind. I can tell you, that others, more robust than you, have not been able to bear it; scarcely had they entered, than they were obliged to abandon it. And what would you do? Your age is tender, you are of a spare habit of body, and your strength is weak. How could you bear it?" These were his uncle's words. I do not find in the Processes, where the fact is related, the exact answer which Benedict made, and I will not speculate upon it myself, being unwilling to relate anything but what is found registered in them. As to the rest, I have no doubt, that whatever his uncle might say with great energy to deter him from the thought of La Trappe, served to give him a greater desire of going, instead of turning him from it, as he had taken the firm resolution to follow, not any austere institute, but this one, which was more so than any other, as he himself declared to others, and especially to his mother in other circumstances. Whoever shall read this first part of his Life, will certainly do justice to what I say. His uncle himself, by the astonishment with which he was seized at the answer given in the Processes, proves more than any other the truth of my words. If Almighty God had granted a longer life to the uncle, even at least till a few years after his nephew's death, he would have been undeceived, and would not have called by the name of weariness the little application which Benedict gave to Latin; on the contrary, he would have thought it a particular inspiration of God, who in Benedict did not desire a learned man, a doctor, a theologian, but a perfect hermit in the midst of the world, who, by his rare examples, and not by his learning, should teach worldlings the contempt of whatever the world prizes. For the rest, a little digression in the eleventh chapter of this first part will come in advantageously, to exempt Benedict from a similar accusation of weariness in regard of the study of logic, imputed to him without reason by a master of philosophy, and therefore I refer the reader to that.

CHAPTER V.

HIS BEHAVIOUR WHILE WITH HIS UNCLE IN REGARD TO EXERCISES OF PIETY: AND FIRST, IN DISCHARGING THOSE WHICH BELONG TO THE WORSHIP OF GOD.

From the time that his mind was enlightened by the use of reason, he gave clear signs of being, as it were, penetrated by the vivid brightness of eternal truths, and the knowledge of the supreme existence of the Creator of the world; hence it was, that wherever he might be, in church, at home, and in the streets, he always appeared composed, grave, and modest, even when he was a little boy, which caused him to be admired by all.

In the house of his uncle at Erin, it was his custom to rise early in the morning, even before the sun, and to employ himself in holy meditations in retirement. Scarcely had he heard the first sound of the bell than he hurried to church, in winter as in summer, on a working day or a feast. He generally served two masses, offering himself with great readiness to the priests, who looked on him with admiration. If some were beforehand with him, though he yielded, he showed himself as much afflicted as a miser who had lost some opportunity of gain. It sometimes happened that some bold person prevented him from serving the priest at the altar: the patience and humility of Benedict were admirable in so unpleasant a repulse; quiet and peaceable, he withdrew in silence, and instead of serving, assisted most devoutly at the great sacrifice. He performed this act of religion, of serving or assisting at mass, not as boys do who are distracted, but with true interior recollection, which appeared by the modesty and reverence manifested in his countenance, to the great edification of every one who beheld him.

He often withdrew from the presence of the servants to go to church; his assiduity, his reverent motionless posture, so contrary to the unquiet and lively disposition of boys, made him an object of admiration of others, and were as a presage of that which he afterwards practised till the last day of his life.

Being resolved never uselessly to waste time, at certain intervals retiring to his room, he employed himself in reading devout books, not rapidly running over the pages, but deliberately enough for meditation, pouring forth holy affections. He went to confession several times a month ; he more than once repeated his general confession, never being fully satisfied with his ordinary confessions, always believing himself to be a criminal and a great sinner. Before he received the sacrament of confirmation at Erin from the bishop of Boulogne, he made his confession with a more fervent disposition. On the same day he received the Holy Communion for the first time, but with admirable affection, devotion, and modesty. After this time he went to communion only once a month, till he was desired by his confessors to go very frequently ; he then obeyed, judging that it was more pleasing to God to communicate through obedience, than to abstain from it through humility. He was so great a lover of the Divine worship, and of whatever appertains to it, that though he was well instructed, and above fifteen years of age, he went willingly to church promiscuously with the little boys to hear the Catechism, as if he required instruction as much as the others. He often visited the Blessed Sacrament in the church, and entertained himself a long time in a very devout manner with his Lord, melting into holy affections. One day having gone to pay Him a visit in the church of St. Pol, where the Blessed Sacrament was exposed for the Forty Hours at the season of the Carnival, he remained there from morning till night immoveable on his knees, and fasting with so much pleasure, that he refused an invitation to dine, given him three hours after mid day, by a devout person who had compassion for him. What I have hitherto related regarding his worship of God is but a shadow in comparison of that which he rendered to God when a pilgrim, and afterwards when remaining in Rome.

CHAPTER VI.

HE PRACTISES OTHER EXERCISES OF PIETY BELONGING TO AN AUSTERE LIFE.

The exercises of piety practised by Benedict while yet a youth living with his uncle, were some of them exercised in austerities on himself, and some in charity towards his neighbour. Here we will only speak of the first, reserving the others for our next chapter.

The austerities which he practised at this early stage of his life were only an attempt at what he afterwards constantly performed till his death; but such an attempt is truly wonderful in the spring-tide of life, which is inclined of itself to pleasures and amusements.

He deprived himself of all those lawful diversions which at certain times were allowed to his young fellow-students: the great pleasure which he experienced in remaining retired in his room, in nourishing his soul with the food of prayer, and with the reading of devout books, had given him a distaste for every other earthly amusement. O how truly do we see verified in him the words of St. Gregory, that when we have once tasted the interior delights of the soul, all the false pleasures of the world leave our hearts; gustato spiritu, desipit omnis caro. When urged by his companions to be present, and jeered at as a rustic and a hypocrite, he did not listen at all to them; on the contrary, he answered boldly, triumphing over human respects, that he found his pleasure in his room.

One day when there were sports in the country parishes, his uncle, the parish priest, urged him to go and divert himself with his companions. He went; but his uncle, well knowing that such amusements had no attraction for Benedict, said to the company, "I lay a wager that my nephew is gone into some corner to pray." Being curious to know the truth, having sought him among his fellow-students and looked in every corner, he found him in the end hidden in a covered barn, where, in a devout attitude, he was praying before a crucifix hanging from a piece of wood, to which he had attached it, and he was so profoundly recollected, that he did not notice the noise his uncle's feet made in entering; and edified and consoled, his uncle quickly shut the door after him, that he might not disturb him, leaving him taken up with his beloved spiritual pleasures.

He did not grant to his body any of those things which flatter the senses. When invited in the most severe winter to warm himself at the fire, he would not draw near to it, being satisfied with the spiritual heat which he drew from his intercourse with God, and with his spiritual books in his beloved retirement. More than once he was observed to sleep at night on the floor, caring nothing for his bed, notwithstanding the great rigour of the season.

He was so sparing with regard to food, that it was necessary to urge him to take necessary nourishment. He chose for himself what was most common and coarse, giving to the servants anything delicious and delicate, and more than once he was secretly observed to give in private to the poor part of his own food. Though he was yet young, and at an age which requires more nourishment, he fasted rigorously, though not obliged to it, the whole of Lent; and at Easter, he said, "Lent is now happily ended for those who have fasted well, but it has badly terminated for the transgressors." He often passed sometimes two, sometimes three days without eating anything.

It was his custom, when he was little more than twelve years old, to rise from table before any one else, as soon as he could. A canon, who was a guest at table, wondering once at this, asked the parish priest why he was in so great a hurry? "Because," he answered, "he likes to remain alone and retired in his room to read devout books; this is his custom."

His uncle had a garden filled with ripe strawberries and sweet fruits of every kind, which by their fragrance alone provoked the appetite of others, particularly of boys, who by their nature, not knowing how to resist such allurements, are accustomed even to take them unlawfully, but it never happened that Benedict allowed himself to gather so much as one, or even to pick up any which fell to the ground through ripeness, or the wind, though he might have reasonably presumed upon his uncle's tacit permission, and even pleasure, as he was very affectionate and liberal towards him. Benedict frankly confessed this one day to him, when having taken to him some ripe fruit which he had gathered by his order, his uncle asked if he had tasted one, "No," he answered with sincerity, "not one, and I know well that I could not do so without your leave."

CHAPTER VII.

HE EXERCISES CHARITY TOWARDS HIS NEIGHBOUR. HEROIC ACTS OF IT ARE RELATED. GLORIOUS DEATH OF HIS UNCLE, THE PARISH PRIEST.

In the same proportion as he was austere to himself, he was kind and amiable towards his neighbour. It is the property of true charity, to despise oneself, while it gives itself entirely to the assistance of others. The poor and the sick were the chief objects of compassion to the heart of this youth, who was so sensible to their miseries, that he willingly deprived himself of his nourishment, dividing it with them; and to keep his charity secret from the eyes of others, he sometimes threw it to them from the window of his room. On this account it was, that several poor people departing with provisions from the priest's house, went away satisfied, saying, "To-day we have had abundant alms from the house of the parish priest, by the hands of his nephew, Mr. Benedict." On the contrary, they sometimes said, "We have to-day been obliged to go without an alms, for neither the priest nor his nephew were at home."

It happened one day, that three poor people of another parish, begging at the parish priest's door, were driven away roughly by the servant, who said to them, "Go and work, you idle and lazy people." Scarcely had Benedict heard this, than being unable to bear to see them go away unrelieved and mortified, he recalled them, and with eager charity, "Come," said he to them, "I will give you relief," and looking kindly on them, he provided them all three with bread.

A more spacious field was opened for Benedict's charity by the contagious epidemic, which in 1766 made great havoc in Erin. He went, burning with charity, along with his uncle the priest to the houses of the sick, never satisfied with assisting them, as people were wanting to help, on account of the domestics being for the most part attacked by the same illness; he did not care for the danger of being attacked by it himself; he thought it would be glorious to give his life for others, the most distinguished mark of true charity, so that his uncle was obliged to moderate his ardour, and expressly forbid him to enter some houses which were more dangerous. Thus, if there had been any one who could have restrained the great zeal of the priest himself, a pastor then necessary to his flock, Benedict would not himself have been involved in the affliction. Despising every danger, caring nothing for himself, he behaved as a true pastor in this dreadful affliction, serving the sick, administering the sacraments, assisting the dying without any regard for himself, with so much fervour, that he was himself attacked by the contagious disease. His nephew Benedict deeply grieved, but united to the Divine Will, waited upon him indefatigably, taking care that the orders of the physicians were executed, and when there was any spare time he did not fail to go hither and thither alone, to help different people. At length his uncle, by the Divine Will, yielding to the force of the disease, died in September, 1766, a victim of charity, an example of a true parish priest, worthy of eternal remembrance; and if it is the will of Almighty God, that every just man should be honoured by the remembrance of posterity, ("The just shall be in everlasting remembrance," Psalm cxi. 7,) how much honour is not due to such a priest, who besides being just, and an example to his sheep, even gave up his own life for them!

If Benedict did not fall into the same illness as his uncle, it was by the dispensation of Divine Providence, who preserved him to be an example of contempt of the world, at these times, principally when the world by its flattering pomp draws after it a great many, who, allowing their eyes to be fascinated, follow it blindly, to their own eternal damnation. He was also preserved to continue the offices of charity in the course of this disease, which increased after the priest's death. In fact, charity made Benedict to be all eyes to mark the needy, all arms to serve them, all heart to render them every charitable aid, however abject the person might be; to some he gave alms for their subsistence; he went at certain intervals to the neighbouring field to bind up grass to feed the cattle of the sick, which would otherwise have also fallen victims, not to the disease, but to hunger, there being no one to give them their necessary food. His charity shone forth particularly in the assistance which he gave to a whole family, who were abandoned by all at this critical time of the epidemic. When this came to his knowledge, he ran eagerly to help them with his services, to administer to them what was necessary, and he went every day with a fervour of charity greater in proportion as he saw their abandonment and necessity to be greater.

CHAPTER VIII.

HIS UNCLE BEING DEAD, BENEDICT RETURNS HOME. HE TAKES MEASURES TO OBTAIN HIS PARENTS' LEAVE TO RETIRE TO LA TRAPPE. THEIR MANNER OF PROCEEDING, AND THAT OF BENEDICT.

BENEDICT, in great affliction, but fully resigned to the Divine Will, in the loss of such an uncle, returned home in the eighteenth year of his age. Here he followed constantly the course of a rigid life which he had undertaken, being entirely averse to everything which regarded worldly things or his own convenience. Retired in his room, he was continually employed in holy prayer, spiritual reading, and other exercises of piety. Very sparing was his food; rigorous and frequent were his fasts; he was more assiduous than any other in remaining in church, where he was admired by all for the reverence and modesty with which he adored Almighty God, assisted at the adorable Sacrifice, and frequented the sacraments. Fervour in him increased equally with age.

His great pleasure was all in mortifications, which he took care to try to hide from the eyes of others. He begged his parents in the beginning to prepare him a very high bed; but he used it only to lie under it, disarranging it on purpose in the morning, to conceal his uncomfortable repose. His attempts were all directed towards persuading his parents, who still resisted, to give him leave to abandon the world entirely and retire to La Trappe, whither he believed himself called by God. He had consulted wise and enlightened persons on this resolution, and they had unanimously approved it; therefore with very great prudence he took the opportunity of circumstances to declare himself resolute, and to extort the desired permission from his parents.

Being once scolded by his mother, because she had surprised him one night on the floor, "Mother," he said, "do not be troubled; God calls me to a very austere life, which I believe to be that of La Trappe; to correspond to my duty it is proper that I should exercise myself well in it before I undertake it." He declared himself thus clearly on other occasions, sometimes to his mother, sometimes to his father, and sometimes to both together.

Judge now yourself, whether they were willing to consent; paternal affection, the valuable qualities of such a son, the severities of La Trappe, which were well known everywhere, made them stand firm in their refusal, and they made use of persons of authority to turn him from his design. Benedict remained firm against the representations of every one, more firm than a rock against the assaults of the impetuous waves, and to that degree, that he openly declared one day before his parents themselves and the whole family, that even if his father should place himself across the door to prevent him from going to La Trappe, he should not have any difficulty in passing over him to obey God. The mediators could obtain nothing further from Benedict, so resolutely firm, except some delay at the request of his parents.

In the meantime they greatly desired that he should go to his other maternal uncle, by name Don Bonaventure Joseph Vincent, at this time vicar of Conteville, afterwards parish priest of Pesse, a most exemplary ecclesiastic and beloved by all, that he might proceed with his studies, which had been interrupted. Benedict went willingly only through obedience, but with his views directed towards his beloved La Trappe, waiting for the desired permission from his parents, and offering to God fervent prayers that He would vouchsafe to move them to it.

It is certainly an astonishing thing to see a youth, at the brightest period of life, do so much, suffer so much, and subject himself to more inconveniences than the most passionate lover of the world will go through to attain the object of his desires; as if La Trappe were a garden of delights, when it is only a wilderness of great austerity, calculated to terrify any one. But let it not surprise us. Benedict loved nothing but God, heavenly and eternal things, and the salvation of his soul; thus nothing else was of any importance to him, however serious it might be. "Hunters do not consider as troubles the pains and difficulties of the chase," says St. Augustine; "on the contrary, they take pleasure in them, because they like hunting. It is the same with a soul that loves God." He manifested several times how much he loved the retirement of La

Trappe, not only by his actions, but in letters written to his parents, in which he calls La Trappe "An abode which I so much desire, and have for so long a time desired." In the house of this uncle, instead of decreasing he much increased the rigid tenor of life which he had elsewhere followed. He did not fail to continue his studies, but, like one who has another object in view, he remained for the most part either in the church absorbed in God, or at home employed in reading spiritual books. From this system of his his uncle clearly understood that Benedict was a flower which was not to remain in the open field, but to be transplanted into an inclosed garden; he knew also from his sentiments what were his designs. He was more persuaded of it when he saw his devout employment of following spontaneously some fervent missionaries, who were preaching in three parishes a few leagues distant from Conteville, in Boyaval, in Brias, and in Ruillecourt. He followed them on foot, undismayed either by the rigour of the season or the inconveniences of the journey, eating nothing more than what sufficed for the necessary nourishment of his body. Benedict had the pleasure of seeing his resolution of retiring to La Trappe, which he had made known, approved by them. Benedict did not remain longer than a few months with this uncle. The letters which he wrote to his sister, Benedict's mother, and the accounts which he gave of her son's austere mode of life and of his wishes, incline me to believe that they contributed much to induce Benedict's parents to grant the desired permission.

CHAPTER IX.

HE OBTAINS HIS PARENTS' PERMISSION TO GO TO LA TRAPPE. HE IS NOT ADMITTED: FOR WHAT REASON?

Benedict, after his return home, did and said so much, and took such measures, that at length he succeeded in persuading them. They could no longer resist either his earnest and repeated entreaties, or the pain which the distress of their son caused them; they at length yielded, making to God a sacrifice of their first-born, who by the virtues and talents with which God had adorned him, had gained their love more than any other of their sons; they at last gave him the desired permission for La Trappe. A valiant warrior does not rejoice more in gaining the triumph after a long and perilous battle, than Benedict exulted in the victory he had gained. Without any delay, he joyfully presented himself to his parents, thanked them, asked their pardon for the grief he had caused them, not by his own fault, but through the necessity of obeying the holy will of God, by whom he felt himself called to a very austere life, which he believed to be that led by the monks of La Trappe. Receiving the blessing of both his weeping and afflicted parents, he departed happy, being very desirous to reach the limits of his journey. The ardour of his holy desires, made him entirely disregard the difficulties which might have deterred him from undertaking such a journey at that time. The season was very severe, the rains were continual, the roads bad and dangerous, the distance long, being nearly sixty leagues, and his strength not very robust. Entirely disregarding all this, he arrived at last.

He thought the bark had already reached the port, when an unexpected wave drove him back into the storm. These religious, taking into mature consideration his youth, and his spare habit of body, would not receive him; they promised indeed to receive him some other time, and at a more robust age, more suitable to the austerity of the institute. Deeply grieved, the servant of God submitted; he adored the Divine dispensations, he fully acquiesced, and set out to return to Amettes. He arrived in such a state that he excited the compassion of all, and particularly of his parents. He was benumbed with cold, exhausted by his spare nourishment, fatigued with his long journey, again made on foot, and little less than naked. The great pain of his parents was in some degree alleviated by seeing him at home again and in their company. This comfort was not of long continuance; it was not long before Benedict, feeling the desire of La Trappe always strong within him, and judging it to be a Divine inspiration, renewed his entreaties to his parents, flattering himself, that he was sufficiently robust to be admitted. How long a time he suffered to elapse I do not find in the Processes, but I think without doubt that it was less than a year, as any one who reads what follows will unite with me in believing.

The renewal of his petition was unexpected by his parents, who fancied that he had given up the thought; they took all means to deter him from it; they at last declared that they were willing to allow him to go to La Chartreuse, that he might no longer think of La Trappe; but seeing him constant in his resolution, they at last engaged the curate of Amettes, Signor Don Jerome Thoret, afterwards parish priest in Burbure, to dissuade him from his design.

Whatever pains he took in managing it, he could not succeed in making him yield. One day he reproved him with some sharpness, but seeing the tranquil and humble expression of countenance with which he received reprehensions, he was sorry for having had recourse to them, and judged it seasonable, with a mild and benignant countenance, to bring under his consideration the great grief into which he would plunge his mother, who was then near her confinement, and to whom the consequences might be injurious. He advised him rather to follow the counsel he gave him, which was, to write to the abbot of La Trappe, to hear if he would receive him. The advice pleased Benedict, he moderated his wishes, and wrote, but received no other answer than this, "That as the same reasons for which he had been first refused continned to exist, he must not think of moving."

CHAPTER X.

HE SEEKS TO ENTER AMONGST THE CARTHUSIANS: HE DOES NOT SUCCEED. HE AGAIN ATTEMPTS, IS ADMITTED, BUT IS OBLIGED TO LEAVE.

BENEDICT, grieved at this answer, thought he would avail himself of his parents' leave to go to the Chartreuse, at Neoville near Montreville. He went thither in May, 1767, but unwillingly, La Trappe being always his beloved object. He heard from these fathers that it was necessary for him to learn their chant first, and a little of logic. Benedict being resolved to be entirely remote from the world, in the best manner he could, placed himself by the wish of his parents under the guidance of the parish priest of Auchi, Don Jacques Dufruse, to pursue these studies. Benedict gained his good opinion so completely while with him, and pursuing his rigid course of life, that in the Processes he gives his testimony of him as a saint at the age of eighteen or a little more. Being urged by him one festival-day of his parish to go and amuse himself with some of his relations and friends in their innocent gaiety, he answered, "That he found his delight in remaining retired in his room, and that being on the eve of quitting the world, he would only go to see his parents to say farewell to them at a time when there was less bustle."

The only thing which displeased the priest, was to see him indifferent about study; he was for the most part employed in reading devout books, and in the exercises of piety. Having tried mild measures, he one day spoke more roughly, reproving him with severity. But he was obliged to discontinue his speech at the sight of the serenity and humility with which he listened to him. From that time he knew that study did not suit Benedict, but rather the science of the saints, and that the Almighty desired another manner of proceeding from him, and knowing him to be not only blameless of every sort of fault, but endowed with even heroic virtue, he could not call blameable that disrelish which he showed for every other study. Here let a little digression be permitted to me, in order to defend Benedict from the accusation which some inexperienced person might fix upon him, of being guilty of a fault by this disrelish for study. Having related in the preceding chapters the little application of Benedict in learning the sciences, and the reproofs by which his uncle and others mortified him, any one might think him guilty of disobedience. But what disobedience, what fault can there be, if it were all the dispensation of Almighty God, who having other designs upon him, guided him, inciting him by His sweet attractions, to follow that path which would make him a particular model of sanctity? God willed him to be a perfect anchorite in the midst of the world, not a learned man, an example, not a preacher, which, according to St. Thomas, is more efficacious in persuading men than words, "Homines magis exemplo trahuntur, quam verbis." God willing him to be an anchorite, what necessity had he for study and knowledge? How could they have agreed with the neglected, humble, penitent, and solitary state, in which God willed him? St. Theresa likewise forbade her Carmelite nuns to study Latin, or anything little suited to their state, and she declared herself desirous, in a letter written to the prioress of Seville, that her daughters living entirely apart from the world, should have the holy ambition of appearing simple and ignorant, as many saints have done, rather than of being female rhetoricians. Thus after some years, when Benedict knew as much of Latin as sufficed to understand the sense, and to nourish his soul with the frequent reading of the Holy Scriptures, Almighty God entirely took from him the duty and the wish to proceed farther with the sciences, drawing him totally to the true solid science of the saints; He infused into him a great pleasure and a sweet unction in reading devout books and the Holy Scriptures, and with sweet violence He thus drew him to the knowledge of Himself, and of eternal things, which is the science of the saints. Being ordered to apply to study, he did all he could to obey, but transported, if we may so speak, by God, who is the absolute Master of His creatures, to the contemplation of His greatness, and to the knowledge of eternal truths, how was this application possible to him? Of what fault can we accuse him? If any inexperienced person should pronounce him guilty, we must also pronounce the same judgment on the beloved spouse of Jesus Christ, St. Theresa. She was forbidden to pray by one of her confessors, and yet she prayed a long time, transported by God, the absolute and independent Master, with strong impulses, which sweetly immersed her in God. Who can accuse her of a sin? "I obeyed," the saint writes, "as well as I could, but I could do little or nothing in that way; it was not in my power to divert myself from prayer, however much I wished it, and tried not to think of God; for the more pains I took not to think of God, so much the greater was the increase of His graces and faveurs in me." The same has happened to other contemplative saints in our time, to the Ven. servant of God, Sister Maria Gertrude Salandri, foundress of the monastery of Valentano, who was forbidden to pray by her confessor, but she was nevertheless drawn by God with sweet violence, and in an ineffable manner, which she knew not how to explain.

For these very solid reasons, which could be easily perceived by his uncle in Erin and by others elsewhere, I fancy that, after these proofs, they became quiet at last, leaving him at liberty and declaring themselves very well satisfied with him, and always greatly edified by his blamelessness, and by the heroic virtues which they admired in him.

After having freed Benedict from the unmerited accusation of being culpable, let us proceed. Scarcely had five months elapsed, than, thinking himself sufficiently instructed to be admitted amongst the Carthusians, he first returned to Boulogne, where, to put himself in a better disposition, he renewed his general confession to the rector of the college, then presented himself to the bishop to obtain the necessary certificates, to whom he also ingenuously avowed his greater inclination for the institute of La Trappe, as more austere than that of the Carthusians, asking his advice on the subject. The wise prelate asked him if his parents would be pleased with it. Hearing his answer to the contrary, he replied, "Obey your parents, my son; go to the Carthusians." Benedict promptly obeyed, gaining the victory over himself through the repugnance which repelled him from La Chartreuse, and being returned to Amettes, his native place, he prepared for his departure, but in taking leave of some persons he said clearly, that he went to the Carthusians only through obedience to the bishop and his parents; for the rest he did not think he should remain there, this institute not being in accordance with the inspiration which he felt to embrace one more rigid. To his parents he openly declared that he should not return, and that they would not see him again except in the valley of Josaphat. He departed in effect for La Chartreuse at Neoville near Montreville; he was well received there

He did not remain longer than six weeks in this probation. Almighty God, who designed him for another state, gave him at that time such interior agitations, such pains of mind, that the father-prior, fearing with reason that a longer residence might render him entirely useless, judged it proper to dismiss him, with these words, which clearly show the Divine will: "My son, Divine Providence does not call you to our state; follow the inspirations of God."

Benedict, conforming himself to the Divine dispensations, first fortified himself by the reception of the Bread of Heaven; then he departed on the 2nd of October, 1769, with attestations of great encomium given by these fathers in regard of his virtue. Remaining a short time at Montreville, he wrote a letter to his parents, in which he makes known to them his departure from La Chartreuse, and his other designs. I will copy it here, that the conduct of Divine Providence in his regard may be made known.

Letter of Benedict to his parents:

"My very dear father and mother,

"I make known to you, that the Carthusians not having judged me suited to their institute, I left them on the 2nd of October. I regard this as an order of Divine Providence, who calls me to a more perfect state. They said themselves, that it was the hand of God which drew me away from them. I am going then to La Trappe, a place which I desire so much, and have done for so long a time. Be not uneasy on my account. Even if I had wished to remain, I should not have been received. I rejoice much at this, for it is the omnipotent hand of God which guides me." Here he thanks them for their goodness towards him, for the services they had rendered him, and for his excollent education; then he adds, "Do not afflict yourselves because I have left the Carthusians; it is not permitted to us to resist the will of God, who has thus ordained it for my greater good, and for my salvation. I have cost you a great deal, but be assured, that, by the help of the grace of God, I shall profit of all that you have done for me. Grant mo your blessing; I shall never be again a trouble to you. That good God whom I received before my departure, will assist me and conduct me in the undertaking with which Ho has inspired mo. I greatly hope that I shall be received at La Trappe. In any case I have been assured, that in the order at Sept Fontaines, where there is not so much severity, they receive younger persons, &c., &c.

"I am your very humble servant,

"BENEDICT JOSEPH LABRÈ."

CHAPTER XI.

NOT BEING ADMITTED AT LA TRAPPE, HE ENTERS THE MONASTERY OF SEPT FONTAINES. HE IS EXCLUDED BY THE WILL OF GOD.

BENEDICT went again without delay to La Trappe, and not being admitted for the motives which still existed, and had been already alleged to him by the father-abbot, he presented himself at the monastery of Sept Fontaines of the Cistercian order, celebrated in France for austere regular discipline, being always desirous to live in the continual maceration of his flesh, by as rigorous a system as he could, as it seemed to him that in this he was directed by the Spirit of God. He was speedily received on the 11th of November, 1769, to the great joy of his heart, as he declared himself afterwards to his confessor, the parish priest, D. Maria Paggetti, in giving him an account of his conscience, and being clothed with the habit he received the name of Brother Urban.

But God clearly made known, not only to him, but to these solitary fathers also, that this was not His will, nor the manner of life which He had destined for him; for scarcely had he entered than he was seized with so great and painful an illness, that the superiors and physicians judged that the institute did not at all suit his weak constitution. To bodily diseases

d so intense and continual, that he wa
to the thinness of a skeleton. Thus,
x months and twelve days, it was judged
nt, on his own account, as also on that
nonastery, to send him away with mutual
Benedict was afflicted, for he greatly
to lead there a penitential and solitary
; he quickly submitted his desires to the
ill of God, nor were other words heard
is mouth than these, "Fiat Dei voluntas,"
he shed many tears, which flowed from
terness of his heart. The grief of these
s was not less at being deprived of sc
ary a subject, and who was so beloved by
account of the virtues observed in him;
ey give in the Processes very high testi
of his holy conduct. The great charity
father-abbot, and of all those holy reli-
nen, did not permit that he should leave
he had recovered his health, which wa
estroyed, and therefore a place was given
the hospital of the house, where he wa
with distinction. Every one admired th
love which when convalescent he showed
yer and for the reading of devout books
ch as his strength permitted, and hi
for his neighbour, serving the other sick
s of his own accord. Solitude and silence
practised by him in this hospital with
exactness, that all believed that he wa
united with God, and considered him a

a saint; hence they strove with one another in their ambition to know him, saying, mutually, "Pius Juvenis Labrè sanctus est, eum ergo adeamus visuri. Let us go and see Labrè, who is a holy youth."

Leaving the monastery of Sept Fontaines, after a residence of about six months, and the above-named hospital after two months, he wrote to his parents on the 31st of August, 1770, from Guiers in Piedmont, relating everything to them in an edifying and very respectful letter, which was his last: he would not again return home, believing for certain, that this was not the will of God, as he himself stated to the before-mentioned parish priest of St. Venanzio in Fabriano, Don Maria Paggetti, who was then his confessor. In the meantime he felt himself always more strongly urged by new interior impulses, to undertake a constant and very austere system of life, totally opposed to the system of the world. He prayed fervently to God that He would discover it to him, offering himself as ready to embrace it whatever it might cost him. At length God vouchsafed to hear him. We shall see in the second part what this state was, and with what perfection it was fervently embraced by him, and constantly practised till his death.

PART II.

NEW AND CONSTANT STATE OF LIFE UNDERTAKEN BY BENEDICT IN ACCORDANCE WITH THE SPECIAL WILL OF GOD

INTRODUCTION TO THIS SECOND PART.

Before I proceed to explain the new and very austere state of life followed by Benedict till his death, it is necessary to remind the reader, that it is usual with Almighty God to inspire some of His dear servants with what He requires from them, but not distinctly, nor at first. He inspires it in the beginning in a general manner, that they, being desirous of pleasing Him, may exercise themselves in frequent prayers, in fervent oblations, and in other acts of piety, that they may afterwards understand it distinctly and clearly; thus, by increasing their merits, He disposes them better for it. Then He gives them some sensible and clear sign, that they may execute it with pleasure. The sacred histories are full of similar cases, of which some are very clear in the divine writings. Let it suffice to make use of two only, one in the Old Testament, which occurred to Abraham, the other in the New, to the spouse of the Blessed Virgin, St. Joseph.

As to the first, God willed that Abraham should sacrifice to Him his beloved son Isaac; but He did not at the same time reveal to him the mount on which he was to sacrifice him; He only commanded him to sacrifice him on a mountain, which He would show him: "Go into the land of vision, and there thou shalt offer him for a holocaust upon one of the mountains which I will show thee." (Gen. xxii. 2.) But which mountain shall this be, out of the number which lift up their heads in that land? Abraham does not know. God only expressed it to him in general, upon one of the mountains. Abraham promptly obeys and sets out, but with an uncertainty as to the place. He makes two days' journey in doubt. On the third day, casting his eyes first on this, then on that mountain, he saw the place afar off, which God had commanded him. God showed it clearly to him, by the sensible sign of a little pillar of fire, on the top of Mount Moria, as the text is explained by the Rabbis: "Signum fuit columna ignis, in cacumine Montis Meriæ."

As for the New Testament, the angel commanded in the name of God, St. Joseph, who was an exile in Eygpt, that as the tyrant Herod was now dead, he should return into Israel with his spouse and the Child Jesus: "Arise and take the Child and His mother, and go into the land of Israel." (Matt. ii. 20.) The saint, obeying, prepares immediately for the journey, but to what city or part of Israel is he to go? Israel contained Judea, Galilee, and many cities and countries. The angel did not reveal it distinctly to him; he only said to him in general, "Go into the land of Israel." To go into Judea was a great risk, as Archelaus, son of the persecutor Herod, then reigned there; "He was afraid to go there." In this perplexity the saint has recourse to prayer, and God hears him; He makes known to him by the ministry of an angel that he is to go to Galilee, to the city of Nazareth. "Being warned in sleep, he retired into the quarters of Galilee; and coming, he dwelt in a city called Nazareth." (v. 22.) Now the same thing occurred to Benedict Joseph; he had from a boy the inspiration of God to lead a very austere life, as he himself declared to his parents and to his confessors, but he did not know in what manner, in what religious order or solitude. Being grown up, he made two attempts to enter La Trappe, but was obliged to give up the thought of it, understanding from his parents and from the bishop of Boulogne, that this was not the will of God. He then tried La Chartreuse, but was rejected, for these fathers knew, and said to him clearly, that God did not will him to be one of them. No other remained to him but the very rigid cloister of the Cistercian Fathers at Sept Fontaines. He goes with great eagerness; he enters, satisfied, believing that he has at length ascertained the will of God; but Almighty God begins to afflict him in such a manner with continual illnesses and interior trials, that these religious men tell him openly, that God wills him in another state and not amongst them, though they knew him to be a youth of great perfection. What will Benedict do? What will he follow? When will he lead that very austere form of life to which God always inclined him by His holy inspirations? This will form the subject of the present second part.

CHAPTER I.

A GENERAL DESCRIPTION OF THE VERY RIGID LIFE OF BENEDICT, WILLED EXPRESSLY BY ALMIGHTY GOD.

Benedict, having left the cloister of Sept Fontaines in doubt where and in what rigid manner he should lead the rest of his life, turned with greater fervour towards Almighty God, multiplying his prayers in order to obtain a clearer light from heaven. Our Lord heard him and consoled His servant. God is accustomed to make Himself clearly heard by some of His servants, by means of an internal voice, in speaking of which the mystical doctors assert unanimously, that He makes Himself heard in this manner with such clearness, that the exterior sense itself could not give it in a greater degree, and at the same time He gives them a strong inclination towards what He requires of them. St. Theresa was thus favoured in the commencement of her spiritual career, and she confesses that by means of this real internal voice, He eradicated entirely from her heart every earthly affection, even though innocent, which was not agreeable to God in her, and He entirely calmed that great tempest of fear into which certain directors who were not well versed in mystical theology had thrown her. God favoured His servant Benedict with this real internal voice. He made known to him by a very clear illumination of mind, joined to a sensible inspiration of heart, "that it was His will that he should follow the traces of St. Alexis, abandoning entirely his country, his parents, conveniences, and whatever is flattering in the world, leading a new sort of life, the poorest, the hardest, and most penitential, (which shall be described in this second part and in the third,) and that he should lead it, not in a desert, nor in a cloister, but in the midst of the world, visiting celebrated places of devotion by pious pilgrimages, as much as he was able." Thus spoke the interior voice, giving him at the same time a great inclination to prepare himself for the undertaking.

Interior peace, which is the characteristic of the true spirit of God, the movements and interior affections of his heart, in virtue of so clear an illustration and knowledge of the holy will of God, might have been sufficient for him. But as it was his custom, always and in all things to regulate himself by the direction of confessors furnished with the Spirit of God, he made known the whole to a confessor whom he knew well, who was wise, prudent, and very well versed in the science of mystical theology. He approved of his design, and animated him to the execution of it. Afterwards all the other confessors to whom he went in Rome and in various cities, knowing by the Divine light, that God willed him in that very austere state of life, also gave their approbation of it, encouraging him also to pursue it till his death. I met with only one in the Processes, who, regulating himself by the maxims of human prudence, showed at the first conferences he had with him in Rome some difficulty in approving of it, not liking to see a young man of an age adapted for labour living in idleness, remaining in churches the greater part of his time, and he commanded him, chiefly to put his spirit to the proof, to apply himself to some employment, which he should prefer before any other. He answered, that there was not any. Being advised to seek the occupation of a servant, he showed himself very ready to obey; "But to whom shall I go," answered he, "for I know no one?" "Speak to some countryman of your own," replied the confessor, "and return to tell me the result; in the meantime I will do what I can to find some master among the number who are known to me." Benedict, who was most obedient, showed himself ready for anything, remarking to him, however, as he went away, that his miserable ability would reach no farther than to the washing of dishes in the kitchen. Leaving his confessor, he speedily executed his orders, making useless efforts; then when he returned to confession, he said frankly, that he had not succeeded, for all turned their eyes elsewhere, seeing him begging, so ragged, and so thin; some even dissuaded him from seeking further, because he would find no master in whom his mere appearance would not cause horror.

The sincerity of this account, and his ready obedience, joined to the useless efforts made also by his confessor, and to the knowledge he gained from private discourses with Benedict, clearly made known to him, that the course he had undertaken was entirely the will of God; therefore, instead of dissuading him from it, he encouraged him to persevere in his plan of life, as it was the will of God.

He judged it proper to advise him only to mitigate in some degree the austerity of his life, specifying to him his sleeping in the open air and on the bare ground at all times, never retaining anything for future subsistence, and the like. Benedict showed himself most ready to follow this advice, and ready to execute it when he should be commanded, but he brought forward so many texts of Holy Scripture, which were the rule of the plan of life with which God had inspired him, the sensible divine light which urged him to it, and so many other reasons, that the confessor at last knew clearly that Benedict was guided by God in the difficult path of the most sublime perfection. Then giving him his entire approbation, he left him at full liberty, exhorting him, however, to remain constant in following that God who guided him.

Another confessor at Loretto, who was very wise, and well versed in mystical theology, hearing in the first conferences he had with Benedict of the tenor of his life, judged it well, in order to put his spirit to the proof, to treat him as a vagrant, on account of the idle and wandering life which he led, a life which, without an extraordinary inspiration from God, approved by a skilful director, could not be persevered in without a scruple of conscience, and to this he also added harsh reproaches. The servant of God listened with an humble and placid countenance, and was silent. Being obliged by a formal precept of holy obedience to answer, he did so with tears in his eyes, showing that he had to overcome great repugnance in doing so. He said at last, that having left the monastery of Sept Fontaines, while he was begging from our Lord help and light to know His divine will, regarding the manner of life which he was to embrace, he felt a very sensible interior inspiration, and a very vehement impulse, which moved his heart tranquilly, inclining him precisely to his present system of life; in this, however, trusting little to himself, he had consulted a very skilful director, who had not only approved of it, but had also animated him to be constant in his undertaking. This was sufficient to induce the wise confessor also to leave him to follow the divine guidance.

Besides these confessors, there were also persons, who, fearing for Benedict's perseverance in the holy and rigid plan of life which he led in the world, through the occasions and risks which everywhere abound therein, sought to persuade

a harbour, he would be less exposed to dangers. To which he replied, "that this was not the will of God, for if God had willed it, He would have disposed events differently, but God willed him to remain thus in the world. God would assist him by His grace, and he could do all things, and could remain unhurt in the midst of the fire, like the three holy youths in the furnace of Babylon."

There was another kind person in Loretto, who, compassionating the hard life which he led, exhorted him to remain constantly at Loretto in the employment which he would procure for him, of serving masses in that church, or to make himself a Camaldolese monk in the hermitage situated on the mountain of Ancona, a few miles distant from Loretto. Benedict, lifting up his eyes to heaven, as he was accustomed to do in giving his answers, and having thought about it, answered in a resolute manner, "That is not the path in which God wishes me to walk." He was very sure that the severe road he had taken was the will of God; the interior light which he had received from God, and the exterior approbation of his confessors, gave him this security.

HIS PILGRIMAGES TO HOLY PLACES. HIS DEVOUT MANNER OF PROCEEDING IN THEM. REPUTATION OF SANCTITY AND EXAMPLES OF HEROIC VIRTUES LEFT BY HIM EVERYWHERE.

In the same year 1770, in which he left the monastery of Sept Fontaines, in accordance with the Divine inspiration of which his confessors had approved, he began the course of his pilgrimages to holy places. The manner in which he performed them was on foot in a miserable and ragged dress, which he never changed for the variation of the seasons, without any provision, confiding in Divine Providence, caring nothing about the inclemency of severe and snowy weather in winter, and the very hot and uncomfortable weather in summer, often leaving the beaten roads and going by solitary and rugged paths out of the way to avoid any commerce with travellers or pilgrims, satisfied with that God alone who guided him, and with whom he was always united wherever he went. "The omnipotent hand of God guides me;" thus he wrote to his parents on leaving La Chartreuse. He chiefly slept on the bare ground in the open

long and painful journeys. Though he only appeared before men as a poor man, abject, and a beggar, yet before God and the angels he made as noble and grand an appearance as his exterior was despicable, through the train of virtues which everywhere accompanied him. He walked always with great modesty; he never allowed his eyes to look upon those beauties which attract the curiosity of travellers; always absorbed in God, who granted him very sublime lights of the understanding and very ardent affections of the will.

In passing through some cities and countries, he imitated our blessed Saviour when He went about all the cities and towns, doing good, and healing every disease. Our blessed Lord however went "healing all," Benedict only some persons, according to the circumstances in which God placed him; here consoling the afflicted, there healing the sick; in one place giving wholesome advice for the good of the soul, in another obtaining favours from God to reward those who sometimes lodged him through charity; everywhere he gave examples of mortification, humility, strict observance of the Divine commands, and of other virtues, of which I shall speak separately in the third part. Some little, however, will be mentioned in speaking of some of his pilgrimages, that the simple narration of them may not be too dry.

We shall see verified in Benedict the three promises of God in Ps. xxxi. 10, "I will give thee understanding, and I will instruct in this way, in which thou shalt go; I will fix My eyes upon thee." The first is, that God will give to any one who walks in the path which is pleasing to Him, understanding to know and avoid the snares of his infernal enemies: "Intellectum tibi dabo." The second is, that God Himself will be his conductor, that under His guidance he may not deviate at all from the right path, and by the help of His grace may preserve in every place the purity of his morals: "Instruem te in via hac, qua gradieris." The third is, that He will always behold him with a loving eye, giving him at all times the interior assistance of His grace, and of His lights, and external help, that the means of subsistence may never be wanting to him: "Firmabo super te oculos meos."

In the first place, Benedict directed his view to the Holy House of Loretto, which is the most celebrated and venerable Sanctuary, and the most frequented by all, on account of the very sublime mysteries operated by God therein, during the residence of the holy Mother of God, the Queen of the world, and through the prodigies by which Almighty God has been pleased to authenticate the veneration paid to so singular a Sanctuary. The first time that he visited it, in the beginning of November, 1770, there being yet no knowledge of him, and a great crowd of pilgrims, his conduct was not particularly noticed; still there were not wanting some among the servants of the holy place, or those who were present, who from only seeing his continual and very devout behaviour, formed a good opinion of him ; nevertheless the impression made on their minds, was like the impression that a switch makes in still water, which speedily disappears. In later years his singular devotion, his continued residence, his modesty, and his whole behaviour, made him shine forth out of the numerous crowd of pilgrims, like the moon amongst the stars; and for this reason some persons of great discernment, having noticed him, began to observe his proceedings, to examine him closely, and mark his conduct minutely, from morning till night, in and out of the church, and they gave very high testimony of him in the juridical Processes. These will be read with great pleasure and admiration when they occur in the course of the history.

He went from Loretto to Assisi, to proceed afterwards from thence to Rome: he arrived on the 18th of November, 1770. He venerated the memory of St. Francis of Assisium ; with great devotion he procured to be inscribed in the arch-confraternity of the Cordigeri of the saint, founded by Sixtus V. the Sovereign Pontiff, and according to its rules, he first made his confession ; then he received with very tender devotion the Bread of Heaven, and began to wear from that time a little cord on his bare flesh, which was not known till the body was unclothed after death. From thence he went to Rome in the beginning of December in the same year, 1770, and was received into the hospital of St. Louis of the French for three days, according to custom. He remained in Rome for many months, till the September of the following year, 1771. Here his manner of life was to spend the day in the churches, and sleep at night in the open air. Of the manner in which he visited the great places of devotion, the sacred memorials of our Divine Redeemer, and the churches dedicated to the Blessed Virgin, we shall speak more seasonably in another place. In Rome, as in Loretto, he was not noticed the first year, except in common with the crowd of pilgrims and strangers who are accustomed to flock thither; but in the years of his constant residence, the tenor of his holy life attracted the admiration of all, who began to observe and notice his conduct minutely, and they afterwards gave depositions in the Processes of the heroic virtues practised by him; his invincible patience in the ill-treatment he received; his great contempt of himself; his very long prayers, not only of several hours, but of whole days, and all his other virtues, of which an account will be given elsewhere.

rather we should say, God was pleased
st him to the world as His beloved
After some months devoutly employed
; the sanctuaries in Rome, he left to
n the Holy House of Loretto, which
ne his delight, about the month of
l.
rning he went to the city of Fabriano,
ie body of St. Romuald, abbot, founder
amaldolese monks and hermits. The
and devotion which he showed during
veneration of the saint, began to draw
n from every one who beheld him.
to a higher degree in the church of
s the Greater, where on the 13th of
feast of St. Anthony of Padua was
l with very great pomp. He was in
h by the time the doors were opened
he morning. There he began to pray
ices, but with such devotion, modesty,
ur, that the parish priest, Signor D.
ggetti, who had the direction of the
ntering early, was struck at the sight,
ved him attentively while unseen by
he had the opportunity several times
him on his knees, motionless and reve-

the day, when there was no one in the
he had prayed for a long time with hi
extended in the form of a cross. The
admiration increased exceedingly at this a
in considering the devotion of this poo
so indifferent about himself that he h
even thought of taking refreshment, bei
ployed in prayer, and he judged him in
mind to be a saint.

His admiration rose to an extreme de
the evening when the doors were going
closed, on hearing from the sacristan th
poor man had begged of him to allow
remain in the church that night. Thou
condition of the poor man was quite u
to the priest, he could not suspect him
a rogue or a hypocrite, for no one can
so high who has not the true Spirit
Urged therefore by his generous charity, i
to give him accommodation for sleeping at
he told the sacristan to offer him a lod
a little hospital above the church itself,
provide him with food, with some money
he gave him, it being very plain to him t

On the following morning when the priest returned early to his church, he found him kneeling there with his hands joined in the act of prayer. Soon after, going into the sacristy, Benedict went to him, and very humbly and modestly asked him to hear his confession, to allow him to serve his mass, and to give him the Bread of Angels. Having heard his confession, he was confirmed in the idea he had conceived of his sanctity, not having found in him sufficient matter for absolution. His reverence, devotion, and fervour in serving at mass and communicating were so great, that not only the priest, but those who were present, were moved by them, and some afterwards congratulated him on having communicated a saint, and on having had him as a server at mass.

A few days after he made to D. Maria Paggetti a general confession of his whole past life. The confessor was greatly moved, and exceedingly edified to find in him, First, baptismal innocence faithfully preserved till that time. Secondly, abundant grace bestowed on him by God. Thirdly, his fervent correspondence with that grace at all times. Then with the same edifying devotion with which he had first received the Divine Sacrament, he remained fifteen days longer in Fabriano, in the course of which time he received again twice the Sacraments of Penance, and the Blessed Eucharist. Every morning he went early to church, assisted at mass, prayed the whole day, and only returned at night to his lodging.

Such a holy system of life could not be so concealed in any manner by his humility, as not to be known to many in Fabriano; hence it was, that when he left the church many pointed him out, and amongst them he was held for a saint, and was beheld by them with an astonished and respectful eye. Absorbed in God, and plunged into the abyss of his own nothingness, he went to other churches, remaining there usually till it was time to return at night to his lodging.

On one of these fifteen days, which was the 23rd of June, the fame of his sanctity extended itself still farther in Fabriano through something which happened at the house of some devout females. One very pious woman, named Vincenza Rocca, on a very wet day saw him pass near her house quite wet and dripping with rain. Moved by compassion she offered him shelter in her house; Benedict accepted the kindness, and saluted her by saying, "Praised be Jesus Christ," but with his eyes cast down and head bent. She was struck at the first sight of him; his poor dress, the crucifix on his breast, the rosary round his arm, his words, his demeanour, every thing breathed devotion, so that she not only felt pleasure in having him in her house, but took courage to mention to him certain griefs which rather distressed her. Benedict, who was filled with the Spirit of God, brought under her consideration the confidence which we ought to have in the infinite goodness of God and His fatherly Providence; the wrong which we do to God by not casting all our cares upon Him, who is a 'ather of infinite love; and he expressed so many entiments in such a manner, that he wonderfully ıoderated her distress; and being consoled she ent on to ask him to recommend her and her hildren to God. These were at a little distance. Benedict, with a loving countenance and amiable ıanners, called them to him; he told them kind-y, that if they wished to be children of Jesus Christ, they must be very careful not to tell ies, or be disobedient, that they must always ive in the fear of God, with other instructions uitable to their age. The pious mother formed high opinion of him, and seeing him ready o go away, she begged him to come again; he romised and departed. Vincenza ran immedi-tely full of joy, to relate the whole minutely o a young woman, Vincenza Fiordi by name, who was her neighbour, and for nine years had een confined to her bed by a disease of the tomach: she was well known in Fabriano for er piety, and her entire resignation in her long nd painful illness, and she mildly complained ecause she had not brought Benedict to her ouse, and she begged that when he came back he would do her that charity.

He returned, in fact, the following day, which vas the feast of St. John Baptist. Being re-quested to accompany her to her sick neighbour, e consented, to satisfy the desire of both. Hav-ng entered the room, he saluted the sick person nd those who were present, by saying, with his ead bent and with an humble voice and demea-our, "Praised be Jesus Christ." The mere sight of him infused consolation and great respect into the sick person's heart, so that she took courage to explain to him her very painful state. The sentiments of soul with which the servant of God endeavoured to animate her to bear willingly the cross of Jesus Christ, were so lively, and suggested with so much sweetness, that the invalid said that she had never heard any servant of God speak in so lively and consolatory a manner as Benedict; adding, that in listening to him it seemed to her that she heard Jesus Christ Himself, or a saint, and that she had received more comfort and consolation from him than from any one else in so many years.

Her consolation and opinion of him were increased at the time of dinner. It was near midday, and the sick person requested, in order that she might not be so soon deprived of his presence and spiritual sentiments, that he would dine in her house. Benedict did not refuse; being an imitator of Jesus Christ in accepting similar invitations, he imitated Him also in the end for which he did it. "Jesus Christ went to banquets," says St. Anselm, "that He might have an opportunity of teaching, and might bestow spiritual food on those who had invited Him." Benedict accepted it, not for the sake of feeding his body with meat; he cared as little for it as if it were a putrefaction; but to feed the mind of the guests with instructions and spiritual maxims. His manner in dining, the small quantity of food he took, and the discourse he held during the time, are a proof of this. With regard to his manner, he first lifted up his eyes, hands, and mind to God, and thanked Him for the love He has shown towards man in creating so many things to nourish him even delicately. He practised politeness, and the civil manners usual to those who are well born. The sparing quantity of his food astonished those who were at table with him; he took only a few mouthfuls of the meats which had been prepared, and being pressed to take more, he answered sincerely, "A little suffices for me; a superfluity given to the body serves for nothing but to feed the worms." His conversation was all regarding God and salvation, and he spoke with so much agreeableness and fervour, that all were moved, and thought more of feeding their souls with his holy words, than of nourishing their bodies with meat. When dinner was finished he gave thanks to God, standing for this purpose in a very devout attitude. Having thanked this devout company, he wished to give them a proof of his gratitude; he wrote there himself the prayer which I copy below, addressed to our Lord Jesus Christ; and told them that if they devoutly recited it, their house and the neighbouring ones would be exempt from the scourge of earthquakes, thunder, and lightning. The effect verified the promise and authenticated his words. A few years later, when Benedict was still living, a terrible earthquake took place in Fabriano on Easter Sunday, overthrowing many houses, but this and the neighbouring ones stood firm and uninjured, which was attributed to the promise made to them by the hol man.

Prayer against earthquakes, thunder, and lightning. "Jesus Christus Rex gloriæ venit in pace. Deus homo factus est. Verbum caro factum est. Christus de Maria Virgine natus est. Christus per medium illorum ihat in pace. Christus crucifixus est. Christus mortuus est. Christus sepultus est. Christus resurrexit. Christus ascendit in cœlum. Christus vincit. Christus regnat. Christus imperat. Christus ab omni fulgure nos defendat. Jesus nobiscum est. Pater, Ave, Gloria." This prayer was printed and distributed in Fabriano while Benedict was still living.

Having left this prayer he took his leave. One person accompanied him down stairs, and in that short time manifested to him some internal agitations which kept his mind in continual affliction. He, in a few words, strengthened by the Holy Ghost, changed the storm into a perfect calm.

Everywhere the servant of God left in all persons a great desire of his presence; all spoke of him in every place with praise and great admiration, publishing what had happened to them during that short time he spent in their house; every one strove to have him in his house, and to speak with him on things relating to the soul, and they esteemed those fortunate who were honoured with his presence. It is truly surprising and a thing for which we should praise God. Benedict was not come from any desert clothed in the respectable dress of a hermit. He was not a religious of a considerable order, nor a prince, nor a gentleman with fine and splendid clothes, attended by numerous servants. He was a secular, covered with rags, thin in countenance, of despicable appearance, humble, modest, and retired. And yet we see him greatly respected by all who beheld him; we see his presence and the opportunity of speaking to him sought after. So true it is, that even on earth God wills that the sanctity of His servants should be honoured and venerated. "Thy friends, O God, are made exceedingly honourable." (Ps. cxxxviii. 17.) "Better is one that is poor and wise than a king that is foolish, who knoweth not to foresee for hereafter," (Eccles. iv. 13;) a poor and ragged man who has true wisdom, which consists in loving and serving God, being much better in every way than a great personage, who making a considerable figure in this world, wants the most valuable prize in the fear of God, and of providing in time to secure an eternity of happiness.

The servant of God having perceived the signs of esteem given by these persons and others in Fabriano, speedily and secretly departed, abhorring honours more than the world hates insults. He only secretly desired the sacristan to thank the priest for him, for the charity he had shown him, a charity for which God would reward him; and instead of going at night as usual to the hospital, he departed on the 27th of June, quite alone in the dark, with his little bundle on his back, to pursue his pilgrimages. Our Lord soon verified the promise of His servant to the kind priest, by a legacy left unexpectedly a little after to his Luogo Pio.

CHAPTER IV.

OTHER PILGRIMAGES MADE BY BENEDICT, UNDER THE GUIDANCE AND PROTECTION OF GOD.

Many were the pilgrimages made by Benedict Joseph to the most celebrated sanctuaries, and all of them in the most devout and edifying manner that can be imagined, as we have shown already in the second chapter. This was the inspiration which God gave him, this the tenor of life which God required from him; and it is a very surprising thing, that in so many thousands of miles passed over in this manner, amongst so many insults, inconveniences, so much want, and the most sparing quantity of food, he never fell ill so as to be obliged by sickness to remain in any house or hospital; he was always strong, always well, cheerful at all times and in every place. But my surprise ceases, and that of others should also cease, when we reflect that Almighty God, by His divine Providence, always proportions His graces to the vocation He gives. God called him in a very particular manner to this form of life, and God always assisted him, verifying in him the promise explained in chapter second: "I will fix My eyes upon thee, in this way in which thou shalt go."

To mention here minutely all the journeys which he made after the first to the Holy House of Loretto, from 1771, till the last year of his life, which was 1783, would prove tiresome to the reader. I will therefore proceed in this manner: I will give a short notice of them all in this chapter, and let it suffice to know, that in them all, and in every place, he always left a most agreeable odour of sanctity, that the mere view of him gained him veneration as a saint, and that in none of so many different kingdoms did he at all change his very rigid system. It is true, however, that in some cities persecutions were not wanting to him, through the idea wrongly formed of him in the beginning, as a thief, a rogue, and a wanderer: God permitted this, to give greater lustre to his sanctity, to purify his virtue, and to make him a more lively copy of our blessed Redeemer, who was also held in some cities for a sinner, a disturber of the people, a deceiver, and a criminal.

Having for the first time paid his devotions to the holy mother of God at Loretto, and having visited the sanctuaries in Rome and Fabriano, he went to Bari in 1771, to the much-frequented sanctuary of St. Nicholas. Then he went to Naples, to venerate that great saint and principal protector of the city, St. Januarius. Afterwards he passed into Tuscany, being desirous of paying his devotions to his beloved advocate, St. Francis of Assisium, in the sanctuary situated among the mountains of Alvernia, where the saint was honoured with the real impression of the holy stigmas. From thence he went into Switzerland, to the famous sanc-

of our Blessed Lady in Einsiedlen, he visited five times in the course of years. He went into Germany, then rance, far, however, from his home and ·ents, whom he never sought to see again e left the monastery of Sept Fontaines, told them in the last letter he wrote to 'rom Montreville, that they would never a again except in the valley of Josaphat. ınce and Germany, and wherever he ed to be, though merely passing through, ted the most celebrated sanctuaries. ›ry tender affection towards the Blessed venerated at Loretto, urged him to visit ıce every year, and therefore in his jour-) so contrived as not to fail any year in :hither. He returned to Rome in the ng of September, to avail himself of at treasure of indulgences by the jubi-

his illustrious example, through the very devout manner in which he performed them, and through the heroic acts of virtue which he practised during the whole time that he remained in Loretto.

CHAPTER V.

PILGRIMAGES TO THE HOLY HOUSE AT LORETTO: HIS MANNER OF PERFORMING THEM. THE HEROIC ACTS OF VIRTUE WHICH HE EXERCISED.

His journeys to the Holy House of Loretto were more frequent than to any other sanctuary. They were eleven in number altogether. This is plain from the authentic documents which he carried with him, and from the Processes made in Loretto. He made them in as many years as he lived, after his first journey in 1770. From that first time of visiting it, he was so affected that he could not satiate himself with seeing it, venerating it, melting into tears, and with loving affection kissing again and again those holy walls, and inflaming his heart more strongly with love for the holy Mother of God. In his last journey he himself prophesied that it would be the last of his life, and God also caused it to be foretold by others, and the fact verified the prediction.

The following is the plan to which he adhered in performing them, and it may at least in part serve as a model for any one who might wish to perform it as a duty. In the first place he ardently desired to arrive as soon as possible at the Holy House. Love, when it is sincere, sets the heart on fire, and, as it were, gives wings to the feet; thus, being advised not to hurry so much, that he might not have to undergo greater suffering, he answered, "that through his desire to arrive soon at that holy place, he endeavoured to hasten his departure and travel quickly." He took very little repose on the way, always walking with new vigour. He never thought about provision for his journey, he entirely confided in God, so that when once two pauls were offered to him, as an assistance, he only accepted one, which he received through obedience, it being sufficient for his nourishment that day. This he did always; when more was offered to him for his journey he would never take more than one paul. His heart, inflamed with love for Mary and abandoned to Divine Providence, thought of other things than those which regarded his wretched body, as he called it. Nor did he think more about clothing to defend himself from the rigour of the season, but lightly and poorly clothed as he was and in rags, he travelled on, to the edification and wonder also of a person, who, observing him in this state, attests it in the Processes. Passing once through Cossignano a very pious priest, seeing him so badly clothed, but knowing from his countenance and devout appearance, the spirit which he nourished in his heart, would lodge him entirely in his own house, giving him refreshment, and treating him with that courtesy which is the effect of true charity. Benedict's civil manners, unaffected piety, and agreeable company, so charmed his heart, that he did not know how to separate from him; he wished to deter him from leaving so soon, but overcome by his eagerness to reach the Holy House, he was obliged to leave him at liberty. Notwithstanding, he sought to have the pleasure of his company a little longer, by accompanying him some way on the road from Cossignano, and in separating from him, hearing his lively expressions of gratitude, and seeing his humility, which prompted him reverently to kiss his hand, he was so grieved that he felt, he said himself, as if his soul were detaching itself from his body; he could not restrain his tears, and shutting himself up in his room, notwithstanding the reproofs of his brother-priests and friends, he vented his grief in tears for a long time.

In proceeding to Loretto on another occasion, heavy rain came on towards dark, which wetted him completely, so that he was dripping with water from head to foot. A worthy man with his brother having perceived this from his house situated in the country between Monte Lupone and Monte Santo, speedily offered him a lodging. The servant of God asked for the oven as a charity, but it was judged less inconvenient to place him in their own stable. Though his torn clothes were displeasing to the eye, still feeling themselves inspired with devotion by his devout and humble behaviour, they treated him with civility, giving him some refreshment. During his scanty

object of his journey, the Holy House of They perceived from this that he was nc world, and that he was some good se God; they provided him with straw an under which to sleep at night, and they locking the stable door. Having opened dawn, Benedict was found on his knees, with his arms extended in the form of This devout attitude raised the opinio: sanctity which they had formed the da, Hearing afterwards that he came fron they took courage to ask him to menti bers for the lottery, believing that Gc inspire one who was dear to Him, thus that they understood that the securit, numbers does not depend on the har draws them, nor on human knowledg cannot avail on such a point, it being delusion to believe the contrary, for pressly said in the Holy Scripture, t] depend on God alone, "Sortes mittunt num sed a Domino temperantur." \ God that this were understood by the p lovers of such games! How much moı many cares, how many sorrows would t] themselves by recommending themselve;

question, they asked him if he had ever been present at the drawing in Rome. The servant of God was silent, as if he had not understood. When asked a second time, he answered, "What drawing? What lottery? This is not for poor people." This reply made them blush, and they did not attempt to proceed any farther. Beginning then to take leave of them, a small loaf was presented to him for his journey. He said he would not take it, for God would not let him want elsewhere for a person to provide him with food; at last, being importuned, he accepted it and departed, continuing his hard journey to the Holy House of Loretto.

To the painful manner of performing his journeys, he added another method, which must have given him no little trouble, that was, to go as much as he could out of the beaten paths. Being once asked by a priest, how long a time he employed in his journey to Loretto, he answered, "I do not know, for I always go out of the road." He who is accustomed to travel will understand well, how much trouble such a method of proceeding must cause, for in following this plan, mountains and hills must be crossed, torrents passed, he must walk over loose and sharp stones, go longer distances, and expose himself to precipices. This difficulty must have been more considerable for him, who was so miserably clothed and provided with nothing, with torn stockings and shoes broken into holes, only suitable to admit the rain, not to defend the feet. But he cared nothing for his difficulties, through the love which transported him. Love makes us bear any pain peacefully, it lightens it, and even changes it into delight. The labours of those who love are not burdensome.

In his last journey in 1782, he occupied two-and-twenty days, as he confessed when asked; for crossing a mountain covered with snow, he was obliged to stop, benumbed with cold; then arriving in Loretto at night, he sought no other than spiritual fire to warm himself. The following morning being Good Friday, he went very early to the church, and remained there till evening without eating anything. What was his behaviour afterwards in Loretto, and how many heroic virtues he there practised, the following chapter will inform the reader.

CHAPTER VI.

HIS MOST EXEMPLARY BEHAVIOUR IN LORETTO, BY DAY AND BY NIGHT, IN THE CHURCH AND ELSEWHERE.

His behaviour at Loretto was so edifying, that excepting the first time when he was not yet known, in the second and subsequent annual visits which he made, there was not one of the priests or assistants in that great church who did not consider him as a saint. In consequence of this opinion, an order was given to the soldiers who keep guard at the little door of the Holy House, that they should allow him to enter when he pleased. A priest belonging to the church, reflecting on the conduct of Benedict, on his fervour, his contempt of himself, and his assiduity at all times, said within himself, "This man is either a fool, or a great saint;" nor need this surprise us, for it was said of our blessed Lord, because of the extraordinary works He performed in Palestine, "He is become mad," (Mark, iii. 21,) on account of which even His own friends thought of confining Him as a madman.

This priest knew afterwards clearly, that Benedict's proceedings were entirely the effect of sanctity and not of folly, and he became one of his most respectful admirers, and a zealous publisher of his virtues.

When Benedict arrived in Loretto, he went immediately to pay his devotions to Mary, ragged, tired, and faint as he was, from his long journey, refusing any kind invitation. He remained the whole day in the church, from the time the doors were opened, till they were closed at night, always kneeling, always motionless and in sublime prayer, excepting that he spent part of the time before the most Blessed Sacrament in the church, and part within the Holy House, which is encompassed by the church. He generally spent in the Holy House those hours when the crowd is smaller, which are those occurring between mid-day and vespers, that he might pour out more freely his loving affections towards the blessed Virgin, weeping through tenderness, and esteeming himself unworthy to remain in a place so holy and venerable, in which the Mother of God had dwelt. He assisted at the Litanies and other prayers which are every day recited there, but with a devotion so extraordinary, and answering with so clear a voice, and so much compunction, that he shone forth wonderfully from amongst the others.

In the church he endeavoured to put himself for prayer in places apart and hidden, that he might be less observed, and give a more free course to his interior affections, but the situation itself betrayed his humility; for some persons seeing him every day and the whole day in a retired place, with so much constancy and devotion, felt great curiosity to observe him, to be more and more edified, and to know who he was; and they went unseen by him purposely to see him.

Amongst these, we may remark particularly Don Gaspare Valeri, one of the priests belonging to the church. The doors being fastened one night, he placed himself quietly behind him, to see where he went to lodge at night; he observed that he went to sit near the side door of the church, on the left hand, supporting his head with his hand, in the attitude of one who is meditating on great things, lifting up his eyes from time to time to heaven. Going near to him Don Gaspare asked him if he wanted an alms; he answered, "If I find any thing, and if any one gives me something." He proceeded to ask him where he slept at night. "In no other place than this," was his reply. In effect, Don Gaspare Valeri going about dawn to the church, to fulfil the duties of his charge, found him several times waiting for the opening of the doors, sometimes extended on the cold marble, sometimes leaning on his little bundle. He felt so much compassion for him, that he could not help telling him, that he had better sleep under the porches, or in some bake-house in the country, rather than in the open air, and on those marble stones, which were very hurtful to health. Benedict answered, "A poor man throws himself down where he can, he does not seek a comfortable bed, and I like to be alone, and to enjoy peace." Yielding, however, to his advice, he began from that time to go to some bake-house in the country, at a distance from the Holy House, and from thence he walked every morning about dawn to the Holy House, where he remained the whole day without any food.

One morning he arrived there, from the place where he had slept the preceding night, so weary and covered with dirt, from the heavy rain which had fallen that night and the day before, by which the roads had been broken up and spoiled, that he ingenuously confessed to Sigr. Valeri, that he had suffered much, but that he was particularly grieved, because the distance of the place, and the inclemency of the weather, shortened the time of his remaining in the church, and he begged him to find some place near for him. Signor Valeri found one kindly for him, and went with him thither the following day, ice him to leave off the rags which he wore; it he refused everything, excepting the trowrs, saying that he was not precisely in want anything but these, and that the rest might given to some poor person more needy than was. He took of what was prepared for super only enough for his necessary nourishment, id passed the rest of the night in devout colquies, which were heard by a person who was ear.

But in later years he would no longer use his place of lodging, though it was near, for ie number of persons in the vicinity disturbed ie quiet of his prayers. Lodgings at a disince shortened too much, on account of the ing way he had to walk, the time of remainig in the church, which he considered precious. ignor Valeri would not consent to his passing he night in the open air, and in this perplexity ot knowing what to do, scarcely had he opend his mind to Signor Valeri, than he with rompt charity offered him his own house; Benedict would not, however, avail himself of it, saying, on hearing of the number of persons there, "There are too many women."

Signor Valeri sought then for a more convenient accommodation; he spoke to Signora Barbara and Signor Gaudenzio Sori, a very pious and charitable couple; and scarcely had he mentioned Benedict to them, than they showed themselves not only willing, but very desirous to receive him in their own house. Barbara having seen him one day as a poor pilgrim in the church, full of modesty and devotion, was so moved and edified, that she formed a great desire to lodge him in her own house; and in a similar manner, Gaudenzio, seeing him once under the public lodges, in a devout attitude, with his eyes sometimes cast down, sometimes raised up to heaven, could not behold him without shedding tears of tenderness and devotion. At this request of Signor Valeri the devotion of both grew stronger, and they esteemed it an honour to give a lodging to such a servant of God. They appointed a person to wait for his leaving the church, as he usually did at sunset, who was to conduct him to their house. Benedict being arrived, and having saluted them with, "Praised be Jesus Christ," gave a proof of his humility, saying, that he was undeserving of such charity; but full of joy, they led him to a little room prepared for him, and furnished with a bed. Benedict seeing it, said, "Why so many conveniences? they do not suit poor people. It suffices to the poor man to have a roof over his head at night and a little earth to lie upon; there is no necessity for a bed, and I should prefer some meaner place, if there be any." Hearing that there was not, and that the little room prepared was so low that the cellars were immediately under it, that there was no worse place in the house, and that the bed was a poor man's bed, he yielded immediately. Being conducted to supper, in his humility he was astonished at their charity: "Is it not sufficient," said he, "to give me a place for sleeping, will you also give me something to eat?" They knew his humility and reluctance, but being also aware of his obedience, "We wish it to be so," said they, "we wish you to eat." Seeing a whole small loaf before him, he begged that they would give him some fragments. "Poor people," he said, "should eat bits." They were obliged to satisfy him, and yield to the spirit of poverty which was so dear to him. Then raising his hands and eyes to heaven, and blessing God, he took a very scanty supper.

When supper was ended, and he had gone back to his room, he wished to be locked up in it, saying, "I wish you to lock me up, you do not know me, I am a poor man; it is better to lock me in; have the goodness to do so." Thus, through his humility, he made it appear as if some deceit or theft might be feared from a poor man like himself; but in reality, he wished to be shut up in order to pray and proceed with more liberty. In effect, when the door was opened in the morning, he was always found on his knees, as it were out of himself; the bed

, but in every word that proceedeth mouth of God," (Matt. iv. 4,) and when ses He can give support by the Bread which is Jesus in His adorable Sacra- om His servant often received: "I am d of Life," (John, vi. 35;) and by the understanding, which are the bright h which God favoured him, lights which im to remain with great pleasure fixed nees in the church, He supported him interior draught of His wholesome wisdom, a water which quenches every rst: "The Lord our God fed him with d of Life and understanding, and gave water of wholesome wisdom to drink," xv. 3;) and again, "He that shall drink ter that I will give him, shall not thirst " (John, iv. 13.) Benedict could say our blessed Redeemer, "My meat is to do the will of Him that sent me," (John, iv. 34;) and it being God's will that he should follow that path, He maintained him in strength and health like those three holy youths of Babylon, without the polluted meats and drink of the palace, with a few vegetables, and with water only.

They were yet more surprised to witness his detachment from all things, as he never received anything but what was precisely necessary. Several times he was offered stockings, shoes, shirts, and sometimes upper clothing, but he refused everything, and only accepted an old hat and a pair of shoes a good deal worn, his own being so ragged and worthless, that the servant threw them away amongst the dirt as entirely useless. The great charity of his hosts made them wish to give him a new coat of coarse cloth, knowing that he would not have anything elegant and fine, but it was not possible to make him receive it. "I do not want it," he said, "give it to some other poor man." Being commanded and obliged by obedience to receive an old shirt, as his own was torn and filthy, he bowed his head and accepted it. His pious hosts, in their holy solicitude, left for him the night before his departure for Rome a pair of stockings and shoes in his room, saying, that he might use them for his journey. When he was gone, they found them in the place where they had been put.

CHAPTER VII.

BENEDICT'S SPIRIT IS EXAMINED BY A CONFESSOR IN LORETTO.

I CONSIDER it of value to this work, glorious to virtue, and an advantage to confessors, and to any one who may read these pages, to relate here clearly, the trials made of Benedict's spirit by one of the confessors of the penitentiary at Loretto. Such trials and his manner of proceeding, the truth and solidity of spirit, and of the heroic virtues found in Benedict, are so surprising, that whoever has read them, explained at length on oath in the Processes, has asserted them to be sufficient to make Benedict considered as a great saint, and to merit for him the honours of canonization.

The confessor was Padre Giuseppe Maria Temple, a Frenchman of the Conventual Minors of St. Francis, a theologian well versed in ascetical and mystical theology, a penitentiary first in 1766 for the French nation in the Basilica of St. Francis in Assisium, and in 1773, penitentiary for the same nation in the Basilica of the Holy House of Loretto.

One day, which was the 11th of February, 1766, as he was leaving his confessional near mid-day, after having been employed the whole morning in hearing confessions, Benedict presented himself before him, like a poor man as he was, ragged and humble. Being asked if he wanted to go to confession, he answered with his accustomed civility, that he should consider it indiscretion to add to his fatigue at so inconvenient an hour; he only ventured to ask him to listen to a few short words. Being permitted to speak, "Since," said he, with an air of sweetness which breathed devotion, "I find myself happily, by the goodness of God and of the Blessed Virgin, in this sanctuary, I should wish to place myself in all things under obedience to you, and at present it will be sufficient that you give me leave, if you judge it proper, to follow my usual method in taking food." The confessor was surprised at so unexpected and singular a request. Then he asked him in a grave manner, "What is your usual method?" "I am accustomed," he replied, "to nourish myself every day with refuse and cast-off things which I find on the roads, orange peelings, cabbage leaves, decayed fruit, and any useless thing that is thrown out of the windows; I only eat what is sufficient for the day, and at night nothing. If I find nothing, I never ask an alms; I accept it in a limited manner if it is given to me. If nothing is given to me, I go into the country, eat grass and drink the water which I find." The confessor, still more astonished, began to suspect some deceit in hearing things which he had never heard or read of, and frowning, he asked him if such a method had been approved by his directors; he answered with sincerity, "Some have, and some have not, according to the inspiration of God, and I have always obeyed." "Oh, very well," replied the confesser in a rough manner, and with an imperious tone, "in virtue of holy obedience I command you, that in the company of that person," (pointing out one who was well known to him at a little distance,) "you eat whatever he gives you, and come back to me to-day; show me your certificates, and then I will hear your confession." Benedict bowed his head, and with a cheerful countenance obeyed everything promptly.

In the meantime the pious confessor had recourse to God, the Father of Lights, that on so important a point He would give him the necessary lights to know the truth, begging the intercession of the Blessed Virgin as the most efficacious means to obtain it.

Benedict presented himself in the afternoon at the time when two other pilgrims were engaged with the confessor. Father Temple was a little disturbed, for one of the two was trying to deceive him, pretending to be a Frenchman, to get money from him, whereas he was not so, and his papers did not show him to be so. On this account, doubting about some deception in Benedict, he desired him with a harsh and angry voice to show his papers. Benedict immediately offered them with a serene countenance; having observed them, examined them, and found them agree, he began to lay aside his suspicions. Nevertheless, he asked him from whence he came. Hearing from Rome, he asked him for his certificates of confession and communion. Benedict was silent, standing with his head bent, his eyes cast down, and his hands crossed on his breast. This silence again raised suspicion in the confessor, and he began to treat him severely, adding reproofs, and saying that this was not the manner of visiting sanctuaries, without approaching the sacraments, and on that account there was room to doubt that he was a Hugonot, a hypocrite, or infected with some other heresy.

The servant of God listened in profound silence with a tranquil and unmoved countenance, remaining in his devout and humble attitude. Father Temple looked at him attentively, and seeing his serenity, added sharp words to his reproofs. "Are you deaf or dumb?" said he, "do you not understand? do you not answer?" He understood very well, but did not answer for the reason which he afterwards gave. It seems to me that I see in him a copy of our Divine Redeemer Jesus Christ when bound, believed to be guilty, and interrogated at the tribunal, he remained in profound silence, "Jesus autem tacebat." The good confessor did not know how to determine; his tranquillity and his attitude made him think him a saint, while his not replying to a reasonable question was an argument of the contrary. He said within himself, "This man must be a great saint or a devil." Breaking off then the conference with them all, he desired them to prepare themselves well for sacramental confession on the following day. During the remainder of that day he remained in doubt and oppressed, not knowing what determination to follow, though certain glimpses of interior light inclined him to believe him a saint, and therefore he continued to beg greater light of God and the Blessed Virgin.

Almighty God began to give him more the following morning. Finding him at the confessional, he anxiously inquired when he was last at confession and communion; he replied, "Eight days ago, and on the journey I also went to confession and communion another time." Being asked if this was in Rome, he answered, that he often went to confession in the Basilica of St. John Lateran, that he had made general confessions, and as for communion, he went as often as his confessors ordered it. "But why did you not tell me this yesterday when I asked you? Answer me; I order you to do so in virtue of holy obedience." In answering, he first gave deep sighs, and shed tears as he was accustomed to do, whenever he was commanded in virtue of holy obedience; being grieved to discover his interior, which he did not wish to be known to any one but Almighty God. He answered, "I was silent, because others were present." This answer began to calm the doubts of his confessor. His tranquillity increased, when desiring to instruct him, as he was accustomed to instruct pilgrims about those things which it is necessary for a Christian to know, and particularly those regarding confession and communion, he found him not only very well instructed in all, but also deeply penetrated with eternal truths. As nothing further was required, he de-

he visibly trembled in the same manner as a man guilty of great crimes would do before the judge.

The doubts disappearing much more from the confessor's mind, he encouraged him to mention his sins. He said with humility and weeping, that he had not loved God as he ought, that he had been ungrateful for His graces and benefits, that he had put an obstacle to his attaining that degree of virtue to which Almighty God required him to ascend, and to which any other person who had been favoured by God as he had been, would have attained. Thus he spoke, and what he said gave greater tranquillity to the confessor. Seeing however in him very great humility, the characteristic of a true spirit, he wisely thought proper to increase it by reproving him, as one who did not know how to make his confession. "What are all these general accusations?" said he; "mention your sins in particular." He again spoke, but repeated the same, but with more lively compunction, more profound humility, reproaching himself with his ingratitude towards a God of

by a formal precept of obedience to answer sincerely, Yes or No."

He began the examination first upon mortal sins, and the commandments of God, one by one in order; then upon those of the Church, but with that great prudence which such a penitent required. He found him to have been not only exempt from mortal sin from his coming to the use of reason, but that he did not even understand what mortal sin was, especially in regard of purity. The confessor heard and was astonished. He proceeded to venial sins. He advanced to some little indulgence given to our own passions, to self-love, and then proceeded to the duties of a good Christian, "and I found," these are the words of the confessor himself, "to my repeated wonder and surprise, that his pure soul from the most tender age had been exempt not only from every mortal sin, but also from venial sins committed deliberately; so that with all certainty I could perceive in him the preservation of his baptismal innocence, and that he was one of those souls chosen by God and prevented with

he had separately from them all agreed toget
Astonished and greatly edified, they told
that Benedict remained almost the whole da
the church, like a person in ecstasy, always q
and on his knees, without ever turning his h
from one side to the other; that he walked
the streets when he was going to the churcl
leaving it, always alone, modest and compos
that he never asked an alms from any one,
went to the distribution of bread and wine, wl
the Holy House gives twice a day through cha
to the poor pilgrims; that he slept at nigh
the open air on the cold stones; that his clo
were all torn and ragged; that he led a n
poor and penitential life, which could not
continued without a very special grace from (
This was the account they gave.

Father Temple was much pleased with
counts so good and so similar to each ot
For greater security, he wished however

munion that same morning, and to return to him in the afternoon. During the remainder of this day, and during two following days, he had private conferences for more than two hours with Benedict, in a place apart, and without giving him any mark of esteem or of his good opinion; he had the opportunity of learning all the virtuous actions he had practised up to that time, and all that had happened to him, and this by no other means than by employing continually the precept of holy obedience, without which a word could not be extracted from him, and when he answered, it was never without venting deep sighs from the bottom of his heart, and shedding many tears. He took care also from that time to note everything on paper, holding it as certain that if he followed constantly the very rigid method of life he had undertaken, Almighty God would vouchsafe to authenticate his sublime sanctity by miracles after his death, and he thought that at that time to become acquainted with his virtues, they would have recourse amongst others to the French Penitentiary at Loretto, and for this reason he would leave these papers as memorials for posterity.

But Almighty God granted to him the pleasure and honour of deposing juridically in the Processes what he had then written, and what he had gained in his private conferences with him, for Benedict did not live longer than about six years from the time; and when he heard the news of his death, which happened in

1783, together with the fame of his sanctity, which quickly spread even to distant kingdoms, he was not at all surprised, knowing the great depth of sanctity which was contained in his heart.

I cannot restrain myself here from extolling with great praises the very wise conduct of this attentive and prudent confessor. We are indebted to him for the knowledge of many heroic acts, and of the singular virtues of this great servant of God. It would be desirable that certain confessors would walk in his footsteps, who lightly and without mature examination send away from them some soul favoured by God in a particular manner, as soon as this person begins to relate anything extraordinary of himself, judging it a delusion. They should remember that in that tribunal, they are not only judges to bind and loose, but also masters to instruct and correct.

PART III.

OF BENEDICT'S HEROIC VIRTUES, PRACTISED PARTICULARLY DURING THE YEARS WHICH HE LIVED IN ROME, TILL HIS DEATH

INTRODUCTION.

What has been hitherto related in the first and second parts of this work, has been a continual tissue of heroic virtues, sufficient to give a high idea of Benedict's sanctity. Still, as no more has been mentioned than the course of history required, I will explain the remainder in the third part, and especially the virtuous and heroic actions which he performed in Rome during the remaining years of his life. He took up his residence in that city in 1776, and never departed from it again, except to go every year to his beloved sanctuary, the Holy House of Loretto. It seems to have been by a special design of Almighty God, that he was inspired to remain in Rome, the capital of the world, after He had shown him in various cities and kingdoms in his frequent pilgrimages. Our Lord would not keep hidden under the bushel of a desert or a cloister this light shining with heroic virtues; on the contrary, He placed him in the sight of the whole world, upon a candle-stick, that he might shine to all, that by the brightness of his virtuous example some might blush for their coldness, and others might be encouraged to imitate him, if not in all, (for no one could mount so high, without the special grace of God. with which Benedict was favoured,) at least in part, proportionably to their state.

CHAPTER I.

OF HIS EXTREME POVERTY AND SINGULAR PENANCE IN HIS CLOTHES.

The poverty of Benedict was entirely his own choice, as he might have enjoyed at home those conveniences with which the comfortable circumstances of his family would have furnished

was perhaps either because God did not inspire him to do so, as the ways of the Lord are different, or because having engaged himself always to work for God's glory, and to give Him greater pleasure, he thought perhaps he should do this better by acting through pure love, without any chain of obligation, as St. Philip Neri would have his disciples do; or St. Francesca of Rome, not wishing to bind them by vow, saying to them, as it were, what the Patriarch of Antioch, St. Meletius, said to St. Simeon Stylites, when he ordered that the iron chain should be taken off his foot, by which he was closely confined to his pillar, "Let not a chain of iron, but a chain of love bind you. To one that loves God, love is a sufficient chain." However this be, we shall see clearly, that the rigorous poverty of the strictest observers of religious discipline does not come up to what Benedict voluntarily practised.

Religious persons in cloisters, where the observance is most strict, however poor they may be, have a little cell to live in; they have a straw bed, a mat, or a table to sleep upon; they do not want for clothes of rough woollen material; without any trouble of their own, they are provided by others with nourishment; they have some small cups, either of earthenware or wood, to drink out of. Benedict had not one of these things; whence we see that the state to which God called him was a life in the midst of the world, more austere than any other; and as it was faithfully deposed in the Processes by those who had attentively observed his system of life, "his mortifications, austerities, penances, and poverty were such, that he far surpassed all those, who, separated from the world, live in the most rigid and austere religious orders." I shall relate things which will seem to be almost incredible, or at least exaggerated, but I shall mention them with great confidence, for as a contemporaneous writer, I might, if these things were not true, be convicted of falsehood to my confusion, by persons still living, who knew the servant of God, who saw him, and spoke with him and with me; many other persons who are worthy of credit would be found guilty of falsehood, and even perjury, and who have deposed these things, and confirmed them by oath in the Processes. The clothing, the food, the habitation, and the bed of this servant of God, all breathed an extreme and singular poverty. I will speak at present of his clothing.

His clothes were rags, sufficient only to cover the nakedness of his body, for the sake of decency and modesty, of which he was exceedingly jealous, but not at all adequate to defend him from the rigour of cold. His shoes had only the form of shoes; they were so worn out, and open in many parts, that they let in the water and mud to his discomfort. His stockings were not only torn, but so short that they scarcely covered more than half his leg: his trowsers were torn in several places. The cloak with sleeves of a greyish colour, which covered his body, particularly during the last years of his life, was so ragged that the different parts hung in pieces; it was bound round him with a cord, which was knotted together in several places; it looked like a vile cloak worn out with age, and become in several parts a refuge for innumerable insects. The rag of a shirt which he wore was very dirty; his head was always uncovered, his hair neglected, and his beard never shaved. He did not always put on the whole of these clothes; many persons attest, that they have seen him in the roads sometimes without stockings, or carrying them fastened to his girdle, that he might be derided, as he was in effect by worthless people and boys, and sometimes without shoes. The singular condition of these ragged clothes distinguished him amidst the numerous crowd of poor persons, who were all clothed better than he was, so that by merely beholding him, you could say that he was a living portrait of extreme poverty.

No variation of seasons could induce him to alter his manner of clothing himself, or discontinne it for a short time; it was always the same, in the hottest summer and the severest winter, alike by day and by night; and from the time that he knew the very austere state of life which God required him to follow, till the last breath of his life, he was always most constant in it, excepting on some rare occasion, when he was either obliged by obedience to put away some part of this clothing, or constrained by the charity of others. This could not certainly be a light suffering to the servant of God if we reflect on his birth, and the manner in which he was brought up. Still this is little in comparison with another which he suffered continually at all times, and in all places. This was an attack from innumerable little disgusting insects, called lice. The foul state of clothes, and linen never changed or washed, joined with the natural filth of the human corruptible flesh, usually produces these troublesome insects, so much the more troublesome as they are more sticky and penetrating. If a few by any accident were to attack us, what torment would they not cause! Perhaps we should go so far as to break the rules of politeness in conversations, and even those of modesty, to free ourselves from them, and God grant that we might not even give way to passionate impatience.

This then was the greatest suffering, the severest penance of Benedict. As he always wore the same filthy miserable clothes, caring as little for his body as if it were corruption, he was always assailed by innumerable armies of these insects, and never trying to free himself from them, he gave them an opportunity of multiplying and attaching themselves more closely to him; so that they were seen in great numbers together, as it were, victorious over him, and walking in triumph over his person. A very worthy priest, who frequently gave him communion in the Cappella Borghese, in the church of Sta. Maria Maggiore, attests, that seeing him at the altar in order to receive his Lord in the adorable Sacrament, the ragged and filthy clothes which he wore seemed to him on the one side unbecoming, but on the other, the devotion, the fervour, and the modesty with which he received Him were such, that he thought they supplied sufficiently for what in the eyes of men appears unbecoming, but is not so before God, who, penetrating into the heart, sees its purity, and is pleased with it.*

The number of these insects was clearly discovered after his death, for six persons who had orders to clean his ragged clothes, as people strove with one another to have relics, on account of the great fame of his sanctity, which quickly spread through the whole of Rome, attest, that there was not any part of them, however small, in which there were not found nestled a prodigious quantity of these insects and of their eggs, so that when they were got rid of by brushing, they were several times again filled, and thrown from them into the fire. Even the little holes of the beads in the rosary which he wore round his neck were full of them. This cleaning did not cost them a little, for they had to overcome

* It would seem forgetful of the "multiform wisdom" and grace of God, who "divideth to each severally as He will," to shrink from this passage, however different from what we read in the case of other saints and holy men. Benedict was led to follow the pattern of the primitive monks of Egypt, who exposed themselves to the musquitoes, and especially of St. Antony, their patriarch, of whom St Athanasius tells us, that "he did not wash his body with water, no, nor his feet, not even putting them into the water except from necessity." On the other hand, we read of our own St. Philip, "He was a great lover of cleanliness, and held dirt in special abomination, particularly dirty clothes, and he was perpetually quoting the maxim of St. Bernard, "'I ever loved poverty, but dirtiness never.'"

the great repugnance of nature to the disgusting employment, as the persons fixed upon for this business themselves attested.

And yet Benedict, in so tormenting, so continual, and so troublesome an attack, was never seen to make any movement with his hand or body to rid himself of them, or obtain any relief; he remained like a dead person, allowing himself to be eaten up alive, and suffering this new sort of martyrdom motionless during whole days in the churches. If on some few occasions he was seen to move his hand, it was not for comfort, it was rather for greater torment, putting again on his neck some of those insects which he saw walking on his sleeves.

With regard to other corporal austerities, we find no attestation of any in the Processes, as he always sought to conceal his virtuous actions from the eyes of others. At Moulins only, whither he went after leaving the convent of Sept Fontaines, when lodging in a house, he was heard giving himself blows with a discipline of cords, having at the ends small iron nails. Other instruments of penance were also found in his bundle, but how, when, and where he used them no one knows. What penance, however, could be more tormenting, more continual, or more troublesome, than to suffer night and day from the bites of these little animals, who continually fed on his flesh, as in a land of their peaceable possession, where no one drove them away, and where they were not even molested by his hand?

It must have been a still greater suffering to

him to see himself abhorred and shunned by many, and even driven away, on account of these insects. When persons entered the church of Sta. Maria dei Monti, which he frequented more in the latter years of his life, they would give each other warning to avoid such a place, "Because," said they, "the poor man was there a short time ago." Ladies, who are more delicate, showed their horror more especially. A pious lady, who was going to communion one morning, at the rails of this church, had placed herself, perhaps without perceiving it, not far from the place where Benedict was reverently praying. One of her friends came immediately to give her notice of it with an audible voice. "What are you doing?" said she, "you place yourself beside this poor man, who is covered with vermin." The pious lady was much grieved to see the servant of God thus publicly mortified, but those

After having made his confession, he begged him to hear him again at other times, if he would have that goodness. "Willingly," he answered, "if you will cleanse yourself well, on account of the persons who frequent my confessional." "But that will be a difficult thing for me," said Benedict with humility and modesty, and he did not again approach that confessional.

He did not manifest the reason of this difficulty, nor did the confessor require it. I have no doubt that I can guess it, however; for in order to correspond with the inspirations of God, with regard to his very austere manner of life, he would not lose the opportunity with which these little animals presented him by their constant bites. He might easily have raised the siege, and freed himself entirely from them; he did not want for speedy means and kind offers, but he was much more desirous to keep them than a delicate person would be to be liberated from them; in every circumstance he not only sought means of suffering, but chose what was most painful, and while his body was afflicted, his soul rejoiced exceedingly.

This interior satisfaction shone in his countenance, which was never disturbed, never sad or afflicted, but always cheerful and serene to the last day of his life. When he was compassionated or interrogated by others, he answered with sincerity, that he was very well satisfied with the state in which he was It could not be otherwise; God is the source of all contentment and felicity; he who lives with God, and in God, is immersed in this fountain, and though he may have no earthly possessions, he lives happy. He who lives not with God, is most unhappy, though he possess an abundance of temporal goods. Benedict was always united to God. We also may be happy, if we live with God, even amidst wretchedness and misfortunes. We shall be unhappy if we separate ourselves from God by sin, even though we abound in riches, conveniences, and honours. "To be with Jesus is a sweet Paradise, and to be without Jesus a grievous hell;" thus wrote Thomas à Kempis in his golden little book, the Imitation of Christ, and Benedict, who was always accustomed to read and practise the sentiments of this little book, gives a proof of the truth of these words. The sentiment of à Kempis was first expressed by Jesus in these words, "In Me you shall have peace, in the world distress." (John, xvi. 33.) The pleasure Benedict took in sufferings will be more clearly shown by what will be related in the following chapter.

CHAPTER II.

OF BENEDICT'S POVERTY AND PENANCE IN HIS HABITATION, HIS BED, AND HIS FOOD.

A PERFECT imitator of our Lord Jesus Christ, His servant, from the time that he left his home, would never have any abode where he could take shelter ; thus, "he had not where to lay his head." (Luke, ix. 58.) Being asked at Loretto one day where he lived, he answered, "Sometimes in this place, sometimes in that." Being urged to say in what city or house, he replied, "In Rome," where he had fixed himself a few years before his death. As to his house, he only answered by a smile, for though he dwelt in Rome, he had not any house wherein he could lay his head.

For several years he was seen to place himself for the night, ill protected as he was by his ragged clothes, under the niche near the Quartiere di Monte Cavallo. During other years he went to a niche of the Colosseum behind the fifth station. Here he lay upon a little straw, and he was heard by some passers-by reciting prayers aloud. A person who observed him several times from above the entrance of the niche, attests it in the Processes. In one of the long days of August, when the heat of the sun is most ardent, he was seen once after mid-day extended upon a step of the Palazzo Bracciano, in the attitude of one sleeping, modestly composed with his hands folded on his breast, with the hot rays of the sun upon him, which he might have avoided by going elsewhere.

In his long pilgrimages he lay on the ground wherever night overtook him, through his wish to avoid inns. In the first years of his pilgrimage to Loretto, being kindly advised not to sleep in the night air, which is hurtful to health, he took shelter in some bake-house in the country. The charity of individuals made them several times and in different places of an abode with some degree of comfort, teet him from the inclement air. He g ly refused it, saying, "Poor people sho be so comfortably accommodated."

This was Benedict's habitation, this l Even when a boy at home, neglecting provided comfortably for him, he took an repose on the floor underneath the be would certainly have continued to sleep bare ground, if the charity of a certain Grimaldi, who saw him in Rome ab years before his death, very much en and almost like a corpse, had not induced lead Benedict by gentle violence with hin Hospital dei Poveri, built by the great cl the Abate Mancini, that he might at preserved from the inclemency of the ni The remembrance of some advice given by a prudent confessor concurred to eng to let himself be conducted thither: tl "When he found that he positively co continue to sleep in the night air, he ha seek some shelter." And though he the shelter of the hospital, he did not bed, though urged by others, and almost to it by his bodily diseases. Having bee selled, before he received this advice and to seek some place of shelter, for that o he would fall dead in some street, he "What does it matter to me?" Showi his total indifference about his body, and

The food by which he supported himself gives us a better opportunity of knowing clearly his extreme and singular poverty. He began as a boy at home to eat sparingly, though many dishes were prepared for table; and the little which he ate was of the coarsest and most ordinary sort, and satisfied with this, he gave to the servants anything that was more delicate and rare.

When he was his own master in his pilgrimages, in the cities and in Rome, he took only enough food, not to recruit his strength, but to preserve life. His miserable nourishment was composed generally of vile and refuse things which others rejected, and which were thrown out of the windows and on the dunghills, orange peel, hard stalks of brocoli, withered cabbage leaves, useless weeds, and spoiled and rotten fruit. On the day of his death, when seized with mortal fainting-fits, his provision for that day was found in his pocket, a piece of bread, some orange peelings, and nothing more.

The public streets and dunghills served him for a refectory. He left the church generally about mid-day, and wherever he found any of this rubbish, he ate of it moderately. It was a subject of wonder to some people in Rome, how to suit with each other the hour and the place in which he dined; he passed the whole day in the church; he had no house for his own residence; where, then, and when did he take his food? But their wonder ceased when they knew that some had seen him about mid-day eating in the roads, others, seated in a public street, using his teeth as weapons to overcome the toughness of a brocoli-stalk, and others again in different places, eating orange peel, triumphing thus over the world and his own body. When he was praying fervently one day in the church of Santa Maria dei Monti, he was shaken after having been called in vain by a devout and wealthy lady, who invited him with a trembling voice to dinner that day. Recovering himself, to his displeasure, as one disturbed from the enjoyment of something very agreeable, he quickly answered, "Dinner! dinner! I dine in the street!" Thus he also answered another, who, meeting him at the dinner hour, gave him a similar invitation.

Some persons wished through devotion to have him sometimes for a guest at their house, and they made the request with timidity, yet with eagerness. He got rid of them quickly, by saying to them, that he ate in the street.

When obliged in Loretto, through the charity of his hosts, of which I have elsewhere spoken in praise, to sup with them at night after having spent the whole day in praying in the Holy House without breaking his fast, seeing a small loaf placed before him, he would not make use of it, saying, "The poor should eat fragments." It was necessary to put it before him in pieces, if they wished him to use it, and if they wished him to eat more, they were obliged to desire him in obedience to do so. If on some rare occasion a whole small loaf was given to him, he either refused it, or if obliged to receive it, he ate less than the half, and gave the rest to some other poor person. One of these refused it one day, out of compassion for him, but he urged him, saying, that what he had eaten was sufficient for him.

He occasionally went to the door of a convent in Rome, where on some days soup is given at mid-day to the poor. But the cup in which he received it, his attitude, and the affronts which he was obliged to suffer, evidently showed that he went rather to have an opportunity of practising mortification, humility, and patience, than for the soup. His basin was of wood, with a large piece broken out of the edge, cracked in the middle, and joined again with wire, thus allowing the liquor to run out. His humble deportment, and the affronts he endured, will be more suitably spoken of in the chapter on his humility. A wonderful, and at the same time a very edifying action, was observed by one of the attendants of Mgr. della Porta, in the court-yard of the palace. He was in a part of it from whence he could see without being observed. He saw a poor man come in, modest, composed, breathing devotion, who, approaching the fountain, drank a little water. Thinking then that at that hour after mid-day there would be no one to notice him, he knelt down, and gathering up with his hand the remainder of the soup which had been thrown shortly before amongst the dirt, and was mixed with it, he ate it up by degrees. Then cleansing his mouth with his hand as with a towel, he went away very modestly. This person was astonished at such mortification, and was confirmed in the idea of his sanctity with which other events had inspired him. When it was reported in Rome that a saintly poor man was dead, he had no doubt but that it was this man; and seeing his master the prelate go eagerly to the church of Santa Maria dei Monti, where his body was said to be exposed, to see him, he could not refrain from going also. When he arrived, he had no little difficulty in reaching the bier, through the great crowd of people assembled, and recognising him, he kissed him devoutly, shedding tears of tenderness.

He never drank wine, except when obliged by obedience. When he wanted to drink, he put his lips to the public fountains of water, which are everywhere seen in Rome, and after his death these places were besieged by the devotion of the people. His hostess, Barbara Sori, in taking leave of Benedict, who was returning to Rome from Loretto, wished to give him some money to purchase, as she said, a little wine in the inns, to quench his thirst. He could not be induced to accept it, saying, "The poor do not carry money; ditch-water suffices for their drink, and if in your house I have taken a little wine, it has only been through obedience, for I always drink water."

Satisfied with his miserable morning's meal, he never took anything at night for supper, nor drank a draught of water. The last time that he arrived in Loretto, in the afternoon of Maunday Thursday, 1782, fatigued and extremely exhansted by the long journey of two-and-twenty days, still fasting, and benumbed by the snow, he was entreated by his very pious hostess, Sori, to remain in the house a short time, to recruit his wasted strength a little. Benedict refused in a pleasant manner, and leaving his bundle by her permission in her house, he went straight to visit his beloved Mother in the Holy House, promising Barbara that he would return at night to supper. He was punctual in the evening, and a small plate of caviale being offered to him, he put it on one side, saying, "That is not food for poor people, it is too dear;" and he supped very sparingly, observing the fast rigorously.

CHAPTER III.

HIS HEROIC POVERTY OF SPIRIT.

Though those rich persons who abound in temporal goods, yet do not attach their hearts to them, may be called poor in spirit according to the words of the royal prophet: "If riches abound, set not your heart upon them," (Psalm lxi. 11,) still, according to the opinion of St. Thomas, those are truly poor in spirit who neither have temporal goods, nor wish to possess them, being entirely given to God and eternal goods, "Dicuntur proprie pauperes spiritu, qui nec habent divitias nec affectant." Such was Benedict, and what was most valuable in his virtue of poverty was, his perfect detachment from all earthly things; so that possessing nothing, his heart desired nothing. When a little boy at home, he had no thought for himself, no diversions, no chattering, no amusements. Prayer, devout books, retirement, and visiting the churches were his delight.

At that tender age he lived so disengaged from every earthly affection, so attached to God alone, that his confessor attests, that he could never discover in him, even when a child, any attachment to any earthly thing whatever. From the time that he undertook the very rigid manner of life with which God inspired him, he never gave a thought to his country, conveniences, or friends; forgotten by them, he went, like St. Alexis, poor, ragged, and a pilgrim, wherever the hand of Omnipotence guided him, trampling in effect, as well as in affection, on everything flattering and brilliant in the world. His parents deposed that they had never had any news of him since his departure from the convent of Sept Fontaines, when he wrote to them, that they would never see him again, except in the valley of Josaphat: the first notice of him they received was brought to them by the fame of his sanctity, which spread everywhere after his death in Rome.

Despising the world, he lived most happy amongst his rags, miseries, and sufferings; and he judged with St. Paul, that everything the world holds in the greatest esteem was deserving only to be trampled on as dung; never did a miser love his riches as he loved his poverty. Thence came his generous refusal of everything which the compassion of others offered him, his negligence about procuring alms, his distribution of them to other poor people.

Though many of those persons who prize earthly more than heavenly goods, disgusted by his wretched and abject state, shunned him, and even sometimes derided him, there were not wanting, on the contrary, many of great piety, who, moved by edification and compassion, kindly offered him whatever they thought necessary to him. They were without doubt inspired by God, who designed on one side to give His servant an opportunity of advancing more and more in the practice of heroic virtues, and on the other, to show us clearly his voluntary spirit of singular interior and exterior poverty; that by his example we might be encouraged to the contempt of temporal things.

In some towns through which he passed in his pilgrimages, persons seeing his poor and ragged clothes, offered him shoes, stockings, shirts, and even many things together. This happened equally often in Rome, where the spirit of charity flourished wonderfully. Showing his sense of the favours, he refused everything in an agreeable manner, saying modestly and cheerfully, that he had no wants; what he had on was sufficient for him; let it be given to the needy. To others he said, "The poor should not be well clothed; this is too good for a poor man; the poor should live by alms." The testimonies in the Processes of such refusals, and of his edifying answers, are so numerous, that it would be tedious to relate them. Some with holy importunity obliged him to accept something; he did so, not to afflict them, but when he had left them he gave it away, or if he used it, he disfigured it so as to make it truly a poor man's garment.

A good lady, seeing him pass one day with his head uncovered in very severe weather, when the quantity of snow that had fallen had whitened a great part of Rome, beholding him benumbed with cold and ill protected by his rags, offered him a little woollen cap through charity. Benedict refused it, but when entreated, he seemed to accept the charity, but shortly after the lady saw him by chance bareheaded as before, and his cap on the head of another poor person, by which detachment she was greatly edified.

A person once gave him a straw hat covered with coarse silk and very old, only sufficient to cover the head. Benedict unravelled the silk in several places, so that the straw here and there appeared, then he put it on so as to make a ridiculous appearance, to draw upon himself insults and derision in the streets. When pressed to take what he wanted of shoes, stockings, and similar articles, he fixed on what was most ragged and worn, and refusing the others, chose that in his extreme necessity.

An enemy to money, he never asked for a

farthing; when any was offered him he refused it, and if any one spontaneously gave him more than sufficed for his miserable daily nourishment, he distributed it to the poor, or put it in the little box for alms at the church doors. This conduct was noticed with admiration, and attested also by many persons.

Being once reproved by one of his confessors, and treated as a stealer of alms, who took them from the real poor, he was obliged by obedience to break the silence with which he tranquilly listened to the reproofs, and to give an account of his alms. He answered humbly, that he never asked an alms except in the very rare case of extreme necessity, and that he only took what was necessary for his very scanty daily maintenance, refusing the rest, or giving it to other poor people. This sufficed to gain the confessor's approbation of his conduct. His sustenance in Rome for the most part consisted of those refuse things which are thrown out of the windows. Scarcely, on one occasion, had he received eight bajocchi, than he gave them into the hands of another poor person. Other money, whether copper or silver, never remained with him; he quickly distributed it, content with his miserable food for the present day, and never taking thought for the future. Some said that it was useless to give alms to Benedict, for he gave it away; he did not want it. A poor woman strengthened this false opinion; begging amongst the crowd of devout venerators of the Blessed Virgin dell' Archetto in Rome, she received to her astonishment an alms from Benedict, who was more ragged than any other. She was so surprised that she could not help exclaiming aloud with wonder, "One poor man gives alms to other poor people!" It happened several times that some gave him by mistake silver instead of copper. When he perceived it, he ran after them and restored it to them, making known their mistake to them. He never would be induced to accept money to pay for being shaved at Christmas, which was offered him by some. The great charity of a most exemplary prelate, on merely witnessing the great devotion and quiet attitude of Benedict, covered with rags, before the most Blessed Sacrament, which was exposed for the Forty Hours' Prayer, in the church of Sta. Maria in Monterone, made him regularly for several years place one of his servants at the door of the church, to offer him, in the name of a benefactor, a monthly pension for his necessities. Benedict thanked him, saying he did not want it, and with his accustomed modesty proceeded on his way.

What is more surprising is, that he would not make use of the little money which he sometimes accepted in his great need, without first asking leave of his confessor. Hence we may perceive that the virtue of poverty could not be carried to a higher degree of perfection than Benedict carried it, and that his confessor at Loretto, Father Temple, did not at all exaggerate when he wrote and deposed in the Processes, that what St. Bonaventure wrote in praise of the great poverty of his patriarch, St. Francis, suited well with the heroic virtue of Benedict. This singular poverty in his clothes, habitation, food, and bed had reduced him to such an emaciated condition, that it might be imagined an excess of which he should have had some scruple, as a worthy priest at first thought, but he afterwards thought otherwise, reflecting that the ways of Almighty God with His servants are various, that God wished him to walk in this difficult path, that He had given him abundant grace for it, so that he might run in it not only willingly, but with pleasure, as He also gave to St. Peter of Alcantara and other saints.

CHAPTER IV.

OF HIS ANGELICAL PURITY. VIOLENT TEMPTATIONS SUFFERED BY HIM: MEANS WHICH HE ADOPTED TO OVERCOME THEM.

Benedict's purity was so perfect, that many call him in the Processes an angel in human flesh, an angelical youth, another St. Aloysius, and one who might have said with St. Paul, "Though we walk in the flesh we do not war according to the flesh." (2 Cor. x. 3.) Having a great love for this beautiful lily, he guarded it always jealously, and gave clear proofs, from his most tender years, of the desire which he had to preserve it untouched from every pestiferous breath. Such was his horror of the opposite vice, that he was accustomed to say, "If a woman touched me I would immediately pull off the skin she had touched." A young woman, servant to the parish priest of Ligny, who was well aware of his caution, once seeing Benedict in the house with his fellow-students, very modest and composed, said, but only to see if she could disturb him a little, "Hold him; I am going to kiss him." Scarcely had Benedict heard her words than he fled from the place, as he would have done if he had seen a horrible serpent in the act of darting upon him: "Quasi a facie colubri," as the Holy Spirit teaches. This flight was a source of laughter to some, of admiration to others.

To preserve well so precious a lily in the interior garden of his soul, he kept at all times a strict watch over his senses, these being the doors by which the infernal serpent seeks to gain an entrance into this garden, either to root up this flower if he can, or if not, to cause it to wither by his pestiferous touch. Hence he kept his eyes always very modestly cast down. He walked in the streets as if he were praying in the church, with his eyes fixed on the ground, and his hands folded on his breast. The magnificence of the Roman palaces, the variety of the fountains, the obelisks and curiosities which usually attract the eye of all, could not draw his attention in the least; he always walked like a person in an ecstasy, he never turned his head nor diverted his eyes. The sight only of his modesty excited devotion, and sufficed to give an idea that he was a saint.

Judge what caution he used, what care, never to look a woman in the face. Being sufficiently versed in the reading of the Holy Scriptures, he well knew the warnings which the Holy Spirit gives on this subject: "Gaze not about upon another's beauty; for many have perished by the beauty of a woman, and hereby lust is enkindled as a fire." (Ecclus. ix. 8.) Hence, knowing that looks enkindled the fire of concupiscence, he never looked at any woman in the face. All the times that Barbara Sori gave him a lodging in her house at Loretto, it never happened that in speaking to her he once looked her in the face; he always answered with his eyes cast down with such modesty and humility, that he always increased devotion in her, and strengthened her opinion that he was a holy soul. Thus she attests many other times, it was a subject of admiration to those who stopped him by chance in the streets, to give him an alms or to speak to him, to see him with his eyes cast down, and his hands crossed on his breast, answering only what was necessary, in few and well-considered words, and then departing as soon as he could disengage himself, going on his way quite recollected in himself, with his arms folded, and his hands within the sleeves of his ragged cloak.

A woman wished once to see his eyes and hear him speak, and stopping him in the street, she offered him an alms; but he continued to keep his eyes fixed on the ground, and his arms folded on his breast, without listening at all to her. Being urged to receive the alms, he extended his hand a little, and accepted it. Wishing to engage in conversation, she told him to recommend her to God, on account of some troubles, yet she was quite disappointed, for Benedict, without either opening his eyes to look at her, or his mouth to utter a word, gave her a sign that he had understood, by merely bowing his head, and went away. Another, who often gave him an alms, being moved to do it by his modesty and devotion, deposes, "that though she had seen him for many years, she could not tell what sort of eyes he had, as he always received the alms without thanking her, much less looking her in the face." Many other persons who assisted him by alms spoke to the same effect.

Regulating himself by the advice of the Holy Spirit in the Sacred Writings, he not only avoided looking a woman in the face, but even shunned conversation with them. From his youth he never discoursed even with his sisters, except when necessity required it. He once omitted the spiritual reading which he was accustomed to read in the evening to a devout widower who dwelt near his house, to avoid a girl of the house, who was listening to him. He never treated with women during the rest of his life, except when absolute necessity required it. They were all objects which he tried to shun, and if in his pilgrimages he was obliged by the charity of others to accept a lodging, to be protected from the night air, he first asked if there were any women there, and if there were, he could not be induced to accept it.

He was not less cautious in the custody of his ears and other senses, than in keeping a guard over his eyes. An immodest word, which he heard by chance, was a sound which filled him with horror. A little girl of about six years of age was singing innocently one day in public a little song which was rather immodest. Scarcely had Benedict heard the first words, while he was walking along the same road, than horrified he uttered a loud cry close to her, and asked her repeatedly if she knew the Pater Noster, but the poor little girl was so astonished, that she had not courage to answer him. One of the reasons for which he avoided the company of other poor people, and often omitted also to go to receive soup at the doors of the convents, was that he might not hear immodest, profane, or improper words, which such people are accustomed to utter either in jest or through anger in their quarrels.

As to what regards taste and touch, which includes the whole body, we need only remember what has been said in the two first chapters of this third part, regarding his poverty in food, in clothes, in his bed, and habitation. Two remarkable things remain to be mentioned. The first concerns wine, of which he always deprived himself. When asked by his confessor at Loretto, whom I have elsewhere quoted, why he drank water, though he at first answered that water sufficed for the poor, wine was

eing always intent on subduing the insolence he flesh, which rebels when caressed. "In-satus est et recalcitravit, incrassatus, im-;uatus dereliquit Deum Factorem suum."

uch was Benedict's vigilance over all his es to keep his purity unspotted. Can we gine greater caution? And yet, who would eve it? he who was so mortified, so circum-t, and delicate, had, nevertheless, to suffer ent temptations against this lovely virtue, ch was so dear to him. Let not this cause der; it is the way in which God usually deals His dearest and most penitent servants; permits the devil to enkindle the fire of his ptations in their imagination and in their ies, but only so far as to refine more and e the bright gold of their purity, and, con-y to the malignant design of the tempter, nake them thereby gain greater merit: "He make also with temptation issue." (1 Cor. 13.) We have a clear proof of this in the horrible temptations of the most mortified St. Peter of Alcantara in his religious order; of those courageously supported by a St. Mary of Egypt in her solitude for eighteen years; and those of a St. Jerome in his hermitage, who, in his cold body, exhausted by penances and fasts, felt the flames of lust: "In frigido corpore sola ebulliebant libidinum incendia."

This also was the conduct of Almighty God in regard of Benedict. He was tempted by day and by night against purity. The temptations which attacked him in the day-time gave him less annoyance, for scarcely did they appear, than they vanished like a flash of lightning; and this was the effect of the very close union with God, in which he was always happily occupied, and, as it were, absorbed. Those of the night were, however, very troublesome to him. No sooner had the servant of God obtained a little sleep, which he could only do with great difficulty, stretched on the bare ground, and besieged from head to foot by those insects, than the devil was behind him, with wicked illusions, images, phantoms, and rebellions of the flesh, to disturb him, exciting the inferior part of the soul to some consent. Then indeed great was the distress of the servant of God, who on one side abhorred with great horror every shadow of offence against God, and on the other, saw himself, as it were, on the brink of the precipice. Strengthened, however, by the Divine assistance, and confiding in God, he used every effort to repress the impetuosity and force of the temptations. He resisted courageously with a resolute will, declaring himself ready to suffer death rather than offend his beloved Lord. And as this did not suffice to overcome the enemy, he extended himself on the ground, humbling himself, imploring the help of Almighty God; he invoked the most pure and immaculate Virgin; he often made the sign of the cross; he struck his breast; and thinking of the Passion of our Blessed Redeemer, he blushed for those shameful thoughts so opposed to it. Thus he at last succeeded in gaining tranquillity and a complete victory. Such combats did not take place merely on one, or on a few nights; they were very frequent, and lasted for years. In the meantime, not satisfied with the remedies he used at night, he redoubled his precautions by day; a more diligent custody of his senses, longer prayers, more frequent and more severe mortifications. He had a fair, fine, blooming complexion, and his hands were well and finely formed. Hence he never would cleanse himself from the filth of those innumerable insects, nor change his clothes, fearing danger to himself or others, in exposing any part of his body, which during his whole life he never would look upon. He hid his hands as much as he could, to take from the eyes the incentive which the sight of them, though in a passing way, might have been, and to deprive the devil of weapons wherewith to attack him. This is attested by two very prudent confessors, one is Father Temple, the penitentiary of Loretto, who by means of obedience obliged him in his conferences with him scover what I have here related. Ho mend to this confessor, in obedience to his com-, that he had given himself to this austere od of life, and continued it, in order to resist unclean spirit by whom he was attacked, St. Paul, "There was given to me a sting y flesh, to buffet me," (2 Cor. xii. 7 ;) and, fore, in the best manner I can, "I chastise body and bring it into subjection." The was his last confessor, Signor D. Giuseppe oni, in Rome, who drew it from the last gen-confession made by the servant of God, a or a little more before he died.

th these confessors, and all the others whom d in Rome, and elsewhere, attest that they found in Benedict during his whole life fault, interior or exterior, against the sixth andment, and that in temptations the grace od had always made him victorious. This tation is a great encomium on Benedict, makes his purity more conspicuous. It l have been easy for him to commit such he was not in an hermitage, or in a cloister ; ved in the midst of the world ; he passed gh estates, towns, and kingdoms ; he was n subjection to any one who might have

singular virtue ; it is much praised by the Holy Ghost in Ecclesiasticus, "Who is he, and we will praise him? for he hath done wonderful things in his life; he shall have glory everlasting; he that could have transgressed, and hath not transgressed, and could do evil things, and hath not done them." (Ecclus. xxxi. 10.) This was an effect of the very officacious grace with which God prevented him, and which was necessary in the state for which He destined him. This virtue was admired in him by a parish priest his confessor, who honours him for it in the Processes, pronouncing him like St. Alexis and St. Roch.

Besides these attestations, there is another in the Processes which confirms his temptations, and his perseverance to the end in this very austere course of life. This is given by Signor George Zitli, who had been treasurer to the Emperor of Persia, Kouli-Khan, and having fortunately become a Catholic, retired to lead a devout and solitary life in the convent of the father Capuchins at Rome ; he was a friend of Benedict, from the time that he first saw with admiration his modesty, composure, and devotion. Compassionating his destitute state, he several times offered him shoes, stockings, shirts, and whatever he wanted. Benedict modestly thanking him, told him he did not want anything, that he was very well satisfied with his sordid state of life, "Because," he added, "youth is inclined to evil, and we must keep it under restraint;" an answer, which caused

Zitli great admiration and edification; an answer, which ought to make any one blush, who being tempted, should presume on his own strength, and who, while living in warfare with the world, the flesh, and the devil, should stand in the battle like an unworthy soldier, without making use of his arms. Hence it is, that "like a soldier without weapons, he will easily fall in the conflict;" he will be quickly and easily conquered if he use not the weapons of watchfulness over the senses, of mortification, flight of occasions, and prayer.

The time at length arrived when Almighty God, pleased with the vigilance and fortitude of His servant, put an end to the combat. This was in the last years of his life, which terminated in the flower of his youth, at the very time when the passions are most lively, and concupiscence the strongest. In these last years God granted him the very singular privilege of exemption from the strong incitements and temptations of the flesh, verifying in him what the afflicted Sara said to Almighty God in the prayer which she offered up in her tribulation: "After a storm Thou makest a calm, and after tears and weeping Thou pourest in joyfulness," (Tobias, iii. 22.) Benedict being questioned by another confessor in Rome, was obliged, in spite of his humility, to confess this gift. Signor Marconi knew him to be so rooted in virtue, that he believed him invincible to the shock of temptations.

CHAPTER V.

OF HIS READY OBEDIENCE.

THE obedience rendered by subjects to their superiors on account of their vow, was practised without vow by Benedict Joseph, with this difference, that he practised it not only towards those who had authority over him, but towards any one who gave him a command, or, without an express command, merely showed a desire that he should do or omit anything, provided it were not contrary to the will of God, regulating himself by those words of the apostle St. Peter, "Be ye subject to every human creature for God's sake." (1 Peter, ii. 13.)

While he lived as a youth in his parents' house, he always obeyed their signs readily, and for this reason they loved him so much more than their other children, as he was more docile and obedient; they never could perceive any disobedience in him, as the Processes show.

He also obeyed his parents in things to which he had a great repugnance, as in being godfather to a little brother, and holding him at the baptismal font. It seemed to his humility a burden above his strength, to have to instruct

that to oppose the wishes of parents r desire anything contrary to the will s not disobedience, but a duty, and act. Such was the conduct of the Aloysius Gonzaga, when he long re- father's will, who did not wish him a religious order; of St. Stanislas youth of sixteen, who, contrary to 's desire, having disguised himself as undertook the long journey of twelve niles, quite alone, to be admitted at o that religious order in which God willed him to be. It is an action in- by Jesus Christ Himself, when He says, to set a man at variance against his (Matth. x. 35.) To obey our parents ng contrary to the will of God, is to more than God, contrary to the first nent of the Decalogue, confirmed by ed Redeemer, when He said, "He that her or mother more than Me, is not Me," (v. 37,) and merits blame and ent, instead of praise and reward. On ary, it is very praiseworthy to disobey them, when their will is opposed to that of God the Supreme Father, and absolute Master of the children no less than of the parents. This being presupposed, we will relate the action of Benedict which appears disobedience, but it is certainly deserving of all praise, being an act of heroic obedience to God. Scarcely had the light of reason begun to shine in his soul, than God called him to the most austere of all states of life. He was certain of this, through a very sensible interior inspiration, and through the approbation, not of one, but of many confessors, chosen and consulted by him as the most noted for long experience, heavenly light, virtue, and piety. He was so convinced of it, that he began from his boyhood to practise as much of extraordinary mortification and austerity as that tender age could bear; and if his parents surprised him by chance in these exercises, he said to them humbly, that he was endeavouring by these means to prepare himself for the more austere state of life to which he felt himself called by God. He wrote this more clearly to them in the letter which he sent them when he left La Chartreuse: "God will assist me, and will guide me in the enterprise which He has Himself inspired: it is not permitted to us to resist the will of God." These were his words. We ourselves cannot deny this his special vocation, seeing, "a posteriori," as it is said, that God conferred upon him that superabundant grace which was absolutely necessary to undertake and persevere till death in the very austere state of life, which has been minutely described in the first chapter of the second part and elsewhere, and without which grace it was not possible for a young man in the flower of his age, living in the midst of the world, to continue it. Being, then, fully convinced of the will of God, whom was he to obey? God, who desired it, or his parents, who opposed it? "We ought to obey God rather than men." (Acts, v. 29.) Who can then blame him for this, as one guilty of disobedienee? Who will not rather extol his obedience? The virtue of St. Jane Frances de Chantal is praised as heroic, because, being called by God to religion, she had the courage to step over her own son, who stretched himself across the threshold of the door to prevent her egress. Why then should Benedict be blamed, who, to execute the will of God, took no notice of his parents' opposition, and declared himself ready to pass over his own father, if he placed himself in the same manner at the door to prevent his departure.

Though he afterwards lived master of his own liberty and subject to no one, as in the time of his pilgrimages and at Rome, he never let pass any occasion of exercising the virtue of obedience. He was not satisfied with having recourse to God, to obtain light before he undertook anything; he also always consulted confessors and directors who were wise, prudent, and well versed in the science of the soul, nor did he ever depart from their advice. Whithersoever he went in his pilgrimages, he told the parish priest, or some other exemplary ecclesiastic, that he wished in all things to depend on their commands and be under obedience to them. One person attests, that he once travelled fourteen leagues to consult one of them.

The particular acts of his obedience were some of them exercised in interior, others in exterior concerns. In regard of interior things obedience was very difficult to him; yet submitting his will and understanding, he punctually complied whenever he was commanded to discover these things, but he could not help showing by his countenance and acts the great repugnance he felt. Though his profound humility made him most desirous to keep secret what passed in his interior, still, when interrogated by his confessors, and obliged by a formal precept of obedience, he manifested all with sincerity; but the combat in his mind between humility and obedience, caused him to send forth sighs from the depths of his heart, sighs so deep and penetrating, that they even drew tears from his eyes. The confessor desisted then from pursuing his inquiry into the concerns of his interior, that he might relieve him from the distress and dejection of mind which appeared in his countenance, his words, his broken sighs and tears.

In exterior things he flew promptly to execute orders, though he was sometimes obliged to overcome himself for this. A confessor in Rome, knowing by his confessions the purity of his conscience, and being also aware that he was not accustomed to communicate the same day as he confessed, that he might with greater diligence prepare himself to receive the Heavenly Bread on the following day, ordered him to go to the altar on the same morning in which he had been to confession. The servant of God, judging obedience to be the best preparation, having made some acts of devotion, presented himself that same morning at the holy table and communicated. In like manner he obeyed a confessor at Loretto, communicating not only on the morning of his confession, but also the following morning, according to the order which he received. Thus he also obeyed others; but no other of his confessors ordered him so regularly to communicate on the day of his confession. His last confessor in Rome, Signor Marconi, gave him, however, very wisely the order always to do so. He acted thus for two reasons: first, to try his obedience; secondly, to ascertain more clearly if he were exempt from the prejudices which prevailed on the subject of communion in the ultramontane countries (suspected of heresy) through which the servant of God had passed in his pilgrimages. Therefore, having no doubt that he might go to communion, even without previous confession, he gave him the order mentioned. The servant of God, from that time submitting his understanding and all his own feelings, most obediently communicated on the day of his confession.

One year he fulfilled three times the Paschal precept out of obedience. Once in Loretto, where he was at that time, and where a confessor in Rome had told him he could fulfil the precept. The second time was in the patriarchal church of San Giovanni in Laterano, as is the practice of pilgrims, being assured by his confesser that he would there certainly satisfy the duty, for the curate of his parish, not satisfied with the communion he had made at Loretto, ordered him to communicate again in Rome; but seeing afterwards the customary billet, certifying his reception of the holy communion at San Giovanni, he sharply reproved him, desiring him to communicate in his own parish. Benedict, accepting the reproof in silence and peace, promptly obeyed, and communicated in his parish. His obedience was admired and his patience praised by all who became acquainted with the circumstance, and after his death it was commended by the parish priest himself.

That confessor in Rome who ordered him to seek for some employment, or for some master to serve, to withdraw him from idleness, was so much edified and moved by his ready obedience in trying to do so, though in vain, that from this he judged with reason, that the true Spirit of God dwelt in Benedict, and the necessary qualifications for the very rigid state of life he had undertaken; and he left him at liberty.

It is not, however, very surpising, that he

the whole of which he had passed in the church. His hostess being displeased at this great abstinence, earnestly begged one of the priests of the church, Don Gaspare Valeri, to oblige him to eat. He went there at supper-time, and was edified by seeing him rise up in his presence, and not take his seat again until he was commanded; he was more surprised, however, to see with his own eyes, that he scarcely put anything into his mouth of the food prepared, but desiring him in obedience to eat, he saw him take a little more. Perceiving that he had left a small loaf intended for him, and was eating only some of his little bits of bread, he ordered him to practise the advice of Jesus Christ to His apostles: "Eat such things as are set before you." (Luke, x. 8.) This sufficed; he quickly took the knife, cut the bread and eat several slices, adding an egg which he had left. Signor Valeri, not content with this, gave him a command to obey his hosts in all things, specifying that he was to accept clothes, as he saw him in rags. He always obeyed most readily, and the hostess being encouraged to a holy boldness by this order, also commanded him in obedience, when occasions occurred, and she saw the order readily executed, as he accepted some respectable clothing and a pair of old shoes, out of obedience. At the time when he lived in the Ospizio dei Poveri at Rome, he obeyed the warden punctually and without reply, in whatever he commanded him; an obedience which is attested by the warden himself, and is much praised as per-

mand he went towards it, though onl
short time. He never drank wine, but h
it if he were told to do so in obedienc
refused invitations to dinner, but on sor
occasions obedience made him accept the
also eat of everything, though only in
quantity sufficient to comply with ob
These acts of obedience were not exerci
Benedict merely once or twice, they we
numerous. They must, however, have c
not a little, for he had to overcome the h
strong inclination which he had for a very
life. Notwithstanding this, yielding to t
mands of others, he aimed at joining this
ence to the austerity of his life; hence,
sake of example, he tasted wine through
ence, but took little; he ate of all th
dinner, but very sparingly of each; he a
relief, but enough for the day only; h
from amongst the things offered him th
and most ragged.

What I have related is quite sufficient
clearly the perfection of the voluntary ob
practised by Benedict.

CHAPTER VI.

HIS LOVE OF GOD: HE SHOWS ITS STRENGTH BY HIS CARE TO AVOID SIN.

THE proofs of a true love of God are many, and its degrees are also numerous. The first is, without doubt, diligently to avoid offending Him. He who truly loves God takes great care not to offend Him even slightly. Benedict had this care from his first coming to the use of reason, and he put it in practice till his death. From the time that he came to the use of reason till the twelfth year of his age, no fault was observed in him, at home or at school, either by the servants, by persons not of the family, or even by his fellow-students. I find it, on the contrary, attested, that "his behaviour in the age of childhood was so modest, discreet, and sincere, that it announced even then the uprightness of his soul, and caused him to be regarded by his equals, no less than by his superiors, as a person of very exemplary conduct. He was so penetrated with the love of God, that there was nothing to be blamed in his whole conduct."

From his twelfth year, in the house of his uncle, the parish priest, till his eighteenth, when his uncle died gloriously in the cause of charity, his care not to offend his beloved Lord by any fault, however small, greatly increased. He showed at this time that he had by the Divine favour a sublime knowledge of His greatness, whence he derived his interior recollection, silence, and retirement, and his great affection for everything belonging to the divine worship. It increased so much, that there was never observed in him during this time any failing, any omission, or even a small fault, and, what is more wonderful in a young man, not even an idle or useless word, which so easily escapes from the mouth even of men of mature years. One person attests with astonishment, that he had several times given him an occasion of being disturbed and impatient, by sharp and lively reprimands, by which he sought to deter him from the resolution of entirely abandoning his father's house. The deponent always observed such tranquillity in his countenance, and so much constancy, that he was, as it were, disarmed; and he acknowledges that he knew from this his great horror of the smallest sins, and his love of God, whom he preferred before his parents and the comforts of home.

He gave once, however, a clear proof of his dread of small faults, when at his uncle's house. He was one day in the garden, where he used to go at his uncle's command to gather strawberries for the table. A little girl of the house, about seven years of age, who came into the garden, wished to taste them, and asked Benedict for some. He answered frankly that he could not himself give her any, but would do so if she went to obtain his uncle's leave. She came back, saying, she had not obtained it; nevertheless, she added, "Give me some, your uncle will not know it." "If my unclo will not know it," answered Benedict, "God will see it." "What consequence will it be?" answered she; "I do not ask for many, two will satisfy me; it is a little thing, you may do it." "A little thing! what do you say?" pursued Benedict; "anything which offends God cannot be a trifle. Besides, we begin by little things, and by degrees we pass on to great. To-day it is only a few strawberries; presently, things of greater consequenco will bo stolen. You yourself would steal a few pins one day, another day a little pair of scissors, then you would not have difficulty in taking things of more consequence; from little things we go on to greater. Be sorry for such an insinuation, and go to confess it as soon as you can." Thus he spoke conformably to the advice of the Holy Ghost: "Ho that contemneth small things, shall fall by little and little." (Ecclus. xix. 1.) Nor was he satisfied with this, he reminded her of it when she was on the point of going to the church to make her confession. Tho warning of Benedict, and his answers to the little girl, were so strongly impressed on her mind, that she could not forget them; even when grown up and become a nun, after many years in the monastery of the Ursulines, she made this depositiou in the Processes. I can piously believo that sho regulated her conduct by this sentiment. O how useful to children are similar warnings! And how much do those displeaso God, and how much evil do they occasion to their souls, who, instead of admonishing them, yield to them, particularly if they have authority over them!

Benedict practised exactly himself the advice which he gave to others; for as he was walking one day in the garden with his uncle and another priest, the latter seeing the abundance of the strawberries, said, "What a great quantity of strawberries! What a size they are! Benediet can easily satiate himself with them." "He could," said the uncle, "but there is no fear of his touching them."

It was well known to the persons of the house, and to those who were intimate with his uncle, that through the great horror which Benedict had for little thefts, which are very common in boys at the age he was then, that he would never have put out his hand to take a single fruit, not even of those which had fallen to the ground, and that he would rather have trodden them under foot than appropriated one to himself. The garden abounded with exquisite fruit, as beautiful to the eye as sweet to the palate. He might also have presumed on some right, which the affection of his uncle and his close connexion by blood with him gave him. But his affections had a different aim from the vileness of earthly things, and the satisfaction of the appetite, nor did he regulate himself by these reflections when the observance of the Divine Law was in question. It happened one day, that being in the country with some youths of his own age, these boys stole some apples from a neighbouring farm, and thinking to do

Benedict a service, they offered him some. But triumphing over human respect, and refusing to receive any, he said to them courageously, "These apples are stolen, it is not permitted to you to eat them, and I will not have one of them." In like manner he refused some cherries offered to him by a companion who had taken them from his father's larder; and when he told him that his father had allowed him to do so, Benedict unwillingly accepted them, but would not taste them, leaving them hanging by a thread to the window, till they became rotten. The careful vigilance which he employed in his tender and youthful age against every offence of God, became greater and more delicate in the remainder of his life. All his confessors agree in deposing that Benedict minutely observed the commandments of God and of the holy Church, that he never deliberately committed a venial sin, that he always practised the Evangelical Counsels, and that he preserved to his last breath the white robe of innocence, which he received in holy baptism; thus, in his confessions no one ever found sufficient, much less necessary matter for absolution. Whoever wishes to read their depositions, (which are greatly to his praise,) will find the page, the number, and the paragraph of each, mentioned in the summary of the Processes, page 81. It is unnecessary that I should speak of them at greater length; what I have mentioned is sufficient. I merely add, that the confessors chosen by him are well known for their integ-

his pilgrimages led him, chiefly in Loretto and Fabriano, but most particularly in Rome. Besides his confessors, priests, and other persons worthy of credit, attest on oath his irreproachable conduct, in what appertains to exterior behaviour, and these testimonies also are cited in the above-named summary.

The observance of the commandments of God and of the Church, and the avoiding of every small sin, must have cost Benedict not a little. When asked by the penitentiary-confessor at Loretto if he had ever missed mass on days of obligation in his pilgrimages, being obliged by obedience to answer, he said, that in order to sanctify them as he ought, he took care not to travel upon these days, which when questioned he had before said to Signor Valeri, but that in order to be punctually present at church on these days, he had often been obliged to hasten his steps very much the day before, to traverse mountains, endure pouring rain, and walk barefoot over the snow.

To avoid the chattering, idle words, murmurs, and obscene jests of the rabble, he always walked alone, refusing all company, avoiding the inns, and quitting the beaten roads, to his great inconvenience, by the increase of distance and the dangers which are often met with out of the principal roads. For the same reason, he also avoided, as much as he could, associating with other poor people; and he sometimes omitted

never found sufficient matter for absolution, and saw him as contrite and humble, as if he were guilty of enormous crimes. Even at little more than fifteen years of age the delicacy of his conscience was so great, that it induced him to make many general confessions without ever having a deliberate sin to mention. Thus the parish priest of Lepesse, Don Jacques Joseph Vincent, testifies.

He practised afterwards exactly what he proposed to himself in his examinations, particularly in regard of preventing others from offending God, even slightly. In the Abate Mancini's Ospizio at Rome, one of the poor people having begun a conversation which was useless, and might offend against charity if it continued, Benedict interrupting him said, "Let us think of the Passion of Jesus Christ;" thus he put an end to the discourse. In the same Ospizio, some gentlemen who lived near them, wishing to speak to one of the poor people assembled there, named Antonino, asked some of them for him, but Antonino refusing to go, told his companions to answer from the window, that he was not yet come. Benedict being unwilling to suffer this evident falsehood, prevented it, and going to the window answered sincerely, "that Antonino was there, but did not wish to go to him." Then turning with holy zeal to Autonino, he rebuked him, saying, "We are never allowed to tell lies; we ought always to tell the truth, at whatever cost." Being one day in the Basilica of the Holy House of Loretto, in the act of reading a little book of devotion, some Roman ladies approached him, desiring to speak to him; but scarcely had they begun, than perceiving his modesty and devotion, and that he did not even raise his eyes to look at them, very much edified, they only said, "Pray to God for us, Benedict," and went away, without receiving a look, much less a word from him.

He was, in fine, so careful and vigilant against every small fault, he weighed with so much exactness every word before he uttered it, that he seemed to some to be excessive, if one can be so, in such cautiousness. Some persons who relied much on his recommendations to God, begged him sometimes indiscreetly to recommend them in all his prayers. Benedict, that he might not tell an untruth, or that he might not afterwards fail in his promise, first raised his

ord Jesus Christ Himself said, that the obser- ance of the Divine commandments was a proof f the love of God: "He that hath My com- iandments and keepeth them, he it is that oveth Me." (John, xiv. 21.) What can we say f one who observed them with so much delicacy? f one who observed also the Evangelical Counsels, nd observed them constantly from the first use f reason till his last breath? Still this is little, empared with what I shall relate in the following hapter.

CHAPTER VII.

HIS LOVE OF GOD IS MORE CLEARLY SHOWN BY HIS CONTINUAL UNION WITH GOD.

As a foundation for what I am going to say in this and the following chapters, I must premise and make known to every one who shall read this work, that Benedict, as the penitentiary at Loretto, one of his confessors, attests, "was abundantly replenished with supernatural lights and knowledge, regarding the mystery of the most Holy Trinity, as also concerning the Passion of Jesus Christ, for which he had prepared the way by continual prayer and contemplation, and by the mortified and painful life which he voluntarily led; so that I can with all security assert, says the confessor, that through the abundance of supernatural gifts obtained from God, he possessed that right knowledge which the saints possess in the way and pilgrimage of this world." Besides this testimony, he confirms it at greater length in the Processes in another place.

Another confessor, who obliged him by obedience to speak of his interior, asserts that in speaking of the mysteries of the most Blessed Trinity, and of the Passion and death of our Divine Redeemer, he expressed himself in terms which showed him to be possessed of great knowledge, "Insomuch that as I have," he adds, "some acquaintance with the spiritual works composed by St. Teresa, it seemed to me that what he said agreed with them. When urged to tell me if he had studied theology, he answered that he had not. Hence I understood that God had favoured this His servant with this high knowledge illuminating his mind with supernatural light, for it was not possible that a person unacquainted with theological subjects, could have expressed himself as he did." These are his words. The deposition of another confessor in Rome agrees with this: "From the few words which he uttered in answer to my questions made in confession, I understood very well," he says, "that he was penetrated with the tremendous majesty of God, and that he had a very lively knowledge of the Divine Attributes, particularly of the greatness, majesty, and goodness of God; hence it was, that knowing his own nothingness, he broke out into most humble expressions."

In like manner, a parish priest who was his confessor in Rome, deposes, that he drew from the conferences that he had with him, that Benedict was favoured by God with lights of the understanding, intellectual visions, and other supernatural gifts which are called "Gratiæ gratis datæ," or, gratuitous gifts. And though at first this confessor feared some deception, yet in time he knew and acknowledged the above-mentioned lights, visions, and gifts to be true and solid, and that they came immediately from God.

Oh, if this last confessor had not been so humble, and the second so reserved, how many more important things would have been transmitted to posterity, glorious to God, honourable to His servant, and useful to all! This last confessor, judging himself through humility incapable of directing so great a soul, and in matters so difficult, wished to be relieved from the burden, and commanded him to provide himself with another confessor well versed in mystical theology, and who had not the care of a parish, that he might with greater ease apply himself expressly to his direction. The second, moved to compassion by the great pain which he knew the servant of God felt in overcoming by obedienee the extreme repugnance of his humility, would not persevere in his questions.

This being premised, it will not be difficult to believe what I shall relate of his union with God, his raptures, contemplation of Him, his ardent transports of love, his ecstasies, and supernatural favours. These are effects which follow from the knowledge of God, illustrated in a lively manner by heavenly light.

As to his union with God, there was no impediment to oppose his closely uniting himself with Him. The obstacles are an affection to earthly things and to ourselves. His detachment from worldly things was perfect: what is related of his singular poverty in the three first chapters of this third part, clearly shows it. His detachment from his own body and from his own will, which is more difficult than any other, is shown by his angelical purity and by the very exact obedience mentioned in the fourth and

from whom he could not separate hin even in thought. He himself, in spite ol humility, was obliged through obedience to order given him by his confessor, to acknowl this close and continual union. Hence, what the confessor drew from him in his co ences with him, and from what he saw witl own eyes, and heard also from others, he dec that he could not find terms to express the of love which burned within him, and ent filled him with its flames; so that what St. aventure left written of his Seraphic Father Francis, may with truth be said of him, "' he was like a coal, entirely penetrated with fire of Divine love, and absorbed by it."

This union, being completely interior, can be known to us through the exterior. The tivity of a fire burning within a furnace, only be ascertained by the flames which out from it. I will, therefore, describe the fla which, being contained in his heart, appe through his exterior senses, from whence we judge of the vivacity of this fire

streets, he kept his eyes constantly cast down, never raising them to look at the people, much less at the magnificence of the buildings, and whatever usually attracts the eye of the curious; he always walked with so much modesty and composure, that those who met him, greatly edified, thought him in an ecstasy; and if any one wished to speak to him, it was necessary to call him by name, and in a loud voice, for he never turned his head or his eyes here and there. Some depose in the Processes, that meeting him in the streets of Rome, they always saw him alone, with his head bent, his eyes cast down, and with such a demeanour, that they judged him, with reason, to be quite immersed in the contemplation of God, insomuch, that in the streets of so populous and magnificent a city as Rome, he seemed a perfect hermit. Others attest, that he was everywhere seen to be absorbed in the continual presence of God in so sublime a manner, that he resembled a person in an ecstasy. Whether he were in the church or walking in the streets, his mind appeared to be so penetrated by the Divine presence, that it was evident he had nothing in view but God. The devout and modest manner in which he walked, was a subject of admiration and edification to every one who beheld him. The attestations of others on this point are very numerous, and agree in stating the same, not only as far as regards the streets of Rome, but of every town where he happened to be. Those we have mentioned will, however, suffice.

In the country while travelling, he was no less modest and united to God than in the towns. He now and then looked at the pleasant fields, the plants, the mountains, and hills; but they all served him as steps to ascend to God. "He made use of all created things," thus deposes his confessor, Father Temple, who had examined Benedict's interior, "to increase more and more his knowledge of the omnipotence, the wisdom, and the goodness of God, which caused him to burst into expressions of the praise and love of God, exactly as it happened," he says, "to my Patriarch, St. Francis, who exulted in all the works of God." The brightness of the sun, the verdure of the fields, the beauty of the plants, the birds, the grass, the flowers, all carried him to God, and made him burst forth into fervent thanksgivings, and rapturous admiration of the divine attributes; enlightened by celestial light he read them distinctly, as in an open book, in all creatures, a book which is closed for us miserable creatures, because we have little love of God, who ought to be the sole object of our love.

This was the cause of his going always alone through the streets of the town; and in all his long journeys, this made him refuse the company of others. The charity of the Abate Mancini, thinking to afford him some comfort in a pilgrimage from his Ospizio dei Poveri, in Rome, to Loretto, induced him to offer Benedict a companion. He refused, however, with thanks. When asked the reason, he answered with sincerity and humility, that he did not wish to be disturbed in his prayer.

Even in Loretto no one could boast of having had him for a companion, for he always loved to remain alone united to God, in order to practise the advice which the apostle St. Paul gives us of praying in every place: "I will that men pray in every place." (1 Tim. ii. 8.)

In the use he made of his hearing, he also gave proofs of his union with God. He would never listen to news about even indifferent things; hence, if the poor of the Ospizio, when the prayers were ended, brought forward such discourse, Benedict quickly retired to his little room to converse with God; but on the contrary, he remained amongst them when conversation on spiritual matters was introduced, putting in some word seasonably himself to carry it on. To speak to him directly of Divine Love, was like touching the string of a musical instrument in good order, which immediately vibrates and sends forth sounds; his face became inflamed, he was filled with a holy eagerness, and uttered sentiments and affections which clearly showed the great fire contained in his heart. On the contrary, he was filled with horror on hearing a word against charity, against truth, or against Almighty God. He hastened with holy zeal towards the person, whoever it might be, he admonished him in the spirit of evangelical charity, and when this was of no avail, he retired to a distance, grieved at the offence of God. On such occasions he had sometimes, however, to endure great ill usage, as we shall see in another place.

The tongue, however, which is the most faithful index of the human heart, manifested most clearly the great fire of Divine Love which burned in the breast of this servant of God. It was his custom when a child to speak very little, for fear of offending God or saying something against fraternal charity; before any word issued from his mouth, it was well considered in his mind, according to the advice of St. Bernard: "Omne verbum prius veniat ad limam quam ad linguam;" and every one admired this in him exceedingly. Whenever the occasion presented itself, he spoke with great fervour of the truths of our holy faith; he insinuated the contempt which we ought to have for earthly things, in order to possess those of heaven; he spoke of the means of practising it, insisting principally on the mortification of the senses, which was so dear to him; and he was heard not only with pleasure, but even with wonder and great emotion. But his fervour shone forth particularly when he began to speak of the love of God towards man, and of the return of love which man owes to God. He showed himself to be pierced to the soul with grief, seeing how ill His love is corresponded to. He complained precisely as a son would do who should see his beloved father neglected and despised by others; he said, like St. Ignatius of Loyola in one of his ecstasies, "O Lord, if men knew Thee, they would not offend Thee." "We offend God," said Benedict, "because we do not know His goodness; he who knows God, does not commit sins." Some persons attest in the Processes, that they had felt great emotion in hearing him speak on similar subjects; it is the property of fire to enkindle fire; that they had much regretted his brevity, and had never been tired of hearing him, nor had they ever at other times heard Almighty God spoken of with the fervour and persuasiveness of Benedict. He inculcated always, to every one who spoke with him, the necessity of living in the holy fear of God and in His grace, the abhorrence of even venial sins, as an offence of God, evincing always the greatest desire that God should not be offended in the slightest degree.

When on some rare occasion he accepted an invitation to dinner, whether it were with other poor people, invited also by the charity of the Abate Mancini, or whether he alone were invited in some town during his pilgrimages, it was his custom first to raise his eyes and mind to God in the act of prayer, then to take the dish of meat in both his hands, and holding it up to entertain himself for a little time with his eyes closed, in fervent prayer to Almighty God, acknowledging it to be His gift. While taking his scanty food, he blessed God, thanked Him, and broke out into acts of ardent love for His goodness in creating so many things for man's benefit. From time to time he raised his eyes to heaven, then casting them down, he urged the guests with affectionate sentiments to praise God; after the meal, he thanked God in a devout manner, thus keeping his mind and heart united to God, even while he refreshed his body with food. His whole conduct, his constant modesty, his serene and devout countenance, his hands always joined, the words he uttered, and everything about him, even to the rags which covered him, and were more prized in him than a royal vesture, showed him to be always united with God and always in contemplation. Wisdom, who is God Himself, and who has the greatest horror of entering and dwelling in a heart stained with sin, for "Wisdom will not enter into a malicious soul, nor dwell in a body subject to sins," (Wisd. i. 4,) was proved by Benedict's whole conduct to be resident in his heart. "The wisdom of a man shineth in his countenance." (Eccles. viii. 1.) Even in the answers which he gave to those who questioned him about things sometimes of little moment, his union with God appeared, for he first lifted up his eyes to heaven, begging light and direction from God, and then he answered.

Even at the time of his nightly repose, those who surrounded him perceived his union with God. In the Ospizio de' Poveri, while the others were in a profound sleep, one of the watchmen heard him often repeat, raising his voice a little, "Miserere mei, miserere mei." Another on different nights heard his repeated exclamation, "O bon Dieu! O bon Dieu! Miserere mei!" Others when awake heard ejaculations which they could not repeat, partly because they were in French, which they did not know, and partly

ause they could only remember this more
ımon one, "Domine miserere mei;" and they
ıtioned it afterwards to the director of the
ɪizio, Abate Mancini, who on hearing these
ıgs conceived a higher opinion of his sanc-
' than he had had before. Also when he was
ɪping in a bake-house in the country, when
Loretto, he was heard to give utterance to
y exclamations and affections.

But the most authentic testimony of his close
on with God in the night time, was given
Benedict himself when interrogated, and oblig-
by obedience to answer, by that excellent
fessor, Father Temple, in Loretto. He drew
n his answers, that every time he awoke
ing the night, his thought was to turn his
ıd to God and call Him to his assistance. On
ıking, he sweetly complained of the Spouse
his soul, as if He were at a distance; but
ieving Him to be present with him, he ex-
ded his arms towards him, exclaiming in these
similar terms, "Ah, my God! I have thought
Thee this night, and Thou hast caused me
ly sorrow and tears; I thought that my ingrati-
e had obliged Thee to listen to Thy justice
to depart from me; I sighed and ran after
ɪe, and saw nothing but darkness. Do not
bt, O Divine Saviour, that I am all Thine,
ɪn Thou seest that the first movement of
heart on awaking tends happily to persuade
that Thou lovest me also to-day, and that
ɪu art not so far from me as I have deserv-
by my defects, and had imagined to myself

His confessor drew from this, and from the whole tenor of his life, that during both night and day, he always kept his mind elevated to God; he thought of God, and delighted in God.

Having asked him in a conference how he understood this passage of the Canticle, " I will lead her into the wilderness, and I will speak to her heart," (Osee, ii. 14,) if in a literal or mystical sense, and if he practised it, he gave as his answer, that he executed it even literally, though he lived in the midst of the world. With great reason this confessor finds no difficulty in considering him always as a seraph of love. With great reason we also may call him an anchorite in the midst of the world.

What is most admirable in his union with God is, that it never relaxed in fervour; on the contrary, it increased day by day, for it was not confined within limits, on account of the infinitude of the Object of union, who is a God of infinite perfections. When he drew near the end of his days, it augmented in such a manner that it seemed to all that his soul must in a short time burst the bonds of this mortal life, to unite itself eternally with its Lord, to whom alone he aspired. This we find deposed in the Processes.

From what has been related, every one will with facility perceive how ardent a love of God burned in the breast of Benedict. "Union," says St. Thomas, "is all the work, all the effect of love. 'Unio est opus amoris.'" If the union which His servant had with God was so close, so continual in every action, in every place, what must his love have been? Still this is but little compared with what I shall set forth in the following chapter.

CHAPTER VIII.

HIS LOVE OF GOD SHOWS ITSELF TO BE VERY LIVELY BY HIS CONTINUAL PRAYER AND RAPTUROUS CONTEMPLATION OF GOD.

PRAYER, whether mental or vocal, when duly performed, is a means of increasing love in the soul towards God, with whom it familiarly treats, as St. Augustine defines it: "Prayer is the affection of the will of man, uniting himself to God, and a familiar conversing with Him." The length of Benedict's prayer, and his manner of performing it, showed clearly that his love of God was very great, and that he had increased it to the highest degree. As to vocal prayer, one of his confessors by examining him found that he did not spend much time in vocal prayers, but gave his whole attention to mental prayer. We only know that he recited the Divine Office of Priests, and the Rosary of the Blessed Virgin, which he always wore round his neck, besides the prayers which were said in common in the Ospizio dei Poveri in Rome, or in the churches before the most Blessed Sacrament, when it was exposed. But the small number of his vocal prayers shows in him a greater love of God than if he had recited many.

It is a very solid doctrine of the angelical doctor, St. Thomas, that vocal prayer is a means of raising the mind to God. "In prayer, words, and such like exterior signs, are to be used only inasmuch as they help to excite the interior feelings of the mind." Hence comes the advice which St. Francis of Sales gives to every one: "If, while saying vocal prayers, you feel your heart drawn towards mental prayer, do not refuse to follow, and do not trouble yourself about not having yet finished the prayers you had proposed to say, for mental prayer, which you make in the place of them, is more pleasing to God and more useful to your soul, with the exception of the Divine Office of obligation."

St. Ignatius of Loyola, a great spiritual master, agrees with him, in the little book of his Spiritual Exercises, where he speaks on the second method of prayer. This may serve as a warning for those, who, loading themselves with vocal prayers to be daily recited, are in such haste to finish them all, that they hurry them over without any devotion. This is a mistake into which St. Teresa acknowledges herself to have fallen in the beginning of her spiritual career. "What is the use of so great a number? Why such haste?" says St. Francis of Sales. "One single Pater Noster said from the heart and with feeling, is worth more than many said in a hurry."

This was the practice of our servant of God.

after reciting some Psalm or Lesson, he put the Office-book on the rails of the high altar, where he prayed and gave himself to contemplation, pouring forth holy affections to God. He understood Latin well, having learned it when young; and the little book of à Kempis, which he read daily, was in Latin, as Father Temple gathered from his answers; but he understood the meaning more clearly through the great light with which God favoured him. After pouring forth his affections for a long time with his eyes fixed, either towards heaven or the beautiful image of the Blessed Virgin, without ever turning them elsewhere, still remaining motionless and on his knees, he began again to read, then again to contemplate, continuing this devout occupation for many hours; and a very pious priest, beholding him attentively, blushed at the difference which he saw between his manner of praying and that of Benedict, and, much edified, he interiorly recommended himself to him. It was the same in regard of the Rosary and other prayers said in common, in which he distinguished himself from others by the attention which showed itself in his devout attitude.

In regard of mental prayer, it far surpassed in Benedict what is common and ordinary. I will show here how he commenced, in what manner and for how long he continued it, and how he concluded it. We shall see clearly that his prayer was not a meditation, it was contemplation.

He had not any great difficulty in beginning it. Powder which is dry is no sooner brought near the flame, than it takes fire. We unfortunate sinners are like green and damp wood, in which fire cannot at once begin to exert its activity; we are obliged first to make use of efforts of the imagination and reasonings of the intellect, that we may be capable of feeling some spark of fire. Benedict was like dry powder; he had scarcely begun, scarcely approached the Divine Furnace, for "Our God is a consuming fire," (Deut. iv. 24,) before he broke forth into loving affections, and felt holy flames within his heart. Let the reader call to mind here what was mentioned in the beginning of the seventh chapter, as a foundation for the singular gifts of his prayer; let him remember that he was plentifully enriched with supernatural light and knowledge, that he was penetrated with a lively sense of the Divine attributes, and was favoured by God with illustrations and mental visions, which are less subject to deceit than those which are visible. Hence it was that he had a great facility, as it is deposed in the Processes, in raising his mind to God, a manifest sign of the union of his soul with the Divine Majesty. He then began to pray, with the gift of rapturous contemplation, in considering the greatness of God, His divine attributes, the ineffable mystery of the Blessed Trinity, and the love shown to man by our Divine Redeemer in

of the truth." (S. Aug.) Those truths of Faith, which the soul at first, by the ob light of faith alone, firmly believed, but not clearly see, she then knows with clea without a multiplicity of acts, by one s glance of the mind, illumined by divine l she knows, she rejoices, admires, and loves so much interior sweetness, as to remain and immoveable in this consideration for and for whole days ; precisely like a person having heard others speak of the beautifu presentations of a famous theatre, believes and figures them to himself, as well as he by the help of his imagination ; but if he ha to be himself a spectator, and to see them self, when the curtain is drawn up, in the b ness of many lights, he then at one look see clearly and distinctly, and he continues t hold, admire, wonder, and enjoy, while pass away unperceived by him. This was ly the case with Benedict. Scarcely had he begun to pray in the churches, than he was introduced into "the cellar of wine," as it is called in the Canticles, wherein the Heavenly Bridegroom is accustomed to introduce those souls who are His spouses, and are very dear to Him. Then fixing his interior eye on the infinite perfections of an Omnipotent God, on the ineffable mystery of the most Blessed Trinity, on the infinite love He has displayed, or on the Passion of our Divine Redeemer, he continued to pray for many hours, sometimes for the whole day; thinking neither of refreshing his body with food, nor of anything else, being entirely occupied in beholding the very sublime things which the divine light granted to him by Almighty God discovered to him; in admiring them, and bursting forth into interior affections of praise, delight, and love, with so much interior peace, and so great an abhorrence of everything but God, that he judged with St. Paul, that all the grandeur and pleasures of the world are worthy only to be despised as dirt by the human heart.

The length of his prayers was well known in Rome, and many persons, in attesting it, speak of them as prayers, while they were, in effect, contemplations and divine favours. It was very common with him to spend in them the entire day, without taking any corporal food, for he was well satisfied with the spiritual nourishment he received from Almighty God: "He fed him with the bread of life and understanding, and gave him the water of wholesome wisdom to drink."

(Ecclus. xv. 3.) "Not in bread alone doth man live." (Matth. iv. 4.) This was observed for the first time at Moulins, immediately after he left the convent of Sept Fontaines, while yet young. Those with whom he lodged there, after having given testimony in the Processes to his great mortifications, in his refusal of a bed, being content to lie on straw, and his abstinence from every sort of food, excepting at night, when he took a little piece of bread soaked in water, to which he sometimes added not more than three or four walnuts; after all this, I say, they attest that he left the house at break of day to go to the church, and remained there till evening; and the parish priest of St. Peter's at Moulins adds, that in the church he was like a person in an ecstasy.

He was noticed in Fabriano to be in continual contemplation for one whole day; in Loretto, for as many days as he remained there; and in Rome, in several churches, but especially in that which he frequented most, Santa Maria dei Monti. All those who uniformly attest the length of his prayers, equally give testimony to his admirable manner of praying. Some call it ecstatic, others speak of him as an angel, immoveable as a statue, a saint, as one absorbed in God; some say that they never saw him during this time blow his nose, move his hands, or spit. Some placed themselves secretly behind a confessional, or in some hidden part of the church, particularly at the most solitary hours, on purpose to watch him: they saw him quiet, ecstatic, motionless, always the same. It was not the human eye that made him act thus, it was the love of God. He who beholds with admiration a majestic sovereign on his royal throne, does not trouble himself about the insects which he is trampling under foot. He generally remained on his knees, excepting some few times, when he stood up, but he did so like a person in an ecstasy, only for a short time, and chiefly towards the end of his life, when he was obliged to it by his severe sufferings. His prayer was so long and so ecstatic, that every one admired it. Some on only beholding him motionless, with his hands crossed on his breast, his eyes fixed, without moving his eyelids, and turned either towards the most Blessed Sacrament when exposed, towards heaven or the image of the Blessed Virgin, feeling great tenderness in their hearts, could not refrain from weeping through devotion, and recommended themselves interiorly to him, believing him to be a saint. Many went expressly to the church of Santa Maria dei Monti, or elsewhere, where they were sure to find him always in contemplation, to be edified and moved to compunction. This a very devout person, who held a benefice in the patriarchal Vatican church, used to do, going often for this purpose to the church we mentioned, and placing himself as near as he could to him in the place where he usually prayed, for he felt comfort in being so near a saint, as he believed him to be; and seeing him in this attitude of devotion, he felt such interior motions and affections as kept him more recollected in his prayer; and he sometimes blushed for himself, considering his example, and sometimes imagined to himself that on the day of universal judgment, our Lord would constitute this poor, dirty, and abject man as his judge to reprimand him for his tepidity in prayer, in serving God, in acquitting himself of the duties of his ecclesiastical state, and corresponding with the graces of God; then humbling himself and exciting himself to contrition, he prolonged his usual prayers, and encouraged himself to a more fervent life.

Father Don Biagio Piccilli, one of the "Pii Operarj," and consultor of the Sacred Congregation of Rites, who heard confessions indefatigably in his church of Santa Maria dei Monti, and who was accustomed in familiar conversation to speak of him as being like St. Alexis, poor by choice, often said to his penitents, that Benedict served him for a model and a stimulus to prayer.

If the method and duration of Benedict's prayer were admirable, as they would be in any servant of God, they were yet more wonderful in him, on account of some circumstances which were peculiar to him. He was continually assailed and tormented by those innumerable insects which he allowed to remain and multiply at their ease. It will be well here to recollect what was minutely described in the first chapter of this third part, regarding this singular sort of penance. One of these insects alone would be sufficient to disturb our tranquillity, our prayer, and perhaps our patience. What then must have been the effect of so innumerable a quantity on Benedict? What torment, what annoyance must they have caused him! What temptations to leave off prayer and free himself from so troublesome, painful, and close an attack! He had also in both knees tumours as large as a small loaf, which were not hard, but so soft as to yield to the touch of persons who noticed them and touched them several times after his death. How much must they have added to the torment he already suffered in his body! Still neither this attack nor this pain prevented him from praying quiet and motionless on his knees, not for one or two hours only, but for the whole day, adding to it a complete abstinence from food. What shall we say of it? Either that he was a corpse without a soul, or a piece of marble, or rather, that he was a saint of extraordinary patience, ecstatic, and so absorbed in God and in His greatness, that for His love he did not care what pain he suffered in his body, as was the case with the holy martyrs, who were absorbed in God and strengthened by Him.

We have yet to consider the servant of God when his contemplation was finished. In the same manner as Moses, (allowing, of course, for the proportion,) when he had ended his long and sublime colloquies with Almighty God on Mount Sinai, and descending from thence, was seen by Aaron and all the people with his face surrounded by brightness imparted to him by the divine and inaccessible light; thus though the countenance of Benedict when not in prayer was like a corpse, pale and thin, still it appeared after prayer quite different, being inflamed and coloured. Others depose, that many times when his prayer was ended, his face appeared so inflamed, that it seemed as if the fire of the love of God which he nourished in his heart, would manifest itself exteriorly. Almighty God has sometimes by a special favour shown in the countenance of His saints the interior flames of their hearts and the great light of their minds, to authenticate their sanctity by an unusual prodigy. Thus St. Philip Neri saw the face of the patriarch St. Ignatius shining while he was alive; and St. Anthony the abbot was distinguished from his monks in prayer, by the reflection which his interior light cast upon his countenance; thus also St. John of the Cross was twice

illuminate in this manner the countenance of Benedict, to show the interior flame which burned in his heart, and the great brightness of the heavenly lights with which He favoured him, and of which we have spoken elsewhere. A person of great piety, being one morning before sun-rise in the church of Santa Maria dei Monti, saw Benedict in contemplation on his knees in his usual place, with his face raised up towards heaven, and suddenly he saw his countenance so bright and shining, that he was struck with surprise and admiration, and the more, because at this time this unusual brilliancy, which lasted some time, could not proceed from the rays of the sun, which had not risen, nor from lights in the church, nor anything else, and he attested this in the Processes. A priest, most worthy of consideration on several accounts, attests that he saw him with his face surrounded by most brilliant rays as he left the church of the Holy Apostles, where he had been a long time in prayer, which rays shed brightness over his body from head to foot, and he was so astonished that he could not take his eyes off him for the space of an Ave Maria, experiencing at the same time within himself various affections of tenderness and respect, and an increase and confirmation of the judgment he had already formed of him, as a man entirely of God, and wholly inflamed with divine love. From what has been said in this chapter regarding the contemplation of Benedict, we may easily understand how lively and active was his love of God, for, according to the saying of St. Thomas, such contemplation has no source but love: "Ad contemplationem movet præcipuè charitas."

CHAPTER IX.

HIS LOVE OF GOD. ITS GREATNESS SHOWS ITSELF BY ECSTASIES, TRANSPORTS OF LOVE, AND OTHER DIVINE FAVOURS.

If his sublime and rapturous contemplations show clearly the interior fire of love, which consumed his heart, the ecstasies with which Almighty God from time to time favoured him, demonstrate it more distinctly, for St. Thomas says that nothing causes an ecstasy in man, but love: "Divine love is the direct cause of ecstasy," differing thus from simple contemplation, for love urges indeed to contemplation, but does not directly cause it. Ecstasy, as it is commonly defined by mystical theologians, is a total suspension of the senses, caused by a very lively knowledge of the greatness of God and the force of His love, and this with so much sweetness, that there is in it nothing of that violence which is the property of rapture. Such ecstasies were very common with Benedict, and they were mistaken by the vulgar for corporal diseases, fainting fits, arising from his known abstinence and weakness of stomach, and the like. Let it not surprise us, for at other times many persons who professed to be spiritual have fallen into this error.

The ecstasies with which our Lord favoured His beloved servant Ven. Sister Gertrude Salandri, were thought to be bodily illness, and epileptic fits; thus when before the foundation of the monastery of Valentano she was staying in Viterbo at the monastery of St. Catherine, falling into an ecstasy, she appeared like a dead person; and the nuns in their confusion calling in a medical man, who had the same false idea as themselves, it was judged proper to apply the remedy of blisters and fire. Sister Gertrude remained insensible to everything. The ecstasy being ended after many hours, she was asked how she felt, and she answered, "I have no pain but what you have caused me while I was sleeping; you have hurt me much, but let it be for the love of God." Thus St. Philip Neri answered on a similar occasion.

Benedict being penetrated with that clear knowledge and those bright lights which discovered to him the greatness, the majesty, the infinite goodness of God, and His other divine attributes, had sometimes scarcely begun his prayer, than suddenly penetrated by the interior brightness of the heavenly light, he was absorbed in God by a most sweet ecstasy; and as in ecstasy the senses have no power to perform their natural functions, the ecstatic person is insensible to the effects of fire or sharp iron when employed to arouse him. Thus I am of opinion, that Benedict at these times did not feel the furious bites of these insects, nor the pain of the tumours, nor the shakings given by other persons.

circumstances, thus describe the manner of his ecstasy, which they for the most part believed to be a fainting-fit: "Being on his knees, with his head bent, and his hands crossed on his breast, he gradually raised his head backwards, and remained with his face turned towards heaven, and immoveable, but in so unnatural a manner, that one would have thought he must fall, as it was an inclined position which human strength could not keep." Some thought of going through charity to support him, thinking he was fainting away, but they did not do so, as they saw him after some time return to his former attitude. To some who were edified by this devout posture, it seemed as if he wished to rise into the air. One person deposes that when he was immersed in contemplation, he bent his body considerably, and leaning his head backwards, he seemed to be ready to fall down on the ground every moment, but on looking at his face he seemed out of his senses and in an ecstasy. It happened one day, that a person, little accustomed to the manner of prayer of this servant of God, seeing him in a position which it appeared to him might cause him to fall backwards any moment, made a sign to the person who guarded the church of St. Ignatius, in which he was, to go quickly and support him; but the man removed his anxiety by saying, "That is the way in which that poor man prays."

He was many times favoured with such ecstasies in the church of Santa Maria dei Monti, and one person, who was doubtless versed in such matters, did not, like inexperienced people, attribute such a position to bodily indisposition, but to what it really was, an ecstasy, and he thus gives his testimony in the Processes: "When I saw him in the church of Santa Maria dei Monti, in that profound contemplation, and in that attitude, with his body bent backwards, at a distance from the rails, remaining so for a considerable time, I felt certain that the servant of God was then out of his senses, and in a sweet ecstasy, as it was not possible that a person could naturally be in the position of Benedict without falling backwards."

He fell to the ground once in the church of San Teodoro, in the Campo Vaccino, on the day when that very exemplary congregation, called in Rome Sacconi, celebrated the feast of the Sacred Heart of Jesus. Many persons ran to lift him up, thinking this fall was an effect of abstinence from food in a poor ragged man. When lifted up, he did not seek or ask to be relieved from his want, as he might naturally have done, had it been an effect of hunger; but he went to the altar rails, and kneeling down, continued his prayer. A priest who was present attests the fact, having at first thought it an effect of abstinence, but from the circumstances he changed his opinion, and said that it was a swoon of love, caused by the contemplation of the Sacred Heart of Jesus, all burning with love for man, expressed in a very lively manner, in the beautiful picture which is there venerated.

If fire quickly communicates itself to dry substances, it is not wonderful that the divine fire in the adorable Heart of Jesus should have enkindled its flames in the heart of His servant, which was so well disposed, and entirely detached from everything but God.

I also believe it to have been a swoon of love, as the attestation does not mention the usual inclined position of the body, but only the loss of the senses, and because I do not find the usual marks proper to an ecstasy, but only to a swoon caused by love, in which I have read similar cases of falls in the Lives of the Saints.

His experienced confessor, Father Temple, wisely judged a similar posture, in which he himself observed Benedict in contemplation at Loretto, to be an ecstasy, and he thus attests it in the Processes: "I perceived, that in time of prayer he was not only entirely absorbed in God, but like a person in ecstasy, he seemed, as it were, out of his senses, and in fact, his disposition denoted this. He went on pouring forth his interior affections to our dear Lord, without uttering a word, or even moving his lips, his hands crossed on his breast, his head inclined backwards, his body bent, and his eyes turned towards heaven. It seemed to me that at any moment his head might separate from the bust. I do not know how any one could naturally remain in such a position for a long space of time, and out of the natural equilibrium, except by a supernatural gift of Almighty God, who by His strength supports the body." Hence it was, that being well acquainted with Benedict's interior, and skilled in mystical theology, he did not go himself, nor send any one to support him, according to the advice given by the Divine Spouse in the Canticle: "I adjure you, O daughters of Jerusalem, that you stir not up, nor awake my love till she please." (Cant. viii. 4.) A worthy priest gives his testimony in the Processes, to a great number of transports of love, swoons, and ecstasies. As Benedict sometimes went to the church of the Minerva, he followed him softly, placing himself not far from the place where Benedict was praying on his knees, and he heard this holy soul break out from time to time into ardent sighs, indicating the love which consumed him. Sometimes these sighs, caused by a more lively degree of love, made him burst into transports, insomuch, that through the violence of the interior movement it seemed as if he would dart towards God, the sole object of his desires; and he kept a little open the rags which covered his breast, to give vent to the vehemence of the interior impulse. Sometimes he sweetly fainted away, seeming as if his strength left him. Sometimes in emitting these ardent sighs, he raised his head softly, inclined his body, and seemed as if he wished to raise himself up on high, being in so extraordinary and uncomfortable an attitude, that it would not have been possible to retain it by human strength, but only by the special favour of God, who sustained him. The same Divine grace was his support, when after remaining some time in the above-mentioned attitude, he let his head fall on his shoulders, and remain thus some time, while the spectators feared he must soon fall.

A witness of authority, professor of dogmatical theology in the Roman College, attests that he saw similar things with his own eyes. He was very often in the church of St. Ignatius, praying in a retired place between two pillars, from whence he could see without being seen; and he saw this poor ragged man come into the church, during the solitary hours after dinner, when he imagined there would be no one who could see or hear him, and place himself near the rails of the high altar. There he began to pray in a most devout attitude. When deeply engaged in prayer, not being able to contain in his heart the fire of Divine love, he broke out aloud, most feelingly, into very tender affections towards Jesus Christ. Several times, looking intoutly at Jesus, as He appears in the picture, in the act of offering His cross to St. Ignatius, he cried out all on fire, "To me this cross belongs, to me, for my sins. It is wrongly placed on Thy shoulders, O my Jesus, nor does it suit the saint who bends to receive it." He sometimes fell into such transports of love, that, agitated with various irregular movements, he appeared almost as if he would take flight over the rails, to place himself under this cross, and see his shoulders laden with it. "I cannot say with certainty," says the witness, "that I ever saw him raised up into the air; I do, however, securely assert, that the position of his body was quite unnatural, it was something extraordinary, and was the index and manifest sign of an internal supernatural fire." He frequently saw him sweetly absorbed in a swoon of love, after the effusions we have mentioned, with no strength in his limbs, and like a person who required some one to support him, as if saying with the Spouse of the Sacred Canticles, "Stay me up with flowers, compass me about with apples, because I languish with love." (Cant. ii. 5.) When he saw him in this state, and continuing therein for some space of time, it appeared to him, that he witnessed in him a renewal of those sweet swoons which he had read of in St. Philip Neri, when, through the excess of love, he prostrated himself on the ground, as one fainting, tore his garments to give some vent to the interior fire of love, and seemed reduced to the last extremity.

In other churches, as those of the Holy Apostle Sta. Prassede, and elsewhere, he received the same spiritual favours, some of which we shall mention more appropriately in another place. What we have already said will suffice for the present, to show clearly to what a degree of strength Benedict's love of God had attained. One of his confessors in Rome with good reason believed him to be, "a soul truly enamoured of God." Another in Rome also speaks of him as "A man of perfect charity towards God. A heart inflamed with the holy love of God." Father Temple, his confessor in Loretto, calls him "a seraph of love, like the seraphic St. Francis of Assisium." Other confessors and witnesses of authority use similar expressions, to explain his very ardent love of God. Their attestations of Benedict's advancement from good to better in the path of perfection, verify what he wrote when a youth to his parents from Montreville after leaving La Chartreuse, giving them in his letter this assurance, "I will always have the fear of God before my eyes, and His love in my heart."

By what I have so far related in these three chapters of his very ardent love of God, I flatter myself that I am not deceived in believing that two affections have been excited in some of my readers. The first is, of wonder and pleasure in seeing in our times so much love in a poor, abject, and ragged man. The second is, of some desire to love God from his example. As to the first, it is reasonable to rejoice with the servant of God and admire him, and to be moved afterwards to entreat him to obtain for us from God by his merits some spark of his great love.

As to the second, if we really wish to know what it is to love God, His servant himself tells us. Being received once through charity at Fabriano, during his pilgrimages, into the house of some devout persons, he remained there five hours; and during the whole time of his stay therein, he spoke to his hosts of the love of God with so much fervour and in so pleasing a manner, that being inflamed, penetrated, and filled with zeal, they requested him to teach them how to love God. Benedict replied, "That to love God,

must be all love for God, speaking always God, thinking of God, working for God. T second must be all love for our neighbour, e deavouring charitably to help him, not on temporally but also spiritually by prayers a instructions The third must be all bitterne towards ourselves, endeavouring to resist our ov will and self-love, chastising our flesh with pe ances and fasting, and overcoming our passions That Benedict had in himself these three hear in one, what we have already said, and what v have yet to say of his virtues, will evident prove.

By this threefold heart, he had attain that high degree of love, proper to great saint which is a love disinterested, refined, a very pure. Not looking at his own advanta even spiritual, nor at the reward which G gives in heaven, he was quite taken up in lovi God for His infinite perfections, and because H infinitely deserves it; and in everything he d and suffered, he had no other view than please and glorify God regardless of himse This Father Temple, his confessor,

earth, and they sufficed to keep him always absorbed, and, as it were, out of himself. For this reason his confessors were amazed in hearing the terms and the propriety of the expressions by which he endeavoured to explain to them the sublime ideas which he had conceived of that mystery, if he were required by obedience to do so.

For this very ardent and pure love of the Blessed Trinity, God now gives him in heaven a special glory, as Benedict himself declared when he appeared surrounded with glory to a dying nun in Sicily, who obtained of our Lord by his merits an instantaneous cure; he was encircled with heavenly splendour, with a very precions gem on his breast, which bore the sign of the Most Holy Trinity, and he told her that this was granted to him by Almighty God in reward for the devotion and love he had shown towards the Most Blessed Trinity.

If we sincerely wish to love God, let us place in our own the triple heart of Benedict; let us correspond with the grace which God gives us, which if it be not as copious as that granted to Benedict, is at least proportioned to our state and employment, for it is of faith that God gives His grace to every one in the measure which is suitable for him: "To every one of us is given grace according to the measure of the giving of Christ." (Eph. iv. 7.) Happy are we if we correspond: "This do and thou shalt live;" but miserable and unhappy are we, if we let the grace of God be fruitless within us: "He that loveth not, abideth in death." (1 John, iii. 14.)

CHAPTER X.

OF HIS LOVE FOR THE SACRED HUMANITY OF OUR LORD JESUS CHRIST, AND ESPECIALLY FOR HIS PASSION.

After the Blessed Trinity, the sacred Humanity of Jesus Christ our Lord was the object of his love. Considering the Divine Word humbling Himself for the love of man, to take human flesh: "Taking the form of a servant, being made in the likeness of men," (Philip. ii. 7,) he was amazed at so great a mercy, and was inflamed with love for God made Man; hence he spoke of it with expressions which had their source in his burning heart, when occasions presented themselves; he desired that He should be loved by all; he grieved at the ungrateful return made by man for so much love, and complained lovingly of it to his confessor, in giving him through obedience an account of his prayer. This love inspired him with the salutatien which he always offered wherever he went or with whomsoever he spoke: "Praised be Jesus Christ;" and with tho answer which he made when others saluted him in the same form, "Praised be Jesus Christ for ever!" From this cause he had often in his mouth the holy name of Jesus and of Mary, and reverently bowed his head when he heard them named in the pulpits.

Love was the origin of the humble, abject,

and painful life which he undertook; he was himself obliged to discover it to his confessor when he questioned him. The humiliation and abjection of Jesus Christ was that which touched his heart most, made most impression upon him, and gave him a very strong impulse to imitate Him.

Hence he adored Him in His infant state with the most tender affections. Every year he was present at the novena of the Holy Nativity, in the parochial church of our Blessed Saviour, "ai Monti," but with that exemplary devotion which is attested in the Processes, and which can be imagined in a soul penetrated by the lively knowledge which he had of the abasement of infinite Majesty to the state of a man and an infant. It was also his custom to visit from time to time the manger in which the Infant Jesus was placed, which is preserved in the Basilica of St. Mary Major. Still more pleasing, however, to Jesus, than this external honour, was the desire he had from his early age to make himself a child in imitation of Him, and to animate by this imitation his exterior marks of reverence. He began from that time to become like an infant, by baptismal innocence, which he always preserved by a profound humility no less interior than exterior, by silence, keeping his tongue in strict custody, and by a total contempt of himself and of worldly things, abandoning himself entirely to Divine Providence, and to His paternal dispensations, like a child in the bosom of its nurse. Therefore, in the letter mentioned in the tenth chapter of the first part, he wrote to his parents amongst other expressions the following: "I greatly rejoice, because an omnipotent God guides me. God will assist me, and conduct me in the undertaking with which He Himself has inspired me."

However great was his love for the Infant Jesus, still the principal object of his contemplations, after the ineffable Mystery of the Blessed Trinity, was the Passion and Death of our Divine Redeemer. This kept him absorbed in a sublime amazement, considering on one side His greatness and majesty, on the other, the bitterness of the insults He received, His torments, and the ignominious manner of His death on the cross. Several times he fainted away and fell into a swoon; and I do not doubt, that from this sorrowful contemplation, the loss of his senses, the extraordinary inclination of his body, and those swoons caused by love, of which I have elsewhere spoken, frequently arose. One of the confessors who examined him on this point attests, that in relating to him, when obliged by a command, his sentiments in contemplating the Passion of our Divine Redeemer, his countenance appeared so afflicted and full of compassion, that he seemed to say with the Apostle, "With Christ I am nailed to the cross," (Gal. ii. 20;) for though our Lord manifested Himself to him with high and sublime communications, still the superior part of his soul was afflicted because he knew himself to be wanting in strength and virtue to correspond with so many benefits, and because he knew how bad a return is made by man to so good a God, who loves man so much, and has died on the cross for him.

Another deposes, that in answering questions through obedience, "regarding the contemplation of Jesus Christ's Passion, he appeared as sorrowful as a very tender mother would be, who should see her beloved and innocent son barbarously murdered by cruel hands before her eyes. He appeared so penetrated by the consideration of the Passion, and so absorbed in it, that he nearly fainted through grief:" and he says, that what St. Bonaventure wrote of St. Francis, may be said of Benedict: "He wept over his Beloved, and his soul was filled with compassion for Him." This contemplation was Benedict's daily bread.

This profound contemplation and lively compassion did not confine itself solely to the interior; it urged him also to two external effects, of which one was, to endeavour to resemble Jesus Crucified, bearing with Him the hard wood of the cross; hence, he wore those vile rags, only sufficient to cover him decently, but not to defend him from the inclemency of the seasons: hence the austerities, penances, and mortifications which he practised continually to the last day of his life. The other was, to offer to Jesus as much exterior reverence as can be offered, by a soul penetrated with compassion for His sufferings. I mention what I find in the Processes. He often visited the Scala Santa, and in mounting all the steps on his bent knees, he shed many tears, though exhausted in strength, besieged by the insects elsewhere mentioned, and tormented by those large tumours. The devotion of the Via Crucis was observed almost daily in the Colosseum at Rome, where all the mysteries of the stations are represented ; and he performed it sometimes alone, and sometimes in the company of other poor people, who were lodging in the Abate Mancini's Ospizio, under the guidance of a zealous priest, and he distinguished himself from them all, particularly by the modesty and composure, indicative of his interior sentiments, which caused admiration in every one who observed this humble troop, insomuch that the priest who reproved first one and then another of these people for their negligence and indevotion in so pious an exercise, never found fault with Benedict, but was as much edified by him as were the other spectators.

Several times he was seen performing the same pious exercises of the Via Crucis in the church of Aracœli, after having first contemplated the mysteries of the sacred Passion in retirement behind a confessional, but so modestly and devoutly, that one person observed him to his great edification, and going soon after into the sacristy, he told some religious who were there, that he had seen in the church a poor man, who visiting most devoutly the Via Crucis resembled our Lord Jesus Christ. He also frequently visited in the church of Santa Prassede the pillar at which our Lord Jesus Christ was scourged, which is placed in a chapel apart, and the crucifix which is also venerated the He occupied himself for a long time in c templating the Passion, and was several tir seen out of his senses in that unnatural p tion of the body, with the head hanging ba wards, which we have elsewhere mentioned, wh caused him to be considered a holy soul those who attentively observed him, and v received great edification from beholding hir

On the Monday of that holy week dur which he died, having bought half a pint of vi gar at the shop which stood near the gate Santa Prassede, he was seen by many pers to begin to drink it. Being advised by sc to desist, as it might do some injury to his w health, he replied, "Jesus Christ drank it the cross first, and during this week He suffe more than I do for the love of man." Say this, he joyfully drank all the vinegar. T Abate Mancini once asked him, while he staying in his Ospizio at Rome, to go every to the Basilica of St. Mary Major, and th at the altar of the manger of Jesus to m an hour's prayer, according to a paper wh he would give him. Benedict candidly refu to satisfy him in this every day, not being a I think to undertake it, on account of the tance, his daily long prayers, and the vi which he was accustomed to make to ot churches, and especially to those in which most Blessed Sacrament was exposed for Forty Hours' Prayer.

He showed himself however ready to ol

any day when he was desired to do it. Signor Mancini did not wish to command him; and it was agreed, that he should go for twelve days only Having received the paper for the prayers, and looking it over carefully, Benedict begged him to give him leave to make two hours' prayer instead of one, and to meditate at the same time on the Passion of our Lord Jesus Christ. The Abate granted this with much pleasure, admiring his fervent devotion towards the Passion of our Lord. The wonderful manner in which he meditated at the same time on the Infancy and Passion of our Blessed Saviour, could only be the effect of the particular lights from God who guided him. I imagine to myself, that he imitated in this the Blessed Virgin, who revealed to St. Bridget, that as often as she looked upon the hands and the feet, and admired the beauty of her Divine Son when an Infant, she felt her heart pierced with the sword of grief, remembering what the prophets had foretold, which was well known to her through her perfect understanding of the Holy Scriptures with respect to her Blessed Son's future Passion. "As often as I looked upon my Son, my soul was overwhelmed with fresh grief, for I thought of the manner of His crucifixion." Whether my reflection be correct or not, I admire in him, not only what the Abate Mancini admired, his fervent devotion to the Passion, but also his obedience, candour, and delicacy of conscience, his love for prayer, after which he always hungered, how much time soever he employed in it.

Finally, his special devotion was to place himself every morning in the wounds of his crucified Lord, "in the clefts of the rock," which are the wounds of the hands and feet, "in the cavern of the wall," which is the wound of the side, and to dwell in them most happily, in the midst of his so great austerities, considering Christ crucified as his life, with the apostle, "To me, to live is Christ," (Phil. i. 21,) and a secure shield from the assaults of the infernal enemy, and the dangers of the world.

He was constant till his death in this tender love for our suffering Saviour. I read in the Processes one act of veneration for the Passion of our Divine Redeemer, which in itself contains many, which was performed by him two years before he died, that is, in 1781. He had performed his usual journey from Rome to Loretto, he had employed twenty-two days therein, travelling on foot, and suffering great inconvenience from the snow, frost, and cold, which were very severe that year, receiving little protection from the miserable rags which he wore, with stockings torn and only covering half the leg, and with worn-out shoes. He arrived in Loretto on Maunday Thursday, in the afternoon. Meeting by chance his kind hostess, Barbara Sori, she invited him into her house, to warm himself, and take a little food. But, generously despising the care of his body, and careless of

visit the Blessed Virgin, promising to return at night. He did so, and supped very sparingly, not even taking as much as the holy Church allows for collation. Hearing that on Good Friday morning there was to be a sermon on the Passion very early in the church, refusing the necessary repose to his fatigued body, he went diligently at that hour to the church, and heard the sermon, and we can imagine with how much interior affection, remaining in the church till the doors were closed at night, and then returning home. Supper was ready, but being plunged in the consideration of the sufferings of our Lord, and devoutly recollected within himself, he did not go near the table. When pressed by the hostess, he answered with a very sorrowful countenance, "Is this a night, do you think, to take supper? Ah! our Lord suffered very much during this day, and do you wish me to take food?" "That is true," she replied, "but if we do not eat, we shall not be able to pray either, so come to supper." In obedience he went, but he would not taste the food which had been prepared; he asked for the charity of some raw herbs, a bit of bread, and a glass of water; this was his whole supper. I have no doubt, that considering his readiness to obey, from the experience his hostess had already had of it, he would have taken the food prepared, if she had commanded him to do so, but she would not do so, as she told her husband afterwards, in order to yield that night to his devotion at so holy a time.

ıdly contemplated, he made a recapitu-
of the sermon to the family, but with so 'ervour that he greatly moved the hearers, ve them a strong proof of his tender de- towards the Passion of Jesus. He spent ole of Holy Saturday in prayer in the , only returning at night to supper. He ıtreated to come the next day, the so- ' of Easter, to dine in their house as a .an, for these good people had the pious of inviting some poor person to dine on ncipal feasts; but not yielding to their entreaties, he humbly begged them to e with him, promising to return at night 'per, which he did, after having spent the day in contemplation in the church, to nder and great edification of his hosts, all who observed him.

CHAPTER XI.

ST ARDENT LOVE FOR THE ADORABLE SACRA- OF THE HOLY EUCHARIST, MANIFESTED BY DAILY LONG PRAYERS IN ITS PRESENCE, AND THER DEVOTIONS WHICH HE PERFORMED.

in Rome alone. but in everv citv through

known. He who loves sincerely, does not know how to separate from his beloved. Benedict passed the greater part of the day, and sometimes the whole of it, in the churches near his beloved Jesus in His Sacrament, either when exposed for public adoration, especially for the Forty Hours' Prayer, or shut up in the tabernacle; and persons who wished to mention him, and were ignorant of his name, pointed him out as the "Poor Man of the Forty Hours." (Il povero delle Quarant' Ore.)

His behaviour before the Blessed Sacrament was so devout, his body, head, and eyes, which were always fixed upon it, were so motionless, that some say in the Processes that he was like a statue, others that he did not seem like a man praying, but an angel adoring, or a person in ecstasy, absorbed in admiration. In the presence of Jesus the internal fire of his heart shone through his inflamed countenance, which was admired by a person who purposely watched him; for his face, when he was not in prayer, being colourless, pale, emaciated, and cadaverous, through his penitential life, it was wonderful to see him before the Blessed Sacrament with a red colour, and often ecstatic and insensible to exterior things. The same also happened when he went to adore in Sant' Ignazio the Sacred Heart of Jesus, represented in a beautiful picture at the altar of the crucifix. And though his countenance had a grave expression, not however unmixed with a certain amiability, still when he prayed before the Blessed Sacrament, with his eyes fixed upon it, such joy shone in his face that there appeared on his lips a sort of joyous smile which seemed angelical.

He remained a long time in this state of adoration, some attest five or six hours, others half the day, and some the entire day, without giving his weak body the least nourishment. A person who noticed him in the church of Sant Anna de' Palafrenieri in Borgo, was greatly surprised at his remaining there from some hours before mid-day till after sun-set motionless, and kneeling in a very devout attitude before the Blessed Sacrament, which was exposed for the Forty Hours' Prayer; and his astonishment was so great, that, as he had the office of conducting from hour to hour the brothers who are associated for the adoration of the Blessed Sacrament, he made a sign to them also to observe him; and he affirms, that he had seen Benedict practise the same in other churches where the Blessed Sacrament was exposed for the Forty Hours. In Loretto, Fabriano, Erin, Rome, and wherever he was, even for a few days, in his pilgrimages, many persons affirm that they saw him in the church from day-break till evening, immoveable, and kneeling before the Blessed Sacrament, and sometimes till the night had advanced several hours, as it was noticed in Rome in the church della Santissima Trinità dei Pellegrini, of St. Ambrose, and elsewhere. This would be wonderful in any other person; but how much more in Benedict, considering the attacks of those innumerable insects, and the pain of the tumours on his knees. Certainly it would not have been possible for weak human nature, if two things had not concurred, one on the part of God, the other on his own. From God came the sublime knowledge and clear lights by which he kept his intellect absorbed and his will immersed in holy affections. On his side there was the love with which he burned for Jesus; he who loves, suffers all things; "Charity beareth all things," (1 Cor. xiii. 7.) We should also bear the inconvenience we may suffer during the short time of our fixed prayers if we loved Jesus: "His conversation hath no bitterness." (Wisd. viii. 16.)

As these long prayers of his, before the divine Sacrament, were the effect of solid virtue, he was greatly on his guard, not to give an annoyance to those who were present, by certain marks of devotion, which have more show than substance; for instance, to weep aloud, to sigh very audibly, to kiss the ground, to speak to our Lord in prayer so as to be heard, and other acts which often disturb the devotion of others, and sometimes foment the spirit of hypocrisy. It happened once, that as he was beginning his prayer, he heard a woman near him incessantly occupied in these exterior acts, so that others were greatly hindered from praying devoutly: turning towards her, he said meekly, "What is the use of this?" And when she ceased all blessed him for it. He prayed in silence, modestly, with his eyes fixed on the Blessed Sacrament, pouring out his affections to that God who does not require us to speak to hear us, but is pleased with the affections of the heart; hence his method of prayer was a good sermon, it inspired devotion and compunction in the beholders.

To pray thus must, however, have cost Benedict not a little. He felt the heat of the vast fire contained in his heart, which increased in strength in the presence of Jesus in His Sacrament, for "He is a consuming fire," (Deut. iv. 24;) hence he was obliged to use great efforts to keep it in confinement, that it might not show itself outwardly. Sometimes he could not prevent some spark from escaping, at one time in sighs, at another in some affectionate ejaculation, which he uttered in a low voice, and usually when he flattered himself that there was no one near to perceive it. If he thought himself entirely alone in the church, during certain solitary hours, he then allowed this internal fire to vent itself in loud sighs and affections. This happened to him in several churches, but God permitted that some one should be there, unseen by him, to observe him, and reap spiritual advantage also from his example.

He was one day pouring forth deep sighs and affections in the church of Santa Maria in Via Lata, at that late hour of the afternoon in which there was usually no one in the church: there were only two priests belonging to it in the choir, which is entirely separated from the chapel of the Blessed Sacrament, where Benedict was devoutly adoring. Hearing these deep sighs, without knowing whence they came, they wished with devout curiosity to find out, and walking softly on tiptoe, they saw Benedict with his arms raised in the form of a cross, and his face turned towards the sacred ciborium, sighing with such a vehement affection and fervour, as clearly indicated that he was interiorly inflamed with holy love. Leaving him with the Object of his love, they retired contrite and humbled, comparing their prayer with that of this poor man. It also happened in another church, that he was heard by a person who had purposely concealed himself at a solitary hour, pouring forth sighs with fervent and humble affections towards our Blessed Lord in His sacrament, retired in a corner of the church. This occurred also in the church of the Holy Apostles two days before he died, in that of St. Ignatius, and elsewhere.

Finally, the clearest proof of his very ardent love towards Jesus in His adorable Sacrament, is his constant perseverance in passing his days, sometimes even whole days, before the Divine Sacrament, till the end of his life. From time to time he was afflicted by corporal diseases, particularly in the latter part of his life, caused by his ill-treatment of his body, his long prayers, and his refusing himself necessary support; hence he appeared exhausted, emaciated, faint, and more like a corpse than a living person. So many sufferings did not, however, keep him from visiting the churches, to enjoy the company of his beloved Jesus, to adore Him, and, if I may say so, to converse familiarly with Him. This is one of the highest degrees of true love, says

St. Thomas, "to endure without wearying." "Love overcometh all things. Charity endureth all things." Notwithstanding his bodily pains, he dragged himself to the churches, to pray as usual in the presence of Jesus. Sometimes, towards the end of his life, he was seen to stand up for a short time with his usual modesty, and then to kneel down again. The compassionate charity of the Abate Mancini, who wished him to stay at his Ospizio in the latter part of his life, on seeing him so exhausted, made him advise Benedict to seek a cure in one of the many hospitals that Rome possesses, or at least, to remain in bed in the Ospizio, as he would take the charge of assisting him, giving him food, and whatever was necessary for his health. Benedict, thanking him, did not accept either offer; love prevailed over him; this attracted him sweetly; he had no care for his body, and that he might not lose the pleasure of remaining with Jesus in the churches, he totally despised his sufferings. His exhaustion became so extreme, that the warden of the same Ospizio one day warned him, that if he continued his method of life he would be falling down dead in the public street. Benedict replied, that it was of no consequence; and he spoke truly, for his only desire was to remain

others at night after several hours' exposition. Benedict was generally seen present at all, regardless of the distance to the church, the weakness of his strength, or the inclemency of the weather. Every day he visited It in those churches where It is usually exposed for public adoration for the space of Forty Hours, and he usually remained there during those long contemplations of which we have spoken.

He was very exact in accompaning the Blessed Sacrament when It was carried as Viaticum to the sick. Being very often in the church of Santa Maria dei Monti, he no sooner heard the sound of the parish bell calling the people to accompany the Blessed Sacrament to the sick, than he hastened with great alacrity and love, and with a ravishing devotion he followed It, his eyes cast down, his hands joined, and his countenance joyful, as if he saw Jesus visibly.

He heard several masses every day with great attention and devotion, uniting himself in spirit with the celebrant in offering the great sacrifice; nor could anything draw his eyes from the altar, or his mind from this great action. Being once told during the time of mass by an ecclesiastic to go into the sacristy, where some one wanted him, he did not answer nor move till mass was ended, when he went into the sacristy.

When he was allowed to serve the priest who was celebrating mass, so great was his modesty and devotion, that we find it deposed by a priest in Rome, that he blushed for himself, in considering the devotion and fervour with which a laic, a poor and ragged man, served at this tremendous sacrifice of the altar, and seeing him when he turned towards the people after the consecration, with his hands joined, his head bent down, and his countenance full of devotion, he was still more surprised, edified, and confused. Another parish priest, whose mass he once served at Fabriano, deposes, that he was not only himself struck by his fervent devotion, but all who saw him were penetrated and moved. When a child at home, and at Erin, those who saw him were moved by the devotion with which he served at mass with his hands joined, his countenance devout, and his eyes cast down.

From what we have related every one will see, that Benedict was with good reason honoured with the name of "Lover of the Blessed Sacrament;" "the Poor Man of the Forty Hours," and a man who employed the greatest part of his life in devotions to the Sacrament of the Blessed Eucharist.

CHAPTER XII.

HIS VERY ARDENT LOVE FOR JESUS IN HIS ADORABLE SACRAMENT MANIFESTED IN HIS FREQUENT COMMUNIONS. THE MANNER IN WHICH HE PREPARED FOR IT. IN WHAT MANNER HE RETURNED THANKS WHEN HE POSSESSED JESUS IN HIS BREAST. WHAT FRUIT HE DREW FROM COMMUNION. HIS CONFESSION BY WHICH HE PRECEDED IT.

THE frequent use of the two sacraments of Penance and the Blessed Eucharist, much desired by the Council of Trent in all the faithful, inculcated by the holy fathers, and most useful to the soul, was dear to Benedict, and practised by him in proportion as Jesus was dear to him. If his love induced him to remain nearly all day with Jesus in the churches, we may easily infer from thence how much more he must have desired to receive Him into his breast, and to unite himself lovingly to Him, by that close union which Jesus Himself speaks of when He says, "He that eateth My flesh and drinketh My blood, abideth in Me and I in him." (John, vi. 57.)

I find Benedict's practice of frequent communion attested unanimously by many persons in all those towns in which he happened to be, either as passing through only, or as an inhabitant. This practice is attested of him when he was a youth in Erin under the guidance of his uncle, the parish priest, with whom he did not remain more than six years, that is, from his twelfth till his eighteenth year, when the priest died, a glorious victim of charity. At that time he approached the holy communion very frequently. It was the same in Moulins after he left the convent of Sept Fontaines. During a fortnight in which he remained in Fabriano at the commencement of his pilgrimages, the parish priest deposes, that he himself communicated him four times, and that his very devout manner of communicating gave great edification to the beholders. In Loretto, during a space of not more than three days, he communicated twice, as Father Temple attests. In Rome, in his beloved church of Santa Maria dei Monti, in S. Gio. Laterano, in S. Martino dei Monti, in Santa Maria Maggiore, and in other churches, he was very often seen to communicate. The attestations are so numerous, that it would be superfluous, and even tiresome, to mention them all. Any one who wishes it may read a compendium of the whole in the Processes, where he will find the numbers and marginal paragraphs mentioned exactly.

Only at one time, as I read in the Processes, did Benedict discontinue the frequent reception of the Holy Communion, and this was when he was in the convent of Sept Fontaines. He was then about twenty years of age, and Almighty God desired to purify his soul, to dispose him for the sublime perfection to which He afterwards raised him. A great crowd of scruples, perplexities, and troubles inundated his soul with a dreadful fear of not having true contrition for his sins. This was augmented by his having read in the Lives of the Saints of their sensible contrition, their tears, and their swoons, and seeing himself deprived of this sensibility, and feeling dryness in his mind, aridity in his heart, obscurity in his understanding, and coldness in his will, he feared that he was not in the friendship of God, and that he should lose his soul. The troubles of his mind and the distress of his heart were so great, that during this time, which was a period of six weeks, he never went to confession, much less to communion, however much he wished it, considering himself quite unworthy. To these interior storms, exterior afflictions were added, sickness, pains, mortifications from the master of novices, and other similar trials. In vain that pious master repeated to him what the Council of Trent teaches, "That contrition, whether perfect or imperfect, does not consist in feeling, nor does its perfection depend upon it; it consists only in an interior detestation of sin, 'a sorrow of heart, not an external sorrow,' with the resolution never more to commit sin, which detestation may exist, and is a true sorrow for sin, though it be not accompanied by tears or any sensible feeling. The sensible grief of David, Magdalene, St. Peter, and others, was a special favour from God, not necessary for the existence of sorrow." But the wise master spoke in vain, and these good religious feared Benedict would go mad. At last, however, he was in some degree persuaded, or rather we should say, God

of life elsewhere spoken of, permitted that interior storms should arise from time to time, and that bodily sickness should afflict him. Hence the Father Abbot, very well satisfied with his conduct, was obliged unwillingly to dismiss him, only from the fear of his losing his senses, believing and saying to him, "That he was not destined for his convent; God willed him elsewhere," as we have already mentioned in the first part.

When he left that place, Almighty God "commanded the winds and the sea, and there came a great calm," (Matth. viii. 26;) he saw himself in the enjoyment of sweet peace, his fears, darkness, and distress all disappeared, lights and graces, and a clearer knowledge of the greatness and majesty of God succeeded; and also that special light, or rather that very sensible Divine impulse which urged him to undertake the very austere method of life, of which we have spoken in the second part, an impulse which received the approbation of a very skilful and celebrated confessor, and afterwards that of others. He also lost that great fear of receiving the Bread of Heaven, and though he knew and acknowledged himself to be most unworthy of It, he failed not, however, to receive It. It is true that those great lights regarding the majesty of God sometimes raised fears in his mind, but manifesting them to his confessors, he regulated himself in all things by their direction, from which he never in the least departed. From that time forward after this storm, he communicated so frequently, that the priest who was sacristan of the church of St. Peter at Moulins sent him away from the altar several times, it seeming to him an unbecoming and improper thing that a layman, poor and young, should receive so frequently that Divine Majesty, whom the angels themselves are not worthy to adore. "Pluries repulsus fuit a Sacra Mensa, a Sacerdote Sacrista ejusdem Ecclesiæ." We must pardon the zeal of this sacristan; he was not then acquainted with Benedict's great virtue, and was perhaps one of those who do not know the great pleasure which it gives to Jesus, when those who are in His grace receive Him devoutly into their breasts, as the holy fathers unanimously assert in treating of frequent communion, and as Jesus Himself declared to His beloved spouse, St. Gertrude, to whom He lovingly complained of the prohibition given by the abbess to several nuns in her monastery of Rodardes, because their frequent communions seemed to her an irreverence and too great freedom with Almighty God. "All My delight is to be with the children of men; on this account I have chosen to dwell in the Sacrament. He deprives Me of My delight who removes from Me, by too great rigour, those who wish to come to Me, when their consciences do not reproach them

sus, and he spoke not of nuns only, but also of secular persons.

On the occasion of the repulse from the sacred table, given by the above-mentioned priest, I admire with great pleasure the patience, silence, and at the same time the holy intrepidity of Benedict. At first when he was sent away he was silent, and bore it patiently, but he did not fail to approach the altar again on other days, hungering after the Bread of Heaven, and ready for further mortifications: "Charity beareth all things." (1 Cor. xiii. 7.) At last the prudent parish priest undertook his defence, edified by his devotion and patience. He disapproved of his sacristan's indiscreet zeal, he reproved him, and left Benedict at liberty to communicate when he pleased.

Benedict's manner of approaching the Holy Communion was not like the ordinary method of devout souls, it was most fervent, and as excellent as he could make it. He made two preparations for communion, immediate and remote. The remote preparation consists in purity of conscience, which St. Paul inculcates in these words: "But let a man prove himself, and so let him eat of that Bread," (1 Cor. xi. 28;) words which are thus explained by the Council of Trent: "Declarat Sacrosanctum Concilium ex Ecclesiæ consuetudine intelligenda esse hæc verba, ut nemo sibi conscius culpæ mortalis, etiam contritus accedat, non præmissa Confessione sacramentali." That is, the Holy Council declares, that we are so to understand the words of St. Paul, as that no one who is conscious of being in mortal sin, even though he be contrite, is to presume to approach the Holy Communion without first confessing his sins. How singular in Benedict was this purity from mortal sin, will clearly appear to every one who has read in this work of his great horror, not only for mortal, but also for venial sin, and for every little stain, even for an idle word. Nevertheless, he generally went to confession before communion, and prepared for it by a very strict examination of conscience. This he practised every night with great delicacy and rigour, as he himself acknowledged to his confessor, Father Temple, in one of his conferences with him, yet he renewed it when he was preparing for communion, calling to mind those things which he believed to be sins, in order to confess them.

Immediate preparation consists in certain particular acts of humility, reverence, desire, love, and lively faith; these were exercised by Benedict at all times and every day in the churches, in which he passed a great part of the day; but he renewed them so much the more fervently the day before communion, as he was nearer to the time of receiving Jesus into his breast. With this two-fold preparation he approached the eucharistic table after having been to confession. Here I think I shall give pleasure to the reader, and promote his spiritual good, by relating in what manner Benedict confessed, and what were the sins he declared.

In making his confession he practised the instruction which he gave one day at Fabriano to some very pious persons, who, having formed a great opinion of his sanctity, requested it of him. He told them that three things principally are to be attended to, a good examination of conscience, a sincere sorrow, and a firm purpose of amendment. He makes no mention of the fourth requisite, which is truth and sincerity in declaring all our sins to our confessor, for this reason, I think, because the persons to whom he spoke, being very devout, were not likely to fail in this duty, or because, judging others by himself, he thought it impossible that any one could have the folly to commit a sacrilege, and expose himself to the danger of eternal damnation, by concealing a sin from the minister of God. He then gave the manner of practising the three things mentioned, and these persons listened to him with great eagerness. He added, that the want of these three things, or of any one of them, was usually the cause of bad confessions and the ruin of souls. That this instruction might be deeply impressed in their minds, he made known to them a vision which he had had, calling it, however, a dream, for he never spoke to any one of the sublime interior favours he received, unless he was commanded by his confessors. "I dreamed," he said, "that I saw three different processions; the first consisted of a few persons all clothed in white; the second, of many in red garments; the last was very numerons, and those composing it were dressed in a black and mourning habit. Not understanding what was signified to mo herein, I inquired, and received for answer," (he does not say from whom,) "that the first procession signified those who at the hour of death, having well purified their consciences from sin, went happily to heaven; the second, those who went to Purgatory, to satisfy the Divine justice, which in life they had not fully satisfied; the third, those unhappy persons who, on account of bad confessions, were condemned by God to the pains of hell." The persons whom he was instructing were so well satisfied with what he said, that they also repeated it to others and deposed it in the Processes.

He examined his conscience very rigorously the day before communion, "and he was accustomed," says one of his confessors, "to prepare for the sacrament of penance with great attention and exactness." Believing himself to be a criminal and a sinner, he broke out into acts of lively sorrow, which we may imagine in a person who was favoured by God with sublime lights concerning His infinite greatness and loveliness. The purpose of amendment followed, which extended to the reformation of his life, and to an increase in fervour, and in the practice of virtues.

Thus well prepared, he presented himself to his confessor, placing himself always the last in the crowd of penitents; and sometimes he was obliged to wait almost the whole morning, which he did with invincible patience and a serene

fesser. He recites the Confiteor, but with so much feeling, that he trembles from head to foot, especially in saying "mea culpa," as if he were loaded with enormous crimes, or as his confessor at Loretto says, "as if he had been the greatest criminal in the presence of his judge." Still he had no sin which was sufficient, much less necessary, matter for sacramental absolution. He usually confessed ingratitude for the benefits of God, failure in corresponding with His graces, and made such-like general accusations, on which account all his confessors were perplexed to find sufficient matter for absolution, and all of them, without knowing it from one another, attest in the Processes that they had never found in him sufficient matter, not even a venial sin deliberately committed; that, on the contrary, they found in him "baptismal innocence," which appeared plainly from his general confessions made from the time of his first coming to the use of reason. With great astonishment they admired in him a soul beloved and penetrated by God with His paternal benedictions. What I have mentioned in the seventh chapter of the second part, as having happened in the general confession which he made in Loretto to Father

Temple, happened also with another confessor, Father Almerici, who had succeeded Father Temple there ; also in Fabriano with the parish priest, Signor Pagotti, in Rome, with many confessors whom he had there, and with the last, Don Giuseppe Loreto Marconi ; they all endeavoured to find out if he had not committed some slight deliberate fault, but all agree unanimously, that they never could find out any.

In renewing at the feet of his confessor his act of contrition and purpose of amendment, after the many others which he had made in his private examination, you would have thought Benedict the greatest of sinners. He seemed to be a prodigal son, who, humble and penitent, was soliciting pardon at his father's feet ; his confessors read in his devout countenance, in the tears which he shed, in his humble attitude and sincere expressions, his great aversion and horror for an offence against God, and his firm resolution of serving Him fervently for the future, and of never even slightly displeasing Him. Let the example of the lively sorrow of so innocent a soul, make those blush and correct themselves, who having sins, perhaps many and grievous, know not how to grieve for them as they ought ; let them fear to find themselves some day amongst the crowd in the third procession which was seen by Benedict.

After confession Benedict hastened to the feet of Jesus in His adorable Sacrament, and figuring himself to be like one of the ten lepers cured by Jesus, he thanked Him fervently for the institution of the saving Sacrament of Penance he renewed his sorrow and purpose of amendment, performed the penance enjoined, and prepared himself to lead a more fervent life. Hence he went on advancing day by day in the path of perfection which he had entered, and in the exercise of virtues: "He went on from virtue to virtue," (Psalm lxxxiii. 8,) without ever relaxing, like the light, to which the Holy Ghost compares holy souls, which "goeth forward and increaseth even to perfect day." (Prov. iv. 8.

Having confessed, it was his custom not to approach the holy table that same day, but the following, that he might prepare himself in a better manner. The acts of virtue by which he most frequently prepared for communion, were two, as his confessor in Loretto ascertained by commanding him to speak in obedience; they were profound humility and very ardent desire both of which include lively faith.

Humility. The great lights of which we have elsewhere spoken, as they made known to him as far as it is possible for a mortal man to be acquainted with it, the infinite greatness of God so they also gave him a clear knowledge of his own nothingness; hence he was in astonishment that such Majesty should condescend to enter the breast of one who was a mere nothing, and a miserable creature, who was as nothing among other creatures; with this reflection he sank into the abyss of his own nothingness, and the humility of his heart showed itself in the exterior attitude of his body. He repeated with the Centurion, "Domine, non sum dignus." He humbled himself still more by reflecting, that besides being nothing, he was a most vile sinner, ungrateful, audacious, and deserving nothing but hell. These reflections had so much power over him, that sometimes when he was not expressly commanded to approach, he abstained from communion, which he acknowledged when questioned by Father Temple. When, however, his confessors gave him the order, he preferred obedience to humility, communicating even two or three days successively, loving to depend always on their direction. Hence, when at Loretto, before he placed himself under Father Temple's direction, Signor Valeri, one of the priests of the Holy House, having offered to give him communion, deeply penetrated with the thought of his own unworthiness, he answered, "How can you wish that I, a poor sinner, should approach to receive the Holy Communion in that holy place?" Nevertheless, when commanded, he obeyed, and went to communion. He gave a clearer proof of his humility and obedience in something which happened with a confessor in Rome. This priest having told Benedict after confession that he was to communicate, heard him answer in these words: "I ought to prepare for it during a few days." This answer convinced the confessor much more of the ardour of his love, and of his profound respect for Jesus in His Sacrament. "I perceived," says he, "that this blessed soul, before receiving his beloved Lord, desired to prepare his heart and soul for

tians." Having perceived in Benedict, one side, a conscience pure, delicate, and even from every venial sin, and on th a profound respect and love also for tl Blessed Sacrament, he ordered him tc communion that same morning. The sei God readily obeyed, adding these words, I will prepare myself a little more this n and then I will communicate." The cc pleased with his obedience, blessed him, sired him to pray to Jesus for him.

Ardent desire. "Reflecting on the infin of this Divine Majesty for men, he burn a lively desire of receiving Him, breakir into expressions stronger," says his cc "than those which are used by a foolish the world: 'My Good,' repeated he, ... Good......my All......sole Object of my l O come......I desire Thee......I sigh aft ......I wait for Thee......every little dela a thousand years...... Come, Lord Jes delay not.'"

"He had," continues his confessor, " hunger and thirst after this heavenly f seemed to me precisely like that thirs described by the Psalmist: 'As the hart after the fountains of water, so my soul after Thee, O God.' (Psalm xli. 1.) He ardently to approach the holy table,

might unite himself in heart and will to Jesus. He desired to have no other heart, but one which was conformable to the heart of Jesus, to wish for nothing but God. The thought of his own unworthiness recurring again to his mind, he preferred love and obedience before it; confessing himself unprovided with the proper dispositions for receiving so great a Guest, he supplied for the deficiency by offering to our Lord the dispositions and affections with which His blessed Mother, the apostles, and saints had received Him."

Thus well prepared, he approached the holy table with so much modesty, and a demeanour so humble, that he drew admiration from all who saw him, wherever he communicated; and sometimes he was seen even to shed tears through the desire of receiving Jesus. A good priest, who gave him communion one day at the altar della Santissima Annunziata, in the church of St. Ignatius, attests in the following words the great fervour he observed in him: "I was overcome by a certain interior sentiment of wonder and tenderness on seeing before me the above-named poor man," (this he did not experience in communicating any other person of the great number who presented themselves;) "I observed by his exterior, a disposition in receiving the Body of Jesus, which interiorly moved me. Thus, on making the sign of the cross, with the consecrated Host, and saying, 'Corpus Domini Nostri Jesu Christi,' &c., I perceived such great fervour and devotion in this poor man, in receiving the Sacred Particle, that I v fected, moved, and astonished by it; and the whole time that I continued to commı other persons, and in finishing the celel of the mass, I had him before my eye considered his excellent disposition."] his testimony. Scarcely had he returne the sacristy, than he began to express tonishment, asking the server who this man could be. He answered that he ha self admired him, and that he had coı to the Signor Abate Marconi. Many oth test similar emotions which they had enced in seeing him communicate at Ron retto, Fabriano, and elsewhere.

What was his manner of thanksgivin what were his affections, he was himself to declare to the above-mentioned coı who required him to do it:—To renew hi in the real presence of Jesus within his to adore Him reverently in union with the and the Blessed Virgin; to be filled with ishment at so great a condescension; into his own nothingness; to confess most unworthy of it: then to make t

me, confugiam ad Te: dignus sim defendi a Te: timeam mihi: timeam Te: simque de electis a Te: diffidam mihi, fidam in Te: obedire velim propter Te: in nullo afficiar, nisi in Te: aspiciam in me, ut diligam Te: voca me, ut videam Te, et in æternum potiar Te." In English it may be paraphrased as follows: "O my Lord Jesus, grant that I may mortify myself, and live in Thee: that I may take from Thy hands whatever may happen, of prosperity or adversity: that I may fight against myself, and follow Thee constantly, that I may always more and more desire to follow Thee: that I may flee from myself, and take refuge in Thee: that I may be worthy to be protected by Thee: that I may fear Thee, who art all-powerful, that I may fear myself, who am inclined to evil: that I may be of the number of Thy elect: that I may distrust myself, and confide in Thee: that I may obey every one for the love of Thee: that nothing earthly may move me, but raise me towards Thee. Cast on me a benignant look, which may excite me to love Thee: call me to Thee, that I may see Thee in heaven, and enjoy Thee as my possession for eternity."*

* Let not the reader be surprised to see described here and in other chapters the interior operations of this servant of God, attested by his confessor in the Processes It would certainly have been difficult to remember them so distinctly and minutely, if he had not given his deposition till several years had elapsed. But this wise confessor had the precaution by a Divine impulse, to note on paper what he drew from Benedict in his long conferences, at the very time in which they took place, prudently reflecting, as he says, "that if he persevered till death in the way of perfection he had begun, Almighty God would perhaps glorify him by miracles and prodigies after his death, and that, as it was everywhere known

As he communicated in so fervent and extraordinary a manner, we can imagine what great profit he would draw from his communions. The ordinary effect of the sacraments is in proportion to the disposition of the receiver. Now from such dispositions as his, what effect would follow? Be not surprised at what I have related of his excellent virtues, his long prayers, his entire detachment from earthly things and from himself, for I have no doubt that they were all the fruit of his very fervent communions. And if after his first communion, which he received from the hands of the Bishop of Bologne, at Erin, when about twelve years old, he was seen to have visibly redoubled his fervour, kept closer retirement, and frequented the churches more; think how much greater advantage he would derive by degrees, from his other communions, which were made with a much better disposition than he could have had in his early youth. Thus it will be with us; the effect of our communions will be in proportion to the dispositions with which we approach; let us not be surprised if we return from communion the same as we were before, and no better, if we do not prepare ourselves well.

that he had paid annual visits to the great sanctuary of Loretto, recourse would be had to the French penitentiary, to obtain a knowledge of the virtues he there practised." Being requested to give this information juridically after Benedict's death, he had nothing to do but to present what he had written during the life of the servant of God, and to confirm by oath what he had then written and afterwards said.

CHAPTER XIII.

HIS FILIAL LOVE FOR THE MOTHER OF GOD. HIS PARTICULAR DEVOTION TO SOME OF THE SAINTS.

How great, tender, and solid was his love for the Blessed Virgin, we may know from the ardent love which he bore to her divine Son Jesus. These two loves always go together. We cannot love Jesus without loving His mother; we cannot truly love the mother without loving Jesus, as the Ven. Father da Ponte well says, reflecting on these words of the Gospel: "They found the Child with Mary His mother." (Matth. ii. 11.) They advance equally, allowing for the difference between them; the love of Mary becomes stronger as our love for Jesus increases. The love of Jesus in Benedict's heart was a strong and perpetual fire, which he could not keep confined within his breast, so as to prevent some visible sign of it from escaping, notwithstanding his desire to keep it entirely concealed: we may infer from this how lively would be his love for the Blessed Virgin Mary.

From his tender age he chose the Blessed Virgin as his mother, his advocate, and special protectress, and in her, after God, he placed all his hopes securely, as he told his confessor, Father Temple. When he had commenced that austere manner of life with which Almighty God inspired him, he thought no more of his earthly mother, and he told her in his last letter that they would see each other no more except in the valley of Josaphat, and he confirmed with greater fervour his choice of Mary for his mother, abandoning himself entirely to her maternal care. He declared himself before the world to be a son of Mary, by wearing always round his neck the rosary, as her livery, till he died; he openly boasted of it, and esteemed it much more than nobles do those distinctions which mark them from the crowd; he always wore it in the public streets, in his pilgrimages, in the churches, and everywhere.

He recited it every day in honour of Mary, not in the common manner, but contemplating the mysteries profoundly, in a devout, modest, and reverential attitude. In the Ospizio of Signor Mancini, when reciting the rosary every night with the other poor people, he distinguished himself from them like the moon amongst the stars. The others continued sitting, through the permission given them by the warden, on account of sickness or weakness. Benedict always knelt, though urged to sit, on account of his many sufferings and little strength. The indifference of others appeared in their frequent yawns, their irreverent position, sometimes even from their falling asleep, so that the warden had to reprove first one, then another. The attention and devotion of Benedict in reciting it were such, that the warden testifies that he received great edification from him: he appeared evidently to be quite recollected within himself and interiorly penetrated; so that some of the poor, who had him before their eyes, said one to another in a low voice, "Look at Benedict, he is going into an ecstasy."

When he was in Rome he went every Friday morning, in the church of St. Mark, to the altar of our Blessed Lady of Sorrows, and there, after a long contemplation of her griefs, he recited with the others, penetrated with the consideration of the dolours of Mary, the Corona, which is usually recited there, nor did he depart till he had received the Benediction of the Blessed Sacrament, which was there exposed, being sure, that with her Son, Mary would also bless him. At night he was ready for the recital of the Litany of our Blessed Lady, in her church of Santa Maria dei Monti, which takes place there every night. Wherever he was, in Loretto, or elsewhere, the spectators were much edified by his extraordinary reverence, modesty, and attention, which were the more admired, as he appeared ragged, poor, and thin. It was his custom frequently during the day, to revive his love for Jesus and Mary, by the invocation of their holy names; which not being known to a confessor who was advising him to it, he heard Benedict reply, that he already practised this, but would do so more frequently to obey him.

Through this fervent love for Mary, he remained for whole hours, contemplating her privileges, before the most celebrated images in Rome and other cities. These contemplations had for their subjects, sometimes her Immacu-

her sublime dignity of Mother of God, her greatness in heaven, and the Mysteries of her life on earth. Before the holy picture of the Blessed Virgin, placed above the high altar, in the church of Santa Maria in Via Lata, when it was uncovered for public veneration, he remained devoutly kneeling, with his countenance and eyes fixed on his beloved Mother, beholding and contemplating her, completely absorbed in this exercise, causing both admiration and edification to all who noticed him.

It will not be necessary to speak again here of his passing whole days, without thinking of food, in the Holy House of Loretto; his sublime contemplations on his knees, his tears of tenderness, his affections, his effusions of love, in reflecting that he was in the same House which served as a dwelling to the great Mother of God; these things have been sufficiently treated of in the fifth and sixth chapters of the second part; and hence we may ascertain his ardent love for the Blessed Virgin. When in that Holy House he was so consumed by love, that being told one evening that the ministers of the Holy House gave away morning and night bread and wine to poor persons, and that he could share in this charity, he showed an entire indifference to partake of it, nor was he ever seen amongst the others; but rather in the church the whole day, being satisfied with spiritual

ourishment, and with the company of his dear
other.

Very long also were his affectionate visits to
id contemplations before the image of the Bless-
l Virgin Mary, in the great Basilica of Santa
aria Maggiore, in the church of the Holy Name
Mary, in that called the church of Loretto,
id many others. It was sufficient, that they
ere pictures of the Blessed Virgin, to excite in
enedict veneration, devotion, and most tender
fections.

He venerated more than any other, * that
pressive and beautiful picture of Mary, which
placed above the high altar, in the church of
e "Padri Pii Operarj," and called Santa Maria
i Monti. Before this he spent for many years
arly the whole morning on his knees, in con-
nual contemplation, with his eyes fixed towards

others, which were not perfectly heard by the person listening. Another says, that he remained on his knees before this picture with so much modesty and devotion, that he seemed motionless as a statue; and his eyes were so affectionately and immoveably fixed on Mary, that he never took them from her, for any noise that occurred in the church, or for any other circumstance. Every one who beheld him felt compunction and tenderness. Many went on purpose to this church, and having adored the Blessed Sacrament for a short time, placed themselves afterwards in a position to observe him, as they felt excited in their hearts affections of compunction, tenderness, and devotion, in beholding this loving servant of our Blessed Lady, which they did not experience in hearing sermons.

Finally, his love for Mary showed itself in the many pilgrimages he made in her honour; those of Loretto, Einsiedlen, Rome, and other places. But his imitation of her virtues manifests it more clearly than anything else; his spotless life, his angelical purity, his contempt of the world and of himself, and the other virtues of which we have spoken in this third part; for he sought, as much as he could, to be a living copy of the virtues of Mary, and his love for her did not chiefly consist in his pilgrimages, visits, and prayers, but in imitating her virtues, as St. Jerome writes: "My beloved, honour Mary for the love you have for her; but it is then that you truly show your love, when you seek to imitate her whom you love."

After relating the love and veneration of Benedict for Mary, it would be proper to mention here the correspondence of our sweet Lady with Benedict's love. Her heart is so sweet and grateful, that she rewards those who serve her with graces and special favours, even in this world. And I cannot doubt, but that she bestowed many on this fervent lover. How can I, however, relate them, as they are not found in the Processes, the only source whence I have drawn what is contained in this work? We do not find them mentioned therein, because the extreme humility of Benedict caused him to keep carefully concealed the graces which he received from God and from Mary; nor did he ever discover to any one what passed between his soul and God, excepting when obliged by a formal precept of holy obedience to answer on certain determined points. He then manifested what he was obliged to declare with so much repugnance, amidst so many sighs and tears, that he discouraged his confessors from making any farther researches, that they might not continue to afflict him. I do not find in the Processes, that any one of the many confessors whom he had in various towns, ever questioned him regarding his visions, or obliged him to mention the apparitions with which he had been favoured of Jesus and Mary, or the graces and favours he received from them. If they had interrogated him, I feel sure that he would have revealed these things through obedience, which he loved so much. Two favours, however, which I find related in the

Processes, will serve as an indication of rest. The first is a circumstance which pened to him in Loretto the first or se year that he went thither as a pilgrim: it a long and extraordinary ecstasy, not no there at that time, for his sanctity was known then as clearly as it was later. He accustomed, after spending the whole day devoutly in the Holy House, to sleep in the air at night during the first years, if we call it sleeping. One night as one of the vants of the Basilica was returning home, a two hours after sun-set, passing in the under the vault near the church, by the] where there is a miraculous picture of Blessed Virgin, he struck against the feet person who was prostrated on the ground u this picture, and he only just escaped fal Seeing that the person did not move at al suspected that it must be an intoxicated pe On the following morning at break of day, fore the church doors were opened, he tho he would ascertain if the person were still th but he saw clearly to his surprise that it Benedict, who was still in the same place,] trate with his face on the ground in the ac venerating the picture. Surprised at this s he was speedily undeceived; and as St. I formerly said to the Jews, who judged the a tles to be intoxicated when they saw them f with holy fervour through the Holy Spirit w they had just received, so he also said in sp ing of him to his confessor, Father Tem

"Non est hic ebrius," with any other wine than that which is heavenly. The confessor testified great pleasure in hearing it, adding, that he was truly a holy pilgrim; "And would to God," said he to him, "that we also were imitators of his example!"

I felt myself struck with astonishment in reading of this event, and I acknowledge that of all the many ecstasies which I have elsewhere mentioned, this caused me most surprise, on account of the open situation, the time of night, the extraordinary circumstances attending it, and its continuance during the whole night. I have no hesitation in saying that the Blessed Virgin then deigned to give him some idea of her heavenly beauty and of her glory, an idea which so completely absorbed him, that it made him insensible to the sudden blow, and sweetly obliged him to prostrate himself reverently with his face on the ground, like the old and young Tobias when the Archangel Raphael discovered himself to them, "They fell prostrate with their face upon the earth," with this exception, that they only remained prostrate for three hours, and Benedict for the whole night.

From this event we may judge how many more favours he must have received from the Blessed Virgin, which his great humility has kept hidden from us.

The other favour is, that our Blessed Lady so ordered it, as that Benedict should come to the end of his life while reverently praying before her much-venerated picture in the church of Santa Maria dei Monti. He had been praying at her feet from an early hour, and had remained till the morning was half over. Being seized with a fainting fit at Mary's feet, feeling himself, as it were, invited by his Mother to her heavenly abode, as he had so often visited her in her earthly dwelling, his strength no longer sufficing to support him, he left the church like a dying person; he stopped on the outer steps of the church, and being carried from thence to the neighbouring abode of a charitable person, he died that same day, as will be related in its place. Benedict also honoured all the saints as the friends of God, and those especially who were connected with his holy Mother, either by kindred or particular devotion. He was particularly devout before others to the spouse of the Blessed Virgin, and reputed father of Jesus Christ, St. Joseph; also to the three archangels, St. Michael, St. Gabriel, St. Raphael, the Apostle St. James, and others. Another to whom he had a special devotion, was St. Francis of Assisium, and he showed the solidity of his devotion, not so much by visiting him at Assisi, in the beginning of his pilgrimages, by inscribing himself in his confraternity, "dei Cordigeri," and by reciting in his honour the daily prayers prescribed, as in always imitating the virtues of this great saint. He imitated him so perfectly, that his confessor, F. Temple, deposes, that with the exception of the Stigmas and the foundation of religious orders, he made himself a living copy of his extreme interior and exterior poverty, of his contempt of himself, his seraphic love for God, and of all those other virtues which so greatly adorned the spirit of St. Francis, and distinguish him amidst the glorious number of the saints.

CHAPTER XIV.

HIS GREAT CHARITY FOR HIS NEIGHBOUR. HEROIC ACTS OF IT ARE RELATED.

THE love of God and of our neighbour always go together; they are like our eyes, which are two, but have only one sight. Hence, from Benedict's great love for God we may infer the extent of his fraternal charity. He was admitted by the Divine favour to the contemplation of the greatness of God, the excess of His love towards man, especially in His sacred Passion; and inflamed with that ardent love of which we have elsewhere spoken, he also loved every man with tenderness, considering him as the living image of God, the work of His hands, and purchased by that infinite price paid by our Divine Redeemer. In order now to prove Benedict's charity for his neighbour we must mention the exterior acts exercised by him, for, as St. Gregory says, "The proof of love is its being manifested in action."

The objects of fraternal charity are two, the body and the soul. As to that which regards the body, Benedict was very attentive from his infancy, never to utter a word, or perform any act, which could cause any injury to the person or reputation of any one, which, as the Apostle St. James says, is a quality belonging to a perfect man: "If any man offend not in word, the same is a perfect man." (James, iii. 2.) This was observed by many who lived with him, and afterwards attested it in the Processes. Still, this is little. To the negative quality of doing harm to no one, he added the positive one, of doing good whenever it was in his power, and with so much loving zeal, that nothing seemed difficult which was proposed to him, when it regarded the service of God and the good of his neighbour.

Perceiving once, while yet young, that a child had fallen into the dirt in going to school, he ran quickly to raise her up, though he covered himself with mud in doing so; and as the child could not find one of her shoes, whatever pains she took in looking for it, Benedict with kind solicitude found it buried in the deep mud; nor was his charity satisfied till he had accompanied the little weeping girl to school. Another little girl being asked by Benedict, when he lived in Erin with his uncle, and was a little more than twelve years old, why she did not come to school in her parish as formerly, replied, "My step-mother will not give me leave," and saying this, she began to cry bitterly. "No, do not cry," said Benedict to her, with a sweet and amiable countenance, "be comforted;" and he conducted her from the priest's house, where he was then, in the company of others, to the neighbouring door of the church, and there making her kneel down, he told her to say a Pater and Ave, and when she came to "Fiat voluntas tua," he made her repeat it three times, telling her that she must resign herself to the will of God in this little trial; then he said the De Profundis with her, for the soul of her mother; and he exhorted her not to persist in desiring to come back to school, nor to be troubled about it, as she must obey her step-mother. "Our good God," he said, "will supply for it: I will pray for you: do the will of God;" and he made her repeat three times while kneeling, "Praised and adored for ever be the most Blessed Sacrament of the altar." Thus comforted, she went away tranquil and consoled.

A lady who was much distressed by many trials, having discovered some of them to him in order to receive comfort, through the great idea she had formed of his sanctity, he consoled her with this sentiment, which is suitable to any one in tribulation: "In this world," said he, "we are all in a valley of tears; we are not to expect comfort here, we shall have it eternally in Paradise, if we bear our crosses on earth." He also wonderfully mitigated the sorrow of another, who related many of his misfortunes to him, by speaking to him of confidence in God, who afflicts us because He loves us, and who is pleased to see us cast ourselves into His paternal bosom. A sick person, who had been for several years confined to her bed by obstinate sickness, was so encouraged by the comforting sentiments expressed by Benedict, with great fervour, and in a very pleasing manner, that she said no one else had ever given her so much consolation.

We must here call to mind what was related in the seventh chapter of the first part, regarding Benedict's heroic charity during the epidemic at Erin, to the great number of persons who were attacked by it, when he was scarcely fifteen years of age, to the evident peril of his life.

This is so heroic an act of charity, that Jesus Christ says, there is not a greater: "Greater love than this no man hath, that a man lay down his life for his friends." (John, xv. 13.)

He placed his delight in a particular manner in the poor. Considering them as his brothers, he used to divide with them food which he received from his uncle at Erin, taking care, with a holy artifice suggested by humility, to administer it secretly. During the course of his after life, it is known everywhere that he distributed to them the alms which he received from others. Every week when he was in Rome he went to a place near the Porta di S. Paolo, to give alms to a hermit who dwelt there. He several times deprived himself of the soup which he received at the convent doors, to give it to others whom he thought more needy than himself; but in doing so he always placed himself in the last rank among the poor, though he had arrived before the others; and being asked why, "Because I fear," he replied, "that it may fail before some ne who came after me has received a portion." In fact, as owing to the great number f poor who went thither there was not always ufficient, Benedict, careless of himself, and solicitous only to supply the want, distributed noney secretly to those who were disappointed. And as he sometimes noticed among the crowd ome poor mother, whose single portion was not ufficient for her large family, he compassionately dded his own share to hers.

There are bold and insolent people sometimes ven among the poor. One of these having cached the door of the convent of Santa Maria opra Minerva, after the soup had been distributed, had the audacity to take Benedict's porion from him, and to empty it into his own orringer. Another person would probably have nade a great disturbance about it, but Benedict as not troubled; he did not resist, but yielded illingly, being ready to give up his cup also. le was a perfect follower of the Evangelical ounsels, and he practised this also, "And if a

The great number of insects with which he was infested, gave him a new opportunity of exercising fraternal charity. He knew the great horror in which these little animals are held: he saw himself shunned by many, and heard the warning which persons gave each other to avoid his place in the church on account of them. Hence he never went near any one, and removed of his own accord if others approached him, for fear of communicating any to them. He did not go to the grate of the confessional when other penitents were there on this account, excepting when his confessor made a sign to him. One priest, in order to make him sit by him, when passing as a pilgrim through Cossignano, was obliged to make use of the precept of obedience, so great was his repugnance; and when asked the reason of it, he replied with modest blushes, "I fear to leave some filthy insect in your house, as I have many upon me." He gave the same answer to another priest in Rome, who obliged him by obedience to sit down in his house.

What we have hitherto related will seem little when compared with the heroic acts which he exercised towards those who persecuted and despised him. To practise charity towards those who do us no harm, and towards virtuous persons, is certainly a proof of charity; but a much more clear and heroic mark of it, as St. Thomas says, is to suffer contradictions which happen to us from the malice or passion of others. "Validior probatio dilectionis, est sustinentia tribulationum." He was much tormented by bold and insolent persons, but he suffered all without complaining, or giving any sign of resentment; imitating Jesus Christ, who called His treacherous disciple, friend: "Friend, whereto art thou come?" And he sought to do them the good which lay in his power, to pray for them, and interpose himself as a mediator with any one who wished to have them punished. Many of these occasions will be related later, particularly when we have to speak of his humility.

When a youth at Erin, two persons in his uncle's house began to persecute him, emboldened by his imperturbable patience. One of his companions insulted him with jests and contempt, treating him as a hypocrite. Benedict bore it in silence; he even interposed in his favour with his uncle, who had been informed

boys made a jest of him, ill-treating him by words and blows, considering him as a fool, and pelting him with stones, cabbage-stalks, and orange peel, without his giving them any provocation. These things gave him no trouble; he regarded derision and insults with indifference; he pitied these persons; he pardoned them from his heart, between himself and God, without feeling any sentiment of hatred or rancour, but experiencing, on the contrary, interior tranquillity. Another confessor at Loretto obliged him to say with what feelings he regarded those who derided and ill-treated him; he answered, "They are looked upon by me as true friends, because they give me an occasion of merit, and of fulfilling the precept of our Lord Jesus Christ, to love our enemies, and pray for them."

And that this was truly his disposition we see clearly from the opposition he made to a person, who, undertaking his defence in Rome, wished to make a complaint to the government of these bold people. "No," said the servant of God, "let no complaint be made; what we suffer for the love of Christ crucified is little." Acts like these are so heroic, that a confessor in Rome, surprised at the sublime perfection of his great soul, thought proper to give up his direction, thinking in his humility that it was beyond his abilities.

As to the other object of fraternal charity, which is the soul, though not called by Almighty God to the rank of preacher, master, or ecclesiastical doctor, Benedict cooperated much in the salvation of souls, in the best manner he was able in his state of life, doing this by his words, his prayers, and the good example of a faithful Christian. As he began to love God from the time that reason dawned in his mind, he also loved the soul of his neighbour from that time, insinuating always, and on all occasions, the holy fear of God and the observance of His divine commandments, in those with whom he could speak in this manner at his tender age. He instructed, of his own accord, children who were younger than himself. He spoke of eternity, the truths of our holy faith, and of the love of God towards man, with so much fervour and energy, that he caused great emotion in those who would listen to him. He instilled into some a lively confidence in God, into others correspondence with the Passion of our blessed Redeemer, and contempt of the world into the hearts of many. Speaking with a fellow-student of the vanity and baseness of temporal things compared with eternity, he induced him to consecrate himself to God in the rigorous order of the Carthusians, whither he himself conducted him as a glorious conquest which he had made. He had the holy custom when a youth of reading clearly and slowly some spiritual book, not only to the servants, but to many persons of the neighbourhood, who listened to him with no less pleasure than profit. In the fulfilment of the duty of fraternal correction, he had the holy courage, while yet young, to correct his brothers at home, when they disobeyed or committed any other fault. He admonished his companions at school when they brought forward improper conversation, or did anything contrary to charity.

In his pilgrimages, and afterwards in Rome, when he noticed any action prejudicial to the honour of God, or to fraternal charity, he did not fear to correct the person, whoever it might be, but always civilly and with a placid countenance. These corrections frequently brought upon him great outrages, blows, and insults, of which we shall speak in the chapter on his humility.

While he was praying one day in the church, a civil person drew near to say something to him. Benedict would not listen to him, making him aware of the respect we ought to show to God in His house, and of the impropriety of talking therein. He once heard by accident, from the mouth of a priest, a proposition which was directly contrary to fraternal charity. The servant of God respectfully showed him the fault he had committed, concluding that when fraternal charity is in question we must sacrifice everything. When occasion offered he never failed to instruct any one who appeared ignorant either of what we ought to believe or practise. It sometimes happened that he had not the opportunity of correcting one who spoke ill of his neighbour in his presence, and in the presence of persons to whom it belonged to give the admonition. The servant of God being unable to do it with his tongue, employed the means which the Holy Spirit gives us: "The north wind driveth away rain, as doth a sad countenance a backbiting tongue," (Prov. xxv. 23,) and he showed so grave and sad a countenance, that the sight was sufficient to impose silence and give a correction.

In the second place, he cooperated by prayer in the salvation of souls, praying to God every day for the conversion of sinners and infidels. In assisting at mass he united in the prayers which the priest said, directing his prayers to God, with a lively zeal for their conversion. Some French pilgrims, being lodged in a place where Benedict happened to have a little room near them, heard a person during great part of the night, not only offering fervent prayers to God, but weeping bitterly for the conversion of sinners especially. Not knowing who this was, they asked the master of the house, and they heard that it was a poor but holy pilgrim. Desirous to see him, they would not leave till he went out, that they might become acquainted with him, for they were greatly edified by his prayers and tears.

He laboured for the conversion of souls, by his example, in the third place. Example has more power than words, to persuade. Even Seneca says, that the shortest and surest way of making an impression on the minds of others is by example, rather than words. "Longum est iter per præcepta; breve et efficax per exempla." Our Divine Redeemer first practised virtues, and then taught them: "Cœpit facere et docere." Benedict's good example was continual, at all ages, of all virtues, and in all places. We find it spoken of in many places in the Processes, as a most perfect model of sublime perfection. In the public streets, in his pilgrimages, in the churches, and wherever he happened to be, the modesty of his looks, his composed appearance, his fixed attitude in prayer, his reverence in the churches, were a mute but efficacious sermon.

So virtuous was his example, that confessors proposed him as a model to their penitents, telling them to look at themselves in Benedict, and to learn from his example a fervent manner of praying, contempt of the world, and respect in the church. Don Biagio Piccilli of the "Pii Operarj," Father Temple, the penitentiary at Loretto, and others in various places, did so. A great number of persons in fact attest, that it sufficed to see him to be affected, moved to compunction, and animated to virtue. Many express the same sentiment that was deposed in the Processes by a person who, witnessing his humble, poor, and fervent method of life, and seeing so ardent and continual an exercise of prayer practised by a beggar, felt himself urged to take greater care of his own soul, being ashamed to be so inferior in piety to a poor ragged man. Whoever shall read in this work Benedict's illustrious actions, will, if he read them carefully and with an upright intention, without doubt be in some degree moved, and hence he may imagine what effect would be caused by seeing, hearing, and conversing with him; it was such, that his confessor, Father Temple, has no difficulty, from the many uniform accounts which he received, in comparing him to St. Francis in the edification he gave.

The souls in purgatory are also objects of fraternal charity, as they are capable of receiving relief from the suffrages of others, and liberation from the pains they suffer there. Benedict was always solicitous to gain as many indulgences as he could for their comfort. He compassionated principally those souls who are most abandoned; applying, as a suffrage for them, his prayers and the holy sacrifice of the mass at which he was present. This exceeding charity towards his neighbour, exercised in behalf of the needy, the sick, and even of his persecutors, clearly shows that in Benedict dwelt the true Spirit of Jesus Christ, who willed that this should be the distinctive characteristic of His disciples and followers: "By this shall all men know that you are My disciples, if you have love one for another." (John, xiii. 35.) By this every one may discern whether he possesses the true Spirit of Jesus Christ, and whether he is His follower. If he has not charity, let him try to acquire it after Benedict's example, and let him remember, that not to have it is, acccording to St. John, a mark of eternal reprobation: "He that loveth not, abideth in death." (1 John, iii. 14.)

HUMILITY is of two kinds, interior and exterior. "Interior humility," says St. Bonaventure, "is a virtue, which, discovering clearly to us our own nothingness and the enormity of our sins, makes us conceive a great contempt for ourselves." This knowledge comes from the knowledge of God. Whoever knows by supernatural light, as far as it is permitted to us in this world, the greatness of an infinite God, with His infinite perfections and attributes, begins also to see in God his own vileness and baseness, and hence he must despise himself as nothing in comparison with this Supreme Being. Benedict was favoured by Almighty God in his contemplations with very clear lights, which showed him the greatness, the magnificence, and the majesty of God. Knowing himself to have been drawn from nothing, to be nothing of himself, to be able to do nothing of himself except sin, to merit nothing but hell, he had formed so low an opinion of himself, that he frequently burst forth into expressions of humility. He called himself "a most unworthy sinner, undeserving to lift up

a most vile and abominable creature, the greatest sinner in the world." To some persons who made known to him that they wished to see him when he was at the house of the Sori in Loretto, he replied, "What curiosity! Do they wish to see a wolf? I am a wolf."

I know very well that similar expressions are used by many who have not the true spirit of humility, who wish to appear humble, but are not really so, and of whom it is said in Ecclesiasticus, "There is one that humbleth himself wickedly, and his interior is full of deceit." (Ecclus. xix. 23.) Should God permit, however, that any one through contempt should make use of some of these humbling expressions towards them, or treat them as being what they say they are: one word, one action suffices to show the truth; one single spark is sufficient to set fire to a heap of powder. But if they proceed from a sincere heart, and from a lively knowledge of our own nothingness, they are a proof of true humility, as in St. Paul's case, when he said, he was the least among the apostles, unworthy of the name of an apostle, the first among sinners.

The austere life which Benedict led, his contempt of the world, his long daily contemplations, his angelical purity, the sublime virtues by which he edified every one who beheld him, evidently demonstrated that his expressions of humility did not come from a deceitful heart, but from a heart that was sincere and deeply penetrated.

But this is much more clearly shown by an

ich occurred in the month of March, a pilgrimage he made to the Holy House o. A troop of dissolute and wandering who were taking their pleasure while ig to the Holy House of Loretto, outraged ur of God by blasphemy and improper . Benedict, who could not quit that roached them, and with mild and affable and a kind and placid countenance, correct them, placing before their eyes of the offence to God, and the injury to souls. These impious persons, making the words of a poor and ragged pilgrim, lead him with abuse, calling him a hypocrite, and a simpleton. The servant suffered in silence, and they, growing hrew him down, and striving with one loaded him with kicks and blows. In time, by the disposition of Divine Pro- some persons of consideration passed on k, and, horrified at the outrage offered fierce wolves to so meek a lamb, who s a lamb before the shearer," without or complaint, they dismounted and d them with chastisement; and being d, these men left him and fled. Rising ground, Benedict said humbly and with il countenance to these gentlemen, that not know how great a sinner he was, they were astonished at such heroic virtue, and made it known to Father Temple in Loretto afterwards, and two of these insolent people, repenting of what they had done, expressed to Father Temple with tears their sorrow for having ill-treated such a servant of God. We shall relate similar facts when we speak of his perfect dominion over his passions. His invincible patience in enduring such outrages would suffice alone to show the true spirit of humility which Benedict possessed, according to the words of the great doctor, St. Jerome, "True humility is shown by patience."

Here, to what has been already said, may be added other proofs, which are equally strong arguments of his deep foundation of perfect humility. The principal of them may be reduced to three, in which Benedict greatly distinguished himself. The first is, in serving others when occasion offered, as an exercise of humility, not by necessity of condition. We must here recollect the great services which he performed in the whole parish of Erin, when a very fatal epidemic caused such ravages, carrying in his own hands, like a servant, food, or some sort of remedy, to this or that house; and working like a stable boy, in providing grass which he himself gathered in the fields, and giving it to the cattle of other persons, which were deprived of every other assistance.

He acted as a servant in his uncle's house on other occasions. A parish priest attests with wonder, that one day when he was dining with

Benedict's uncle at Erin, seeing him preparing the meats for table, like a servant, he entreated him, jointly with his uncle, to come and sit down with them, as the servant man and maid were there to do what was necessary. The humble servant of God, after the example of Jesus Christ, who "came not to be ministered unto, but to minister," would continue to the end what he had begun, trying to conceal his virtuous action by saying, "I have more pleasure in waiting upon you."

The second is, his taking in all things the last place, according to the advice of our Blessed Redeemer: "Sit down in the lowest place." (Luke, xiv. 10.) In fact, he used to place himself last in the crowd of penitents when he was going to confession; the last in the company of other poor people, considering himself the vilest; the last at the doors of convents, to receive the charity of soup, usually distributed to the poor about mid-day. His being the last gained him sometimes reproofs from the porter, who was very sorry to see him, through his own virtuous conduct, occasionally deprived of his portion; but Benedict, silently bearing the rebuke, went away equally satisfied with the loss of his soup and the addition of the reprimand. A person who esteemed Benedict, passing about mid-day by the monastery dell' Umiltà, saw a great crowd of poor people pressing round the distributor of soup, and seeing Benedict standing devoutly leaning against the opposite wall, without any solicitude about going nearer, he thought it advisable to recommend him to do so, "Otherwise," said he, "you will go without;" but he went away quietly, as if he had received a portion. Sometimes our Lord, pleased with his humility, deigned to give him honour at these very doors, inspiring the distributor to call him first to receive the soup, who stood humbly and devoutly in the last place, thus verifying the words, "Friend, go up higher," to him who "sits in the lowest place," as it happened at the monastery of the Ursulines.

The third is, to fly honours and the esteem of men. Benedict had a greater aversion for these than worldlings have for insults and contempt, which were alone desired by him. The example of the Son of God, who was so greatly insulted in His Passion, on which Benedict often meditated, and which was made clear to him by supernatural lights, had so profoundly moved his heart, that it continually encouraged him to imitate it. For this reason he went through the public streets covered with rags; he bore the attacks of those insects, which besides causing suffering, made him an object of horror to others, and he had an abhorrence of everything like esteem and respect.

A lady, who had a great opinion of his sanctity, meeting him one day, ordered her little son to kiss his hand. Scarcely had Benedict heard these words, than, filled with horror, he retreated to a little distance, and hiding his hands within the sleeves of his ragged cloak, he said as if alarmed, "My hand!" and as she insisted and entreated him to allow it, and the little boy drew near him, he concealed his hands more carefully, and repeated, "Kiss my hand! my hand!" and causing her to desist, he went away quickly. Another person seeing his modesty and recollection after receiving the benediction of the most Blessed Sacrament, in the church of Santa Maria dei Monti, approaching him said, "How happy you are, who are so good! recommend me to our Lord." This sufficed; he seemed like one struck by a thunderbolt; his face became sad, he bent his head down more than usual, and turning his back upon her, quickly disappeared from her sight, so completely overwhelmed that her companions repeatedly reproved her for having so much afflicted him. He showed less grief to another person, who seeing him about to depart for the Holy House of Loretto, said to him these words only, "How happy are you, who go to visit these holy places!" There was certainly nothing in these words that expressed esteem; but whether he suspected that she had a good opinion of him, or that she meant something else, he withdrew from her presence, giving her the very same answer that our divine Redeemer gave the woman, when He heard her say, "Beatus venter, qui te portavit," &c. "Blessed," said he, "is he who does the will of God."

Every word, every action, which expressed even remotely some esteem or good opinion of him, was like a mortal wound to his heart. The porter of the Minerva having perceived, that in giving soup to the poor they strove with one another to be first, and that Benedict was always the last, standing in a devout and edifying attitude, thought to do him a service by keeping a little for him, and giving it to him separately. This slight mark of distinction and honour was enough to cause Benedict never again to appear in that place. He fled more rapidly, and with greater horror from a house where he was accustomed to receive charity, when he heard a servant, through the opinion she had of his heroic sanctity, call him one day by the name of St. Alexis.

When persons requested him to pray to God for them, it was his custom either to give no answer at all, considering himself unworthy and devoid of merit, or to utter words of self-abjection, saying, "that he was the vilest of men existing, unworthy to live amongst men, a great sinner." A very pious duchess in Rome thought it a great favour to her, and great humility in Benedict, when having recommended herself to his prayers, she obtained only these few words in reply, "One for the other."

The event which happened to him in the monastery of Santa Chiara di Monte Lupone, in 1781, with those pious nuns, is very pleasing, and shows many virtues, especially profound humility. The Abate Signor Paolo Mancini, administrator of the Ospizio dei Poveri in Rome, where the servant of God then passed his nights, being requested by him to give him permission to go to Loretto, for his usual pilgrimage to the Holy

House, gave him a letter for Monte Lupone, a few miles distant from Loretto, which he was to deliver to the Mother Abbess, of the monastery of Santa Chiara, Sister Eleonora Mazza, with whom he corresponded on the affairs of the monastery. The letter said amongst other things, "I send you a poor and holy man, who employs his life in prayer;" and he had made this known to her before by another letter.

Benedict arrived at Monte Lupone on the morning of Maunday Thursday, and went first, as was his custom, to the church of the monastery, where the sacred function of the day was being celebrated. Benedict assisted all through on his knees, and motionless, though fatigued by the journey, with such fervour, devotion, and modesty, that he seemed like an angel to one of the nuns, though she did not then know who he was, and admiring his great devotion she took several of the nuns to the Coretto to see him, and by the mere view of him they were greatly moved and edified. Still more were they gratified when they saw him following the Blessed Sacrament in the procession which was made to the altar prepared for the sepulchre, walking with his eyes fixed on the ground and with singular modesty.

When the ceremonies were ended he went to the parlour with Signor Mancini's letter. The abbess being informed of it, and having read the few first words of the letter, brought her by a lay-sister, went eagerly to speak to him. To see him, and believe him a St. Alexis, and, as it were, a portrait of Jesus Christ, as she attests, was one and the same thing. The other nuns being sent for by the abbess, hastened to become acquainted with a saint, and seeing him to be the same who had so much edified them by his extraordinary devotion in church, they formed a great opinion of him, and were much moved, never being satisfied with looking at and admiring him.

One of them seeing him standing all in rags, modest and quiet, said to him, compassionately, "Poor man." The servant of God, who had not before opened his mouth, now said, "Call those poor who are in hell, and have lost God for all eternity;" and in naming Almighty God, he bent his head profoundly: those words made a great impression on every one. The charity of the abbess caused her to offer him some little refreshment. He took a very small quantity, and when pressed to eat more, he refused, begging that what remained might be given to the poor. Some of the nuns offered him other food, but he would not accept anything more, saying, "Almighty God has given me what is necessary for this day; I want nothing more." Their charity moving them to beg him to keep something for the following day, Benedict, who never thought of the future, being satisfied with food for the day, replied, "To-morrow, which will be Good Friday, dedicated to the Passion of our Lord Jesus Christ, we only eat a little bread and drink some water, as nuns must know." While he was taking refreshment one

edict answered, "Loving God." "I know very well," she said, and again put her stion, "What is he doing?" "Loving God," ated Benedict. Having perceived that the s flocked to the parlour, showing some good ion and esteem of him, he took leave quietly departed. They were all filled with astonment and admiration at so many virtues pracl in that short space, greatly grieved at his y and sudden departure.

n his return to Rome the Abate Mancini d him for the answer to his letter, and he didly said, "That in coming back from Lo- he had not gone to the monastery to ree the promised answer, for the good nuns recommended themselves to his prayers, and n him marks of esteem, as if he had been I for something, when he did not know him- to be anything but a vile sinner." The e wisely said to him, that the nuns had done harm by this, for as we are all sinners we it to recommend each other to God, that we be saved, according to the advice of the tle St. James: "Pray for one another, that may be saved." (James, v. 16.) While edict was thus humbling himself, the abate ived the abbess's answer, in which she hear- thanked him for the great pleasure he had n them in making them acquainted with the tly poor man.

CHAPTER XVI.

OTHER PROOFS OF HIS HUMILITY.

What has been hitherto related furnishes us certainly with very clear proofs of his profound humility, and it seems as if it could not be practised with greater perfection. Nevertheless, it did extend farther, even so as not to return to those confessors who had shown some esteem or good opinion of him. This was practised by St. Ignatius Loyola, who quitted his confesser, Diego d' Equia, on account of something which he had said, significant of Ignatius's great sanctity. This made Benedict sometimes change his confessor. He would not on the one hand be his own guide in the ways of the Lord, for he knew that a ship without a pilot to govern it diverges from the right direction, and runs the risk of being wrecked: on the other, he had the greatest horror of seeing in any one else a different idea of him from that which he himself entertained, namely, that he was a vile sinner; thus by leaving those confessors who showed esteem of him, he thought to unite direction and humility well together.

His confessor at Loretto, Father Temple, charmed with Benedict's great sanctity, sought eagerly from those among his countrymen at Loretto, who were sincere and pious, for some details of his life, to ascertain if it were con-

to the idea he had formed of him.
hem he drew, "that Benedict was a
ıd that his humility was so great, that
perceived that he was in any degree
by his confessors he left them and
others, and," adds he, "as I had the
s to hear his confession once, perhaps
not have come again if he had seen in
sign of esteem."

kilful confessor was greatly on his guard
oint, and far from showing a good opin-
him, he sometimes purposely reproved
ating him as an undeserving and idle
ut all his caution was of no avail. It
l one day, when Benedict was three or
es distant from his confessor, that
ıch pilgrims approached the priest, and
ıd to him together, "O father, what
saint you have confessed!" "He is an-
. Alexis," said one. "He is another St.
Gonzaga," said the other; and both
extolling Benedict's sanctity, and re-
several times the same words. The fa-
ed why they thought him a St. Alexis,
ysius. "St. Alexis," they replied, "for
mpt of the world; St. Aloysius, for his
and penance." Scarcely had Bene-
rd the first few words pronounced in
e, than making more haste than usual
ly left the spot, as if struck by a thun-
nor did Father Temple again see him at

for he knew that it had been said from the earliest years, that Benedict on this account did not continue long under the same confessor. He accuses himself as being guilty of the loss of so holy a penitent, for having scrutinized too closely the spirit of Benedict by very minute examination, and for not having immediately imposed silence on those pilgrims who praised his sanctity. Father Temple was very desirous to possess him and speak to him again, for he knew from St. Theresa's writings, that penitents of this sort are of more use to their confessor than their confessor is to them. He could never manage it, however; once he called him to give him an alms in the street, but this had no effect, but to make him quicken his usually slow steps, to get out of the way. He thought of calling him when he was at prayer in the church, but seeing him so recollected in contemplation, he had not courage to disturb him. He says that he regretted much that he had not thought of putting him under obedience, being very sure that he would have obeyed immediately. He concludes by saying, that he conformed himself to the will of God, believing that our Lord designed it as a mortification for him, when he deprived him of a consolation he so much desired.

For a similar cause he went no more to the other penitentiary, Father Francesco Maria Almerici, for he perceived that he also had conceived some esteem of him.

The final proof, which shows his profound humility in the clearest light, was the care wl he took to conceal from others his virtuous tions. This solicitude in Benedict did not re from the fear of vain-glory, of which he alw had a horror. He who knows the greatness God, says St. Francis of Sales, fears vain-g less than any other vice. The knowledge of makes him sink deeply into the abyss of own nothingness. The glow-worm which plays its faint light in the darkness of the ni is completely eclipsed by the glory of the n day sun. In fact, in the large volume of Processes, though we read of different temptati which have been already mentioned, there not to be found any temptation of vain-glory. concealed his virtues, therefore, because, lik perfect follower of the Evangelical Couns he was always eager to profit by the warni which our Lord gives in St. Matthew, to p and perform other pious works in secret, t we may not resemble the hypocritical Pharis who loved to pray in the synagogues and pu places, standing up to draw praise from spectators. "Take heed that you do not y justice before men to be seen by them, but p to thy Father in secret." (Matth. vi. 1, 6.)

He usually selected a secret and retired pl in the church to pray quietly; though he not by this means succeed in avoiding being s by others, who, admiring him, went on purp to watch him without his perceiving it. In almost continual prayer, no affectation or ost tation appeared which could strike the eyes others; he prayed with so much simplicity, that nothing showed itself exteriorly of those supernatural lights with which God favoured him; he remained quiet and immoveable, kneeling sometimes with his hands crossed on his breast, sometimes in the act of holding some pious book open, which furnished fuel to the fire of his love of God; never did he turn his head or his eyes; thus his prayer was a great example and a source of edification to any one who fixed his eyes upon him. It is true that sometimes he was seen to make extraordinary movements, but this happened either because, transported by fervour, he was not aware of it, or because he could not resist the impetuosity of the internal flame of love which burnt in his breast, or because, as is the case with ecstatic persons, the soul, entirely absorbed in God, no longer knows where the body is, nor is aware what is done, though others use iron or fire to bring her to herself.

He employed all his diligence, therefore, in keeping his virtues and supernatural gifts hidden from the eyes of others, excepting only his confessors, when they obliged him in obedience to discover his spiritual affairs to them. Yet even to these he made known only sufficient to give an answer to their questions. He sought to make it appear to them that his fraternal charity was the effect of natural inclination, as it has been elsewhere mentioned; but Father Temple by obedienee found out that his charity was far from being natural compassion; he ascertained that he was moved only by regarding his neighbours as

his heart particularly touched with compa
for the poor. When he was obliged by obed
to draw aside the veil of humility with whic
desired to cover his solid virtues, one of his
fessors attests, "that it was a continual ma
dom to Benedict, and a constant exercise of
found humility, to manifest those sentiments
those actions which he concealed from ever
else with great care." That it was a marty
appeared by the deep sighs which from tir
time escaped him; from the few and b
words which he uttered, like a person who
much grieved; and by the sadness which sh
itself in his confused and blushing counten

With the same diligence he sought to
the respectability of his condition: hence
always went covered with vile rags; he
spoke of his relations, of the comfort he
have enjoyed at home, nor ever let a word e
his lips which could in any way redound t
honour. All his care and industry were ex
in concealing himself and his virtuous ac
from the eyes of the world. He loved to a
as a vile, abject, and wretched person. V

into that part of the country. Benedict, always intent on concealing himself, answered, that he was a Frenchman and a vagrant. The priest did not believe him to be a vagrant, for he saw under those rags, with his quick eye, the virtues which they concealed, and he had heard mention made of various actions of Benedict, which had been observed elsewhere. The virtue of the servants of God is like musk, which, even when concealed, betrays itself by the scent which it sends forth; "We are the good odour of Christ," (2 Cor. ii. 16,) says St. Paul. The priest entered no farther into the subject at this time, but having formed a higher idea of his sanctity, he suddenly cast himself at his feet to kiss them. Benedict being thus taken by surprise, great confusion and horror appeared in his countenance, which he also showed in his tearful eyes and anxiety to go away: but the pious priest tranquillized him, by telling him that he had not done it out of respect to him, but to the Person of Jesus Christ, whom the poor represent. The same thing occurred again, when by surprise he kissed his hand suddenly.

He was well instructed in everything belonging to the doctrine and regulations of the Catholic Church, and even when young himself he taught children. He knew and understood the Holy Scriptures well, through his frequent reading of the sacred pages, and through the understanding which a confessor with reason believed to be the gift of God; and when he could promote the glory of God by it, he cited apposite texts from them, and knew how to give the true explanation of them, to the astonishment even of his confessors. And yet, as if he had been an ignorant rustic, he went to hear the explanation of the Christian Doctrine, which on certain days is given to boys and people of little capacity; and he was so modest and attentive, that he attracted the admiration of the catechist and of the others.

From his constant desire of concealing his natural qualities, his virtuous actions, and the gifts of God, it is my belief that he had this end in view when he chose Rome for his permanent habitation after so many pilgrimages, for in this vast and populous city, "a person does good without being observed, and on account of the number of churches we may go from one to another without being noticed, and we may also go every day to the Forty Hours' Prayer," as Benedict said and practised, flattering himself that no one remarked him. But it is impossible to miss seeing the sun, though it is sometimes hidden by dense clouds; its own light discovers it. Works of virtue, in which the human eye is not at all sought, shine brilliantly, as it has been said by our Blessed Redeemer, "So let your light shine before men, that they may see your good

of Almighty God in inspiring him with it was quite different. It was to exalt him much more, "in idipsum," placing him in view of the Holy Church, in the capital of the world, according to His infallible promise, "He that humbleth himself shall be exalted." (Luke, xiv. 11.) And as our Divine Redeemer, because He humbled Himself, hiding His divinity on the cross, was exalted by His heavenly Father, by miracles wrought in nature, by conversions, and by the resurrection of the dead, "therefore God hath exalted him," so Benedict having so profoundly humbled himself, Almighty God (in proportion,) exalted him immediately after death, by the fame of his sanctity, which spread through Rome on the very day of his death, and very soon beyond Rome, and from thence over all Europe. He exalted him by wonderful and frequent miracles, and also by glorious apparitions from heaven, which will be spoken of in their proper place.

From the example of Benedict every one who desires it may learn the practice of the virtue of humility, in order to be afterwards exalted by God in heaven, where none enter but the humble of heart. "Unless you become as little children," (that is, humble, as St. Thomas explains it,) "you shall not enter into the kingdom of heaven." (Matth. xviii. 3.) It seems as if Benedict said to us all from heaven, what St. Paul said, "Be ye followers of me, as I also am of Christ." (1 Cor. xi. 1.) "Learn of Me, because I am meek and humble of heart," (Matth. xi. 29,) says Jesus Christ. If any one wishes to know by what means he attained so high a degree of this lovely virtue, Benedict himself revealed it when questioned by his confessor under the precept of obedience. These means were two in number, mental and vocal prayer. In mental prayer he frequently meditated on the majesty and greatness of God, and hence he derived the mean opinion which he entertained of himself, as a mere nothing, and as a despicable sinner. In vocal prayer, he often repeated to Almighty God with St. Augustine, "Lord, grant me to know Thee, and to know myself; to know Thee in order to love Thee, to know myself, that I may despise myself; and may I never desire anything but Thee. Grant that I may conceive a hatred for myself, and a love for Thee; that I may do all for Thee; that I may humble myself and glorify Thee, nor ever have any other object for my thoughts but Thee."

CHAPTER XVII.

HIS PERFECT DOMINION OVER HIS PASSIONS. VARIOUS HEROIC ACTS ARE RELATED WHICH HE PRACTISED AMIDST CONTEMPT AND INJURIES. HIS CONDUCT UNDER SPIRITUAL DESOLATION.

THERE are two principal sources from which, as from two roots, all the passions spring: concupiscence and anger. The former urges us to the love and desire of earthly things, the latter to rage, hatred, and vengeance. "It is not possible totally to eradicate these two poisonous roots," says St. Bernard; "they may be subdued, but cannot be entirely destroyed." Benedict aimed at subduing them both, and he succeeded perfectly.

Inasmuch as regards his victory over concupiscence, we have already related sufficient in the third part, where his heroic virtues are spoken of. His angelical purity shows him to have been a generous conqueror of corporal pleasures. His singular poverty manifests his contempt for pomp, conveniences, and riches. His perfect obedience proves him to have been victorious over his own will. It still remains for us to speak of his conquest of the passion of anger, and though we have already mentioned several actions during the course of this history, there are still many of the heroic degree which have not been related.

By the continual exercise of prayer, rigorous daily examinations, and his severe method of life, he had so completely subdued and made the passion of anger obedient, as it were, to reason, that one of his confessors had no difficulty in speaking of him in the Processes, as being like St. Bonaventure and St. Francis of Sales in affability and meekness. Others speak of him as full of meekness. Some say again, that he signalized himself wonderfully in the practice of this virtue, and that by contrary acts he had perfectly subdued, and, so to speak, entirely conquered the irascible passions, so that his heart could not conceive fear of adverse occurrences, nor anger or aversion against any one who might be the cause of them. His countenance was always cheerful and serene, always the same, which is an extraordinary degree of virtue possessed by few. Injuries, contempt, blows, or ill-treatment never disturbed the interior peace of his heart, nor diminished the serenity of his amiable countenance. Many unforeseen occasions which happened to him are a clear proof of this; some regard the body, others the soul. As a person of great piety was one day passing through the Piazza di Colonna Trajana, in Rome, he saw a troop of young people, who making game of Benedict, gave him blows, knocked his torn hat off his head, pulled the hairs of his beard, and loaded him with insults. The servant of God, "like a lamb before his shearer, not opening his mouth," showed no resentment nor disturbance in his countenance. When he bent down to take up his hat, they all, to the number of ten, rushed upon him, and throwing him with his face on the ground, they loaded him with scoffs, blows, and spittle. This treatment, which would have moved even a stone, had no effect on Benedict. Tranquil, humble, and patient, he received all without any sign of impatience, without uttering a word. The person who saw this was moved to compassion, for it seemed to him that he saw a living copy of Jesus Christ insulted by the rage of the Jews; and going into the midst of this disorderly rabble, "When," said he, rebuking them, "will you cease to ill-treat this poor man? What harm has he done to you? You wish, perhaps, to renew in him the cruelties of the Jews towards Jesus Christ?" This sufficed to make them cease, but laughing, they boldly excused themselves, saying, "He is a fool, that is the reason we treat him so." This person, admiring Benedict's heroic virtue, conceived a high idea of his sanctity; he gave testimony to this fact in the Processes, and when privately questioned by me regarding it, after the lapse of ten years, he confirmed it to me.

One day when the servant of God was kneeling on the lowest step of the great door of the church of the Holy Apostles in Rome, praying with his head bent down, and his arms folded in the form of a cross on his breast, a rude and insolent boy threw a stone at him, which struck him so violently on the leg, that it drew blood, which was seen by several persons, for Benedict had then no stockings on, and only a pair of wretched shoes on his feet. The spectaters were filled with just indignation against this insolent youth, who ran away, and they began to compassionate Benedict. But he showed no emotion nor resentment, nor did he turn to look at the boy, but remained quietly praying in his devout attitude, indifferent to the blood which flowed, and to the pain, which must have been severe. This was a sublime and heroic action, which excited the admiration of all. Another time his left leg was struck by a stone, which drew blood, even through his stockings, which he then wore, but with his usual tranquillity,

of God had one day given to another poor man for an alms a bajocco, which he had a short time before received in a public street of Rome. The poor man knowing this, suspected that he was dissatisfied with so small a piece of money, and that he gave it away not out of pure charity, but, as it were, out of spite; and in a rage he rushed towards him, and giving him a blow with a stick, accused him of it. Benedict received this in peace; he was silent; he was not disturbed, nor did he exculpate himself, but tranquilly continued on his way. When Benedict was dead, however, this man, hearing the praises bestowed on his heroic virtues, which resounded in the streets, houses, and everywhere, repented, and was so grieved at his audacity, that he went weeping and in confusion to the sepulchre: he humbly asked his pardon, and left his stick there as a trophy of Benedict's virtue, and as a perpetual memorial of his repentance, for having insolently and unduly used it.

He was frequently the laughing stock of impudent boys in the public roads, who vied with one another, in throwing cabbage-stalks, orange peel, and similar rubbish at him, becoming bolder in consequence of his invincible patience. Benedict suffered all; he heard himself called a fool and a ragged fellow, without turning or giving the least mark of resentment; he went on his way as quietly as if he had not received any insults.

fixed position in their church, and not hav known anything of him previously, suspec that he was feigning sanctity in order to cc mit thefts, as it had happened with some othe They drove him away, therefore, from their chur Benedict bore this expulsion with a tranq mind and countenance; and without complaint resentment, he went humbly to beg the par priest of the church of St. Peter, the par of the whole city, to be so good as to adı him into his church, which was very willin granted.

The vicar, however, in consequence of suspicions, would not on any account suffer presence; and yet the life which Benedict l there was sufficient of itself, as is attested his hosts, to gain for him the reputation sanctity. He remained in the church of Peter praying from break of day till evenir taking no food till night, and then only a f pease boiled in water, and a piece of brea refusing everything beyond this which chari offered him. He often passed the whole day a night without food. He never made use of

ıstisement. The servant of God, not at
.bled, thought it best to give way, and
, those who lodged him from anything
ınt; therefore he cheerfully departed and
) Toulon, in the diocese of Clermont,
s about a league distant from Moulins.
morning, after having prayed for a long
the church of Santa Maria dei Monti,
ding his strength exhausted towards the
his life, he went to sit down on a bench
he organ. Seeing a dog there, he drove
'. The dog's master seeing this grew
and began to abuse him, and was so
l that he was near striking him. Bene-
anquillity amidst these insults was admired
spectators; he said not a word; he seemed
statue, with his head bent down, quietly
these transports of rage. His silence
tience exasperated this angry man still
he went into a more violent passion, he
ed against him more strongly, adding
o insult, without regard to the scandal he
hers, or to that God who was near to

contemplating the Passion of our Blessed I
er, the sight of so great a God, endu
the love of man contempt, insults, and su
made so much impression on him, that he
it nothing in comparison, when anything d
able happened to him, through the malice
and he voluntarily procured as many humi
as he could: he valued more the parti
in the insults and cross of Jesus Chris
in all the honours and riches which a d
world can offer.

But even if his confessors had not attest
facts would have clearly shown it. He w
ing one day along the street which leads t
Maria Maggiore, and had already pass
monastery of SS. Domenico and Sisto, w
insolent boy, looking from his window, b
scoff at him in a loud voice, calling him rep
a beggar, a ragged fellow, and otherwise i
him. Benedict listened in silence, and in
quickening his pace, he walked more sh
purpose, taking delight and rejoicing i
affronts, and satisfying his desire of be
spised, in imitation of his Divine Redeen
distinguished religious, who was at a lit

ıce, observed all this, and forming a high inion of our saint's virtue, gave his deposition it in the Processes, being much edified.

In order to be more ridiculed he often appeared ferently dressed in the public streets, sometimes h a pair of ragged stockings fastened to his dle, then with his legs bare without stockings, ain with ragged stockings reaching only half y up his leg, and sometimes with a hat all n, which had belonged to the stage. And en on this account he was made the butt of insolence of boys, he interiorly rejoiced, seeing himself mocked in this manner, like our bless- Redeemer. O my God, how much do Thy vants suffer! how much do they perform, and w greatly do they desire to resemble Thee, our deemer! And I do not know how to bear even prick of a needle, ... nor one little word! is tranquillity in exterior sufferings is certainly nirable, and is a great proof of the height of perfection; but the serenity and cheerfulness ich he evinced under those sufferings, which the Divine dispensation he had to endure in interior life, are a stronger proof, and show ater virtue.

Almighty God is accustomed from time to time suspend in His fervent servants that contemtion and interior consolation with which He first favoured them; either to purify the soul, t it may be disposed for a higher degree of templation; to prove its constancy and fidel-; or to keep it humble, that it may know, by subtraction of these favours, that it is iusuf-

ficient of itself to form a good thought, but t
every gift, whether great or small, comes f
the Father of Lights; or for other ends, wl
doctors of mystical theology explain. Suc
privation is an indescribable pain to the s
when she possesses no longer that sweetness wl
used to be the effect of contemplation; a sw
ness which, according to St. Thomas, "Om
humanam delectationem excedit," far surpa
all human delights. A soul which is not
grounded in profound humility would easily
terrified, give way to diffidence and pusillanim
believing herself abandoned, or at least neglec
by Almighty God, and relax a little in morti
tion and her usual exercises of piety.

But Benedict did not act thus: being
grounded in that profound humility of which

when he had not the favourable wind of the Holy Spirit, he used the oars diligently himself to advance in his voyage. He made use of two means for this purpose: one exterior, the other interior. His exterior practice was, never to relax in his penances or prayers, but, on the contrary, to increase them; which must have been so much the more pleasing to God, as he was obliged to use greater force to overcome his repugnance. The interior exercise, was, to humble himself before God, confessing himself deserving of punishment and abandonment; to conform himself to the Divine will, and often repeat with the priest Heli, "It is the Lord; let him do what is good in His sight." (1 Kings, iii. 18;) and with Job, "As it hath pleased the Lord so is it done; blessed be the name of the Lord," (Job, i. 21;) and other texts of Holy Scripture, in which he was very well versed. Thus he succeeded in tranquillizing and composing his mind as far as he could: and hence it came to pass, that the serenity and placidity of his countenance were never diminished in these storms. But we should never have known these trials or his exemplary behaviour in them, if the prudence of some of his confessors had not obliged him, by command, to discover these things. What troubled him most in this aridity, was, that he believed himself guilty, and that he had given cause to Almighty God to treat him in this manner, through his ingratitude for the graces and benefits with which God had favoured him, and his not making a proper return of love for the infinite love of God;

for which reason he confessed this in general at the feet of his confessors, with those sentiments of grief and confusion which they mention. Still, in this affliction he humbled himself before God, he conformed himself to His holy will: he was never discouraged; he humbly acknowledged that he had done what might be expected from a sinner, and a miserable man. Thus he overcame the storm, and always appeared tranquil, and gained greater merit before God: who with such conduct "Gives also with temptation a happy issue," making use even of our infernal enemies, to promote the spiritual advantage of His beloved children. The devil desires to fish in the troubled waters of their darkness and desolation, by persuading them to abandon the career they have begun, and to despair of succeeding in it. But our good God knows well how to turn their projects to the spiritual good of His beloved souls, "Salvation from our enemies and from the hand of all that hate us," (Luke, i. 71,) as He made use, for the advantage of young Tobias, of that great fish, which on the borders of the river Tigris sought to attack and devour him.

CHAPTER XVIII.

OF HIS LIVELY FAITH.

WHOEVER has some degree of knowledge of the greatness of God, and truly loves Him, believes firmly, as St. Paul says, all that He

nor could they exist without such a faith; for the apostle says, that the spiritual life of the just man is derived from faith: "But my just man liveth by faith." (Heb. x. 38.)

Nevertheless, we have other direct and clear proofs of the solidity and purity of his faith. Born in a family which has always shown the greatest horror for every sort of heresy, especially Jansenism; nourished therein with the pure milk of the truths and maxims of the Catholic faith, educated by a most exemplary parish priest, his uncle, who was always submissive to all the decisions of our holy Church, and who afterwards died a martyr of charity for his flock; always averse to the company of those whose conversation might have instilled into him the poison of error, and always occupied in works regarding the service of God and the acquisition of eternal goods; how could it be possible that he should not possess the most pure and sincere faith that can be imagined? It is certain, and it is attested in the Processes, that none of the many persons who knew him when a youth in his diocese, nor any of those who saw and spoke to him in his pilgrimages and in Rome, ever had any doubt or suspicion of the purity of his faith. His lively faith induced him to remain in the churches for many hours, and even for whole days, with so much reverence, and so humble a posture of body, that it sufficed to see him to believe him to be not merely a true Catholic, but a saint. Considering himself most unworthy to adore and to pray to that God whom he believed really present in the Divine Sacrament, he was often seen in such a position, that his head nearly touched the pavement, looking upon himself as vile dust and ashes, and humbling himself by saying, "Why art thou proud, O dust and ashes?"

If on entering the churches, or on other occasions, he perceived any irreverence in others, talking, or turning their backs to the most Blessed Sacrament, on account of the music, it is incredible how much it afflicted him; several times he made sorrowful complaints about it to others, saying that Almighty God received disrespect in His own house; and being answered once that in the crowd of people who came, rough people must be admitted, he replied, that not only rough people, but people of education also profaned the holy temple, to the offence of God, the horror of the angels, and the injury of their own souls.

When obliged by his confessor, Fath ple at Loretto, at the time he first be quainted with him, to recite the act which he was accustomed laudably tc from the pilgrims, the same confesso that he could not sufficiently express votion, affection, and reverence, with ' recited it, clearly showing that he did cite it simply in the ordinary manner, deeply penetrated with what he utter made of his own accord some additio usual form, saying with sincere and de fection, that he was resolved not onl and die in the faith of the holy Catholic but to shed willingly all his blood in t of torment in its defence. When req manifest the manner in which he was a ed to recite the Gloria Patri, with his and interior spirit in repeating it, he that when in saying it he bowed his made in his heart an act of faith in t mystery of the Most Holy Trinity ; he ly adored it in spirit and in truth, ar

thanksgiving from his early years, and he continued the practice as long as he lived. He showed an inconceivable joy whenever he heard of the conversion of heretics or Jews to the holy Catholic Faith. The treasurer of the Persian Emperor, Kouli-Khan, named Signor Giorgio Zitli, who had been converted to the Catholic faith, and had retired to live a true Christian life in the convent of the Father Capuchins in Rome, attests that having formed a high idea of Benedict's sanctity, from merely witnessing his exemplary conduct, he wished to converse with him; and that Benedict was never satisfied with offering him his sincere and most lively congratulations, because having abandoned his false opinions, he had embraced the true religion; exhorting him very fervently to be constant in that faith in which alone he might hope to save his soul, provided he kept the promises made to God in his baptism. He had a great horror of heresy and heretics, and of all enemies of the Roman Catholic faith; hence he detested those pernicious maxims which now introduce themselves everywhere, poisoning souls that are not upon their guard. He sought diligently in his pilgrimages to avoid those cities and countries which he knew to be infected with heresy, going purposely out of his way, through mountainous and circuitous paths, being quite indifferent to the inconvenience this caused him. When necessity obliged him to pass through them, he did it with great speed. Feeling compassion, nevertheless, for their blindness, and the eternal ruin of thei souls, he offered frequent prayers to God fo their conversion, particularly during the hol sacrifice of the mass, and in performing th works imposed for the gaining of indulgences He was not satisfied with going to confessio and communion, and reciting the vocal prayer enjoined; but being very desirous of their con version, and of the propagation of the Catholi faith, he earnestly begged of God that He woul vouchsafe to illuminate those who were sun in the darkness of ignorance, and would caus the true faith to spread over the whole worlc

In proportion to his horror of heretics, wer his respect and veneration for the Roman Pontif the supreme Head of the true Church, whom h acknowledged as the Vicar of Jesus Christ, an he gave him this name. He respected greatl all the members of the ecclesiastical hierarchy and all priests. If he were seated when a pries appeared, he immediately rose up out of reve ence to the sacerdotal dignity, nor would he si down again, unless he were commanded. Whe pressed by a priest to walk with him a little di tance, he would not keep by his side, but wen behind through respect. He kissed the hand of priests respectfully, and took off his wretche hat in their presence. As our holy faith teache us to pay due respect to monarchs, "Let ever soul be subject to higher powers," (Rom. xii 1,) he greatly honoured his sovereign, nor wa there ever heard from his mouth a word agains any of his superiors or their orders.

These are marks of his lively faith. But if any one wishes to ascertain more clearly its firmness, let him remember what we have said of his ardent love of God, and the clear lights and knowledge with which Almighty God favoured him. As these constantly increased and enlivened his love, they also greatly augmented his faith: "Charity believeth all things." Every true Catholic believes all that our holy faith teaches; but we believe in obscurity, captivating the understanding, faith being "as a light that shineth in a dark place," (2 Pet. i. 19,) as St. Peter says. He, however, who is favoured by God with divine light, knows in a special manner, as far as it is possible in this mortal life, those truths, which before he believed in the dark, "in the obedience of Christ," and he knows them with so much clearness that he begins to say with St. Ignatius, "that even if the oracles of the holy faith had not been written, and if the Holy Scriptures had failed, which is impossible, he would have been ready to give his life for the truths therein contained, simply through the knowledge which Almighty God had given him of them, by his heavenly lights, when he was at Manresa," or with the Ven. Sister Gertrude Salandri, who was wonderfully enlightened by God, and was "so certain of the truths of faith, that they seemed to her to be all rather evidence than faith."

OF HIS FIRM HOPE IN GOD, AND OF HIS CONFIDENCE IN HIM, BOTH IN SPIRITUAL AND TEMPORAL THINGS.

"CHARITY hopeth all things." He who loves, hopes for everything from God; he hopes for eternal happiness, which is the chief object of hope; he hopes for the necessary assistance of grace to the soul; he hopes also for the support necessary to his body, that is, for the means of obtaining it.

Benedict's confidence in God for both one and the other was remarkable. His ardent desire of enjoying God in eternal glory, moved him to renounce, from his early years, whatever he possessed, or might hope to possess, of earthly goods; it induced him to lead a most abject life, poor in the extreme, and excessively rigorous: nor did anything seem difficult to attain this desired end. This desire made him often break forth into the following ejaculations, which obedience obliged him to make known to his confessor: "Tu es, Domine, spes mea: in Te posui certissimum refugium meum. Tu es, Domine, tota spes mea, in terra Viventium. Mihi adhaerere Deo bonum est, et ponere in Deo meo totam spem meam." "Thou, O God, art my hope. In Thee, as in a place of certain refuge, I have placed my hope. Thou, O God, art alone my hope in the land of the living. O how good it is for me to adhere to God, and to place all my hope in Him!" The word "totam, all," which is not in the Holy Scripture, he added himself to express greater fervour. In reciting the act of hope, he expressed himself with so much fervour to his confessor, that the hope which he cherished in his heart was visible in his countenance.

In order to show much more clearly the firmness of his hope, we will mention his answer to two doubts, proposed by his confessor. The first was, "How can man, who is a vile worm, aspire to so great a good as Paradise, and hope for it from God?" He answered, all inflamed with love, "That God is so good and so merciful, that to obtain it, it is sufficient to ask Him from our hearts for whatever is necessary to the soul and body." The second was, "What he would do or say to an angel, who should bring him the dreadful news, that his name was not written in the book of life, or had been blotted out?" He replied, "I would not on that account cease to do good; on the contrary, I would try to do more; I would say that I would not fear; that I should never be eternally confounded: firmly hoping, that the salvation of my soul would not be refused by the Son of God, who died and suffered so much to save it."

The answers which he gave to others on various occasions are clear proofs of his lively hope in God. When asked by the treasurer Zitli, whom we have named before, how he would be able to continue in the heat of his youth the austere method of life he had commenced, he replied, that "he put his trust in God, and though he had been obliged against his will to quit the convent of Sept Fontaines, he still confided in God, that He would give him the necessary help to crush the head of the serpent, even in the midst of the world."

When told by his mother, while he was yet a youth at home, that he would not be able to bear the austere sort of life to which he aspired, and to which he sought to accustom himself by particular mortifications, he answered courageously, "That with God's help we can do everything if we have a good will; and that as He had given to others grace sufficient for the monastic life, He was powerful enough to give it also to him." He used to give similar answers to his uncle at Erin, and to other respectable persons in Amettes, who, by placing before him the austerities of the solitary life of La Trappe, hoped to weaken his resolution; these answers were full of a most lively confidence.

As an evident demonstration of his very firm and lively hope in God, we may be satisfied with his expressions to his parents in his last two letters elsewhere spoken of: "Be not uneasy or afflicted on my account, for the Almighty guides me.......He will assist me and conduct me in the undertaking which He has Himself inspired."

His own heart being full of hope in God, he always sought to inspire others with it when he had an opportunity, speaking with so much en-

pilgrims, before Benedict Labre had been to
that he found solid virtue and the true
of a pilgrim in very few ; and they answered
with sincerity, that this was too true, and
they had known one only, who before
others deserved the praise of possessing sin,
virtue and the true spirit of pilgrimage, f
employed himself when occasion offered in
of mercy, and especially in inspiring others
confidence in God. Describing him afterw
they said, "He is from Boulogne-sur-mer,
wears a cord round his waist, over a grey c
which he called to mind when Benedict
kneeling a penitent at his feet.

Though Benedict's hope in God was so l
it was never separated from that fear whi
inspired not by the goodness of God, but b
wretchedness of man, too prone of himse
fall and to abuse the liberty which God
given him: "He left him in the hand of his
counsel." (Ecclus. xv. 14.) This fear is
opposed to hope. The Ven. Cardinal Bellar
in explaining these words of Psalm xxxii
"Behold the eyes of the Lord are on them

fear Him, and on them that hope in His mercy," says, that fear without hope is a servile fear; hope without fear is presumption; but fear joined to hope is a true love of God. "Timor sine spe servilis est; spes sine timore, præsumptio. Timor cum spe, caritatem veram declarat."

Such was Benedict's hope. He hoped for everything from the goodness of God; but he feared much on his own account, lest miserable nature, which of itself runs more swiftly towards evil than does a river to the sea, might be surprised. A devout person having once said that he feared for his salvation, because he could not do penance, nor suffer anything, he answered that he feared also. "You doubt," said he, "and shall I not do the same? I also fear." This fear made him always keep a guard over his senses, depriving them of everything which might be to nature an incentive to evil, or a weapon to the devil, in order to attack him. He was obliged to reveal this himself to his confessor, who desired to ascertain by obedience the true motive that induced him to abstain from wine. This fear also made him willingly embrace the austere life which he constantly afterwards led to his last breath. He also inculcated this fear to others, saying, "That if there were one person only to be dammed, each one ought to fear to be that soul." Writing to his parents, after leaving La Chartreuse, he made use of the following amongst other expressions: "Meditate on the terrible pains of hell which are endured throughout an eternity for one single mortal sin, which is so easily committed. Endeavour to be of the small number of the elect." This he repeats in the second and last letter written to them after he left the convent of Sept Fontaines, "Think of the everlasting fire of hell, and of the small number of the elect;" sentiments which clearly show the union of hope and fear that existed in his heart.

His trust in God for the necessary support of his body was no less strong than for the assistance of grace to his soul. Many cases which have been related in the course of this history prove it. Having cast all his care upon God for the sustenance of his body, he thought only of providing for the present day, remembering the advice of our blessed Redeemer, "Be not solicitous for to-morrow," (Matth. vi. 34,) being very certain that our good God, to whom all our wants are known, "For your Father knoweth that you have need of all these things," (32,) and who, with His all-powerful benevolence, "giveth to all men abundantly," (James, i. 5,) would also give him what was necessary on the following day. Hence he refused the alms offered him when he had sufficient for the present day, and gave it to other poor people, or put it in the poor box near the church door, when he was obliged by the charitable importunity of others to accept it. A pious priest having offered to provide for Benedict any day when he had not what was necessary, he replied, that Divine Providence had never failed to succour him.

One of his confessors at Rome advised him

once, according to the laws of human prudence, to accept the alms given him, and keep them for the following days, and to supply him with clothes, for his own were becoming worn out with long and rough use. Benedict alleged and placed before him many passages of the Gospel, in which our Lord forbids solicitude for the future, with so much promptitude and resolution, that the confessor knew that his conduct in this respect was the will of God, and he judged it advisable not to trouble or command him further. Nor is the fact of a little money being found in his pocket after death opposed to this determination, as the same confessor remarks, for he had, by the express permission of his last director, Signor Marconi, amassed a few crowns, not for his support, but for the purchase of a new Breviary, as he was accustomed to recite the Divine Office daily, for which purpose he could no longer use the old one, which was worn out and torn by frequent use during so many years, and by the injuries it had received in his long pilgrimages.

He was sometimes reduced to the extremity of having nothing at all to eat. On these occasions he never solicited charity; he only presented himself before some benefactor, to whom the wretchedness of his clothes, his thin face, and weak body spoke clearly, though in mute language. If they gave him nothing, he went away in peace and tranquillity, repeating his usual aspiration, "In Te, Domine, speravi, non confundar in æternum."

The Abate Mancini having one day observed that Benedict had no shirt, gave him one without his asking for it, telling him at the same time that in such a case it was lawful to ask for what was necessary from benefactors, who sometimes do not give because they are not aware of the want that exists, or because relief is not asked; but Benedict replied, that he had received from a benefactor the ragged clothes which he was then wearing without asking for them, and he added, "When God wills that they should be given to me, persons will give them of their own accord."

All that we have written in the first three chapters of the third part regarding his extreme poverty, shows also how heroic were his hope and confidence in God. The same is demonstrated by all that is mentioned in those chapters of the second part which give an account of his pilgrimages, all of which he made without any provision, confiding entirely in Divine Providence, which was never wanting to him. On this account his confidence was judged to be similar to that of St. Cajetan, and the expressions by which he manifested it like those of the Psalmist and St. Lawrence Justinian.

Of supernatural gifts, some are given for the perfection of the person to whom God deigns to grant them, and these are called, "Gratiæ gratum facientes," or gifts making us pleasing to God; they are, the internal voice of God speaking to the soul; contemplation, a close and continual union with God; transports of love; a continual dwelling of the soul on God. Benedict was greatly favoured with these graces, as we must see by the History of his Life, however little attention we give in reading it. Other gifts are granted by God when He pleases, to some of His servants for the good of others, and to serve as a proof of their sanctity. These we call "gratiæ gratis datæ," or gratuitous gifts, and to this kind belong miracles, the healing of diseases, heavenly visions, prophecies, brilliant lights on the countenance, and the like. I have said, "When God pleases," because Almighty God does not grant these graces to all the saints. And this, says St. Augustine, is by the hidden design of His wisdom, to undeceive those who place all their esteem of sanctity in the exterior ornaments which adorn it, such as the gifts we have mentioned, and not in the substance of sanctity itself, which are virtuous works, to which alone, and not to these graces, will the glory of the saints in heaven correspond. "He will render to every man according to his works, not according to the gifts he has received." We have a proof of this in that great saint, than whom "there has not risen a greater;" and who, as it appears from the Gospel, "wrought no miracle." (John, x. 41.)

Our Lord was, however, pleased to adorn Benedict with these graces, as one of his confessors makes known.

We must first call to mind, that Benedict had always a firm resolution to live entirely unknown to the world, and to conceal from every one what passed between himself and God. A person who knew him intimately, regrets that he never could draw from him a word about his interior. To his confessors only, when he was commanded under obedience, he candidly discovered anything about which they questioned him, but in doing this he showed so great a difficulty in overcoming his holy repugnance, that the confessors themselves, as we have elsewhere mentioned, ceased to interrogate him, fearing to increase his trouble. I am inclined to believe that Almighty God deigned to condescend to this his desire in some degree. Sometimes, however, notwithstanding his humility, Almighty God manifested his hidden sanctity, by surrounding him with heavenly brightness, by granting special graces to his prayers, by suffering him to appear in several places at the same time, and several times by the spirit of prophecy. But I have found no account in the Processes of ac-

'isions of heavenly persons, for it does not r that any of his confessors ever asked him uestion; but one mentions intellectual vi- Something doubtless would have come to)tice if they had commanded him to speak s point. But they judged it expedient not so, either because they would not put his ity to the torture, or because they were of)inion of many, who do not make much ac- of such visions, as being very subject to and illusion.

to the graces granted by Almighty God prayers of Benedict, I find in the Pro- , deposed by two persons, the unexpected of their father at Moulins from a long evere sickness. He had been for many oppressed by frequent attacks of colic and symptoms, which were so violent that he not help crying out dreadfully. Bene- eing lodged at their house, in one of his ilgrimages, approached his bed, question- m about his sufferings. Scarcely had he what he said, and offered up secret pray- God, "It will be of no consequence," said couraging him, "it will be nothing;" and t it was so. Having uttered these words pain quickly disappeared, and the day he rose from bed in perfect health, nor ever troubled with the same afflictions ten years which he lived afterwards, died of a stroke of apoplexy.

'abriano, when that great earthquake oc-

down great part of the city, those few houses remained standing and uninjured in the midst of the ruins, to whose inmates Benedict had promised exemption from the scourge of thunder and lightning and earthquakes, if they recited the prayer which he left them in writing at his departure, as is related in the third chapter of the second part, and which was afterwards printed and published. This favour was at that time attributed by them all to the intercession of the servant of God, as it is deposed in the Processes.

His kind host in Loretto, Signor Gaudenzio Sori, was in great trouble on account of a debt of four hundred crowns which he was unable to discharge, through the difficulty of obtaining money due to him, and the scarcity of customers in his shop; he made known his affliction one day to Benedict; but the servant of God heard him in silence, lifting up his eyes from time to time to heaven in the attitude of prayer. Sori soon saw the happy effect of his petitions. During the course of the three years in which Benedict lodged with him for a few days, he freed himself entirely from all his debts, he saw a great increase in the number of his customers and the sale of his goods; and he ascribed it all to the prayers of the servant of God, who thus recompensed him for his charity in receiving him. His devout wife, animated by the opinion she entertained of his sanctity, and by the increase of the income of her house through his prayers, took courage one evening, before he

dict took leave. When the time of c
arrived, she was happily delivered wit
of her usual pains. On this account t
table couple believed for certain, and
to others, that the protection and P
of God had blessed their house since
received the servant of God.

What we read in the Life of St. Franc
and some few other saints, who were se
places at once, was also witnessed in Ben
known for a fact, while he was living in
pizio dei Poveri at Rome. At that tin
was during the space of about two yea
his death, the keeper, the administrator
poor who lived with him, attest that ev
Benedict was in the hospital with the
the fixed hour, and passed the night
nor could he go out till the morning;
doors were opened, after morning pray
did the keeper ever trust the keys to c
Benedict ask leave to go out, a leave
never granted to any of them. And y
attestation of many, confirmed by t
oath, he was seen praying motionless i
churches, not only during the day, but
after midnight, in his usual ecstatic
before the Blessed Sacrament, which

posed for the Forty Hours' Prayer during the night. He was seen four times in the middle of the night praying in the manner we have mentioned. First, before the Blessed Sacrament, when exposed in the church of the Santissima Trinità dei Pellegrini ; secondly, in the church of the monastery of St. Ambrose he was seen in prayer before the Blessed Sacrament, when exposed for the Forty Hours' Prayer, from the morning throughout the whole day, till three hours after sun-set, to the great admiration and edification of the priests of the church, and especially of the sacristan, who, not knowing him at first, suspected him to be a thief, waiting for a quiet and convenient time to steal some of the silver which was displayed in the church ; and having to take his hour of prayer at that time before the Blessed Sacrament, he charged one of the ecclesiastics in the church to watch that poor man ; but he was perplexed in fulfilling this duty of his employment, as he was more inclined to believe him to be a saint than a thief. When his hour was finished, he heard from the ecclesiastic that the poor man, who, while he remained, had appeared always quiet and devout, had left after three o'clock in the night. Thirdly, he was seen praying as above before the Holy Sacrament, when exposed for the Forty Hours' Prayer in the church of Santa Anna de' Palafrenieri in Borgo, from an hour before mid-day till after sun-set, and his departure was not remarked by the person who noticed him while he was remaining there ;

he only testifies that he left him in devout contemplation after sun-set, when he himself quitted the church. Fourthly, it is also deposed in the Processes, that on the night of the Nativity, in 1782, he was seen in the church of Santa Maria dei Monti at the recital of matins, at solemn mass, and at the whole function, to the last devout ceremony of kissing the sacred Infant's feet.

From these facts it is very evident that Benedict had from God the gift of appearing in several places at the same time; for his presence in the Ospizio every single night without exception, is attested on oath and by many persons worthy of belief. Many repectable persons also attest on oath, that he was present several nights in the above-named churches, and this during that very same time. We must, therefore, conclude, that our Lord vouchsafed to honour His servant with this great favour, and thus to recompense and make known Benedict's great love for the most adorable Sacrament of the altar; otherwise we should most unreasonably condemn as guilty of perjury, not women and peasants only, but persons of consideration for the dignity of the priesthood, for their exemplary lives, and for their learning.

Almighty God vouchsafed also to honour him sometimes with the gift granted to St. Benedict and St. Lucian, by giving efficacy to his looks. Benedict never looked at any woman in the face; but on one occasion, inspired by God, he looked twice fixedly on a woman, as if to warn her of what was passing in her conscience. She attests, that these looks of Benedict were of greater service to her soul, and made a more salutary impression than sermons or even missions had caused; and with great emotion she related this to her confessor.

With regard to the spirit of prophecy, which consists in the knowledge of hidden and future things, I find in the Processes many secrets discovered by him. A woman, entirely unknown to the servant of God, stopped him in the street in order to tell him that she wished to provide him with some clothes, but before she had spoken Benedict said to her, "That he well knew her charitable intention, but that he could not receive the clothes she had prepared;" words which astonished her, as she concluded he could only have known her wish by a supernatural light, for she had not manifested it to any one.

He discovered two of the secret thoughts of his last confessor, Signor Marconi; the first, that he had been thinking of giving him a little book he had himself composed, on the best manner of approaching the sacraments of Penance and the Holy Communion, after the example of St. Aloysins Gonzaga, but that he had afterwards changed his mind, for good reasons. The second, that at the sight of the rags which covered Benedict he had at first thought of giving him an alms, knowing very well that he never asked for anything, confiding entirely in Divine Providence; but that afterwards, through good motives, worthy of a wise and experienced confessor, he had judged it better not to give him anything. Benedict told him of these thoughts which he had never manifested to any one, thanking him, and telling him at the same time that he should not have accepted any charity. The confessor was astonished, seeing in him not only the spirit of prophecy, but also the proper intention of going to confession, which was not to obtain a corporal alms, but only for his spiritual good, all of which he afterwards deposed in the Processes. He predicted clearly to a child of ten years old, in Fabriano, that she would be afterwards a Capuchiness, which in effect she was in the town of Castello.

Other prophecies made by him during his life are attested in the Processes, and some miracles are also mentioned therein. The chapter of the cathedral of Tolentino, in eagerly soliciting from Pope Pius VI. of pious memory the beatification of Benedict, as soon as it could be granted, adduce, as a motive for it, besides his great innocence, and penance, and other virtues practised in Tolentino, which were known to every one, the special good-will of the servant of God towards their city, evinced by sending them a medal which has worked, and still works, by the touch alone, many miracles and admirable things. But the greatest miracle of any, is the conversion of sinners, by means of the gift of penetration of the heart, which will be related elsewhere. But what we have mentioned suffices to show, that Almighty God had granted him the gif f l

I cannot, however, pass over the c diction, which, by the Divine impulse, fested to his confessor, Signor Marconi would take place in the church of San dei Monti, after his death, regarding hi This alone is enough to show us in him of prophecy concerning the future, and us to conjecture the numerous other which his profound humility did not gi portunity of discovering in the course of One day in September, in 1782, the ye that in which he died, which was 178 lated to Signor Marconi, but with c sorrow, and great repugnance, that c had shown to him, "that after his d which he did not tell him the day or t "great honours and veneration would l to his body in an extraordinary manne immense number of persons, some even tant countries. with so great a concou

internal inspiration of God. His confessor, however, had the prudence to consult secretly with three very exemplary priests while Benedict was living; and they were all three greatly astonished, when, after his death, they saw with their own eyes the entire fulfilment of his prediction, which was afterwards spread over Rome. The confessor was yet more astonished, when, in hearing confessions, a young man came to him, who with humility and sorrow revealed sins which he had committed in the church against the sixth commandment, when there was so great a crowd of people there; and as a mark of true repentance, he gave him leave to speak of these sins, and to name him as the criminal, though the confessor judged it proper not to do so.

I am going to show how this prophetic revelation was minutely verified in the three following chapters, which all regard what preceded the death of Benedict, what accompanied, and what followed it.

CHAPTER XXI.

THE HAPPY DEATH OF THE SERVANT OF GOD. EVENTS WHICH PRECEDED IT.

It was the well-grounded opinion of all Benedict's confessors, that if he persevered in the

died like a saint, as he had always lived like one, which I will show in the course of the three following chapters, in the first of which we will only relate the events which preceded his death. These were, prophecies of his approaching death; more ardent desires of Paradise; greater fervour in the practice of virtues.

Almighty God placed these prophecies in the mouths of others, as well as in that of Benedict himself. In the last journey which he made, in 1782, to the Holy House of Loretto, he was observed by his hosts, Signor Gaudenzio and Barbara Sori, to be more than usually thoughtful and abstracted, but at the same time serene and joyful, like a person who is thinking of something very pleasing. When only a few days had elapsed, he said he wished to take his departure for Rome. The pious Sori and his wife wondered at this hasty departure, and desiring to enjoy his company for a longer time, they begged him to stay a few days more. "No, answered Benedict, "I have stayed long enough, you do not know the reason I want to go, I must go." "Do not fail then," replied they, "to come next year." Benedict answered with a smile, "If I do not come, we shall see one another again in Paradise." He repeated this also to Signor Gaudenzio when he was leaving them. When asked by the priest Signor Gaspare Valeri, who was very fond of him, if he should come to Loretto in the following year, he answered, "If you do not see me we shall meet again in Paradise."

In the same year, 1782, Signor Verdelli, an

ecclesiastic of the Holy House of Loretto, (to whom Benedict had distinctly foretold that he would not be a religious of the order of St. Francis in Osimo, though he had put everything in train for the execution of this project, a prophecy which was verified,) when giving him some little papers of dust of the Holy House, with other little articles of devotion, at Benedict's departure, said to him, "I hope we shall meet again in another year." The servant of God answered, "I do not think we shall." "Why?" said the other, "will you not return? shall we not see each other again?" "If God pleases," said Benedict, "we shall meet again in Paradise," which was verified when, in 1783, the news of his death reached Loretto.

He answered his confessor, Father Almerici, in the same year 1782, when he was asked by him if he had been to Loretto before, "That he had been more than once, but that he thought this would be his last visit, for he should not be able afterwards to perform this journey on account of the distance of the place to which he was going." Father Almerici did not understand that he meant heaven by this place, but he thought that, being a Frenchman, he was going back to France. These prophetic sayings of his may be taken as a not ill-grounded argument, that Benedict had received from the Blessed Virgin notice that his death would take place in the year 1783. I regard as further proofs of such a revelation, the mutual love that existed between our blessed Lady and

Benedict; the many painful pilgrimages which he performed with so much love in her honour; the benignity of the heart of Mary, which rewards the services of some of her special servants with a similar warning of their death; and the carefulness of Benedict in concealing heavenly favours.

His death was predicted in Loretto by a boy named Giuseppino, son of Gaudenzio and Barbara Sori, who was not more than five years and a few months old: but it was foretold so distinctly and firmly, that all knew that Almighty God made use of his tongue, as He is accustomed to do sometimes, "out of the mouth of infants," to declare it. We shall speak of this more appropriately, when we mention what took place after his death.

A religious woman of great perfection, a fortnight previous to Benedict's death, made known by a letter to the administrator of the Ospizio de' Poveri in Rome, with whom she corresponded, that in a short time the Heavenly Bridegroom would gather from His garden (the Ospizio) a flower, but that it remained to be seen who would be the happy person. The administrator was not long in guessing, for the sight of Benedict in the last stage of emaciation and weakness, and the knowledge of his great virtues, made him immediately fix upon him: and he guessed rightly, as he ascertained by another letter from the nun.

Besides these prophecies, his death was also preceded by more lively desires of a perfect union with God in heaven. It is the property of love to seek a union with the object beloved: "Unio est opus amoris," says St. Augustine. In his long contemplations Almighty God had favoured him with clear lights concerning the greatness of God, and hence he always sighed after union with Him, and the perfect enjoyment of Him, in our heavenly country. Seeing himself at last near the fulfilment of his desires, he sighed after his God more ardently than a thirsty stag seeks the fountain to satisfy its thirst; he wished that the chains of his body, by which his soul was, as it were, fettered, might be broken; he seemed, in his words and actions, to say with St. Paul, "I desire to be dissolved and to be with Christ. Who will deliver me from the body of this death?" On this account he was quite indifferent about his body, and the numerous pains which afflicted it. Hence he answered a person who advised him to seek remedies, that he might not fall down dead some day in the public street, "Of what consequence is it to me?" As if he had said, "Let my body, which I have always considered as an enemy, perish, provided that my soul takes her flight to God to heaven." He repeated more fervently his usual ejaculation, "Call me, that I may see Thee."

Finally, his death was preceded by an augmentation of fervour, and a greater number of virtuous actions in preparation for it. A great number of witnesses testify, that they observed in Benedict at the latter end of his life a greater degree of fervour and diligence in doing good; and that he seemed like the light, which grows clearer and clearer till the full burst of perfect day—"Which goeth forwards, and increaseth even to perfect day." (Prov. iv. 18.) Besides these persons, all his confessors attest the same, and particularly the last, Signor D. Giuseppe Loreto Marconi. This priest was chosen by Benedict about a year before his death, that is, in June, 1782. At this time his other confessor, Father Gabrini, judging himself through humility incapable of directing a soul in which, by the conferences held with him, he discerned such sublime perfection, ordered him to seek out another director, who should not be like him, charged with the care of a parish, that he might more conveniently attend to his direction. Signor Marconi speaks of this last part of his life with no less admiration than satisfaction, and gives his testimony of "the wonderful progress which he continually made in the way of perfection."

But if such attestations had been wanting, his virtuous actions clearly show it. After his hasty return from Loretto to Rome, after the Lent of 1782, of which we have spoken, he sought to make a better preparation for that death which he had himself foretold. Being soon after received by Signor Marconi as his penitent, he began his preparation by desiring to wash away, by means of a general confession, every stain of sin from his soul. This he made to Signor Marconi. But what sins could he have to wash away, when, by the testimony of the same con-none.* He found in him also great tranquilli of mind, and perfect freedom from those tem tations which had at one time so greatly tro bled him. Benedict being aware that his weal ness had reached the last extremity, omitted i 1783 his usual pilgrimage to the Holy House Loretto, thus verifying what he had said tl year before to those who asked him if he woul return the year following: "We shall see or another again in Paradise: this is the last time. But he did not leave off his accustomed prayer nor relax at all in his usual fervour; he kept th Lent more rigorously, insomuch that some pe sons thought that this increase in his penitenti austerities had reduced him to the last stag of exhaustion. It was difficult, however, to ad anything to his former penances, for his ordinar food was very poor and scanty; he tasted n thing at night but a little piece of bread an a draught of water; he suffered continually fro the vermin which covered him, and exercise himself nearly the whole day in prayer, which when it is frequent, is called by the Holy Gho a mortification of the body: "Much study is a

I find that he confessed several times to Signor Marconi, particularly on Friday in Passion Week, and that he communicated in the church of St. Ignatius.

I find also that he asked Father Gabrini for his blessing and leave to communicate (F. Marconi being then prevented from exercising his apostolic duties) two days before he died, that is, on Monday in Holy Week, and he did communicate on that day in the church of St. Ignatius, at the altar of St. Aloysius, but with so much modesty, devotion, and fervour, that the celebrant declares that he felt great compunction and interior emotion in merely beholding, in a passing way, a certain air of sanctity which appeared in his countenance, insomuch that, by his account, he does not remember to have ever afterwards celebrated mass with so much recollection as on that Monday; that he felt great consolation in communicating that poor man, whom he believed to be a saint; and that in the act of receiving the Body of our Lord Jesus Christ, Benedict showed by his extraordinary devotion and singular fervour the lively faith and ardent love which filled his heart.

Having communicated at the altar of St. Aloysins, he remained in the church to hear another mass in thanksgiving. From thence he went to his beloved church of Santi Maria dei Monti, where he was seen on the same Monday morning passing a long time in prayer and hearing masses. In the afternoon he was seen in the church of the Holy Apostles, quite absorbed in God, in a special manner. On the Tuesday he spent great part of the day in the church of Santa Prassede before the Blessed Sacrament, which was exposed for the Forty Hours' Prayer, absorbed in sweet contemplation; and as, after spending a long time on his knees, he could support himself no longer, owing to his exhausted strength, he stood up a short time, as was his custom towards the end of his life. A person who saw him pass after he left the church, testifies that he appeared so exhausted as scarcely to be able to stand, and walked with great difficulty.

It was certainly very extraordinary that bodily afflictions and weakness, which usually diminish vigour of mind, should in Benedict have augmented it; hence all attest with astonishment, that he not only persevered constantly in the length and fervour of his prayers, in the rigour of his hard and penitential life, and in the practice of virtues, but that he went on increasing more and more therein till the last day of his life.

And what is yet more surprising, on the very morning on which he died, Wednesday in Holy Week, he went to the church of Santa Maria dei Monti, as it were, dragging his body thither by the help merely of a stick, and there remained praying in his usual devout manner for a long space of time.

CHAPTER XXII.

EVENTS WHICH ACCOMPANIED HIS HAPPY DEATH.

In the beginning of Lent, 1783, the servant of God had taken a severe cold, with a violent cough, caused by the carelessness with which he treated his body, even at this latter end of his life; for he was indifferent to wind, cold, and rain, remaining a great part of the day kneeling in prayer in the churches, even while dripping with water, and with his feet wet by reason of the holes in his wretched shoes. His cough and cold kept him awake the whole night. He was reduced to such a state by his want of rest, that the very sight of him excited compassion; his face was cadaverous, his strength extremely weak, his step feeble; he seemed, in fact, like a dying person going about. When urged by the charity of Signor Mancini, the administrator of the Ospizio, and of the warden, to go to the hospital, and being told if he would remain there they would take care to serve him and provide him with what was necessary, he thanked them, but would not accept their offer. He had always his mind and heart fixed on Jesus crucified, whom he wished to imitate till his death, through the great lights which he had received regarding His Passion in his contemplations. For this reason he constantly adhered to his rigid plan of life, as if he did not suffer anything; nor would he avail himself of the permission spontaneously granted him by the warden to retire before the general prayers, or to sit down while they lasted; he continued to say them kneeling with the others, with his accustomed fervour of devotion, till the last day of his life.

On the morning of Wednesday in Holy Week, when he left his room, he appeared so destitute of strength, that he could not support himself on his feet; he seemed like a person in his agony. To the repeated entreaties of the warden that he would not go out, for fear he might fall down dead in the street, he replied that he did not care about his body, he only wanted a stick for a support. The warden knowing his desire to suffer more and more for the love of Christ crucified, and to pass speedily to his heavenly country, granted his request. Dragging himself along by the help of the stick, with a feeble and tottering step, he went towards his beloved church of Santa Maria dei Monti. Signor Mancini, who had quitted it a little before, met him almost expiring on the way, and renewed his kind offer. Benedict, though grateful for his charity, pursued his way, and entered the church. Behold him now kneeling before his Divine Jesus in His Sacrament, and before his holy mother, who seemed to wait for this his last visit, to conduct that same day to Paradise this servant who had honoured her so much in this devout and miraculous picture.

Father Piccilli attests that he saw him early in the morning in the church in his ordinary place, and with his usual devotion, (to which he has given his testimony in other chapters,) that he assisted at an early mass celebrated by him, and that many persons told him that he remained kneeling in prayer a long time after his mass. Zaccarelli, a butcher, deposes that when he left it two hours after to fulfil his Easter duties in the neighbouring parish, he left him kneeling as he had found him. He attests this with much astonishment, for he had seen him a few days before with the appearance more of a skeleton than of a man, and he did not understand how he could bear so uncomfortable a position, and for so long a time. It was divine grace, however, without doubt that strengthened him, otherwise it would not have been possible to him.

While Zaccarelli was in his parish church, Benedict, towards about nine o'clock, feeling his strength fail him, and that he could not support himself, sat down for a little time, which was unusual to him. A fainting fit, however, obliged him to leave the church. The bystanders seeing him go out, walking feebly, looking thin and pale, said with compassion, "Poor man, he is really very ill." Scarcely had he left the church, than he sat down, languid and exhausted, on the outer steps. Many persons quickly surrounded him, looking at him compassionately, and offering their houses, striving with one another who should perform this act of charity. The Abate Mancini, who was passing, offered him his Ospizio; Benedict with a faint voice thanked them all, saying he did not want anything, and he made a sign that he did not wish to be removed from that place.

Zaccarelli having finished his devotions in his parish, set out towards the Madonna dei Monti; his curiosity was raised by seeing a crowd round the steps, and drawing near, he saw Benedict in this deplorable state. Feeling great pity, he addressed him by his name, telling him that his house was ready to receive him if he would allow himself to be taken thither. At his voice, which Benedict knew, he opened his eyes and accepted his invitation. It might be that our Lord wished to reward the charity which Zaccarelli had frequently before shown him, by allowing that His beloved servant should die in his house. Zaccarelli, pleased and much affected, raised him up with the help of others, and carried him in the same manner, slowly. But after a few steps they were obliged to let him sit down, for his strength was not sufficient to enable him even to move a foot. With much difficulty they at length reached the house, which was not far distant. He then gave a proof of the delicacy with which he had cherished modesty and purity, for having perceived that part of his ragged clothes were falling off, he would not allow any one else to touch them, as they wished, but took them off himself by degrees; having with much difficulty mounted the staircase with the help of others, and entered a room, his head became so weak, that he did not know where he was, and he asked whither they were taking him. Hearing that they were taking him to bed, he gave signs of regret, and begged that they would lay him on the bare ground, but this was not granted; and he was taken from the arms of those who held him and laid upon the bed clothed in his rags, with a covering placed over him.

The attentive charity of his fortunate host, Zaccarelli, soon thought of taking care of his body and of his soul. For the body, thinking his illness was caused by weakness of the stomach, he prepared a strengthening restorative for him. As for the soul, judging his sickness to be very dangerous, he sent for Father D. Biagio Piccilli, from the neighbouring college of Santa Maria dei Monti. He came quickly full of zeal about eleven o'clock, and entering the room, said to him, "Well, Benedict, do you want anything? Do you wish to go to confession? Is there nothing you want?" Benedict (who had never in his life committed even a small sin, as we know by the authentic testimony of all his confossors, which I have elsewhere repeatedly cited,) calling together his departing strength, said, "Nothing, nothing." Feeling his pulse, he found it so weak that he said, "He is certainly dying. How long is it," continued he, "since you received the Holy Communion?" "A short time," he answered with much difficulty, scarcely being able to utter a word. He had communicated on the Monday in Holy Week, and also on Friday in Passion Week, as we have said before. The father believing that Benedict's faintness was caused by his well-known austerities, and wishing to arouse him that he might be able to receive the Holy Viaticum, tried to do so with another restorative, after which he gave him a little biscuit dipped in wine, which he only tasted. Then he offered him a piece of cotton wool, dipped in perfumed water, saying "Smell, Benedict," but instead of smelling he opened his mouth. Father Piccilli knew by this that he was not sensible, and his fear of his approaching death increased greatly, when on applying the cotton to his nostrils, he saw he had not strength to smell it, and that he let his head fall to the left side. Seeing clearly that he was not able to receive the Holy Viaticum, he said to those who were present, "There is no time to lose, let him receive Extreme Unction," and then he left and was not again sent for. The physician and surgeon pronounced him not only incapable of receiving the Holy Viaticum, but any corporal remedy also; the first, who arrived at three o'clock in the afternoon, and the second at four o'clock, found him with an irregular, varying, and scarcely perceptible pulse, his mouth firmly closed, his teeth clenched, his eyes fixed, closed, immoveable, and visible only when the eyelid was raised by force; insensible to the voice, when addressed or called, and to the touch, and also to mustard-plaisters, which were applied, so that they judged him to be then dying. They ordered, however, that the Holy Sacraments should be given him if he awoke from his lethargy.

But this was not God's will. He willed to

recompense him speedily in heaven, for the merits he had amassed by his rigid and extraordinary plan of life, which he had constantly observed till the last day of his life. The assistant parish priest administered to him the sacrament of Extreme Unction, having judged him entirely incapable of receiving the Holy Viaticum: but Benedict gave no sign that he understood what was going on. In the meantime two fathers, called Scalsetti of the Congregation della Penitenza di Gesù Nazareno, who dwelt in the convent of Sant' Agata dei Tessitori, successively assisted him, for the dying man continued in the same state as at first till night, and many persons came to the house to see him. It was a very edifying thing to see the attitude in which he continued till his death; composed with his hands crossed on his breast as he always had them, even in the streets, but more quiet, more tranquil than usual.

The physician attests that though fainting fits usually cause tranquillity, yet that which he noticed in Benedict, in the two visits which he paid him, had something extraordinary about it, which excited his admiration. It was doubtless an effect of the interior peace promised by Almighty God to the just at their death. "In the sight of the unwise they seemed to die, but they are in peace," (Wisd. iii. 2;) and per-

to the apostles only, but to all the faithful.'" But as owing to his state of insensibility, he was unable to give any sign of it, we cannot assert with certainty, what we are inclined to believe from the extraordinary tranquillity noticed by the physician and the infallible promise of our Blessed Redeemer, which has been verified in so many of His other servants. One of the fathers recited, in union with the bystanders, the prayers for the dying. A few moments before eight o'clock in the evening, they began the Litany of the Blessed Virgin, all being on their knees. While the clock was striking, and the father assistant was saying Sancta Maria, and the others answering, "ora pro eo," he quietly ceased to live, giving no other sign of his departure than the cessation of that weak respiration which he had before made. This happy death took place on the 16th of April, 1783, the Wednesday in Holy Week, when Benedict was at the age of thirty-five years and twenty-one days, and at the very moment when all the bells in Rome began to give the sign for reciting the Salve Regina, and other short prayers, ordered by Pius VI. of happy memory, to move the Blessed Virgin to intercede with Almighty God, that He would vouchsafe to grant tranquillity to the bark of St. Peter, which was then agitated by storms.

a case in which the soul is contained, to be honoured on earth, so that he could say with the Psalmist, "Thou hast cut my sackcloth, and hast compassed me with gladness," (Ps. xxix. 12;) in giving to my soul that eternal happiness which Thou givest in heaven to Thy beloved and faithful servants.

As for his soul, Almighty God made use of a boy's tongue to declare his reception in heaven on the same day in which it was separated from his body. There is great room for astonishment in this circumstance, when we consider the boy's tender age, the distinctness and clearness of the prediction, which was several times repeated, and the distance from Rome of the place where he resided, which was Loretto. The event occurred as follows: Benedict's friends in Loretto, Gaudenzio and Barbara Sori, were discoursing together on Wednesday in Holy Week in 1783, of Benedict's arrival, which used to take place generally in Loretto on Maunday Thursday, and being desirous of enjoying his company again, they were flattering themselves that he was then on the point of arriving. Giuseppino, their son, who was not more than five years and a few months old, being present during their conversation, said positively, and repeated, "Benedict will not come any more: Benedict is dying." Though at first they took no notice of the words of a simple little boy, still, the mother after some reflection showed some doubt whether he might not be ill in Rome, or be staying in some hospital on the road. Giuseppino heard this, and he repeated more firmly, "Benedict is not suffering anything, but he will not come any more; Benedict is dying." Even this second time the parents paid no attention to what the child said, and in the afternoon of Maunday Thursday they were going to prepare Benedict's little room, saying, "That it was nearly time for him to arrive." Then, again, Giuseppino said distinctly, "Benedict is now dead, and is gone to heaven." The mother, wondering, asked him how he knew it. "My heart tells me so," he replied, and he repeated it several times between that day and the Saturday before Low Sunday, before the news of his death had arrived. The parents, astonished, began to be afraid, and in order to surprise him, and to see if he remained firm in what he said, they said to him in the presence of others, when he came back from school, with a firmness above his age, he answere out hesitation, "Did I not tell you that B is dead, and that he is gone to heaven?" then really believed what he said, thinki Almighty God had put these words in th cent child's mouth; and they saw them to their great wonder a few days later, arrival from Rome of the news of his on the Wednesday in Holy Week.

Almighty God also made use of the nu as we have said in the preceding chapt written to the administrator of the Os fortnight before Benedict's death, saying, the Heavenly Spouse was going to ga flower from His garden." After his dea taken place she wrote again, as he affirı ing, "That Benedict was the flower wh been gathered and transplanted into the of Paradise."

As to his body, Almighty God cause honours to be immediately rendered to had not been seen in Rome from the St. Philip Neri, nor do we read of such

desired information respecting him and his vi
tues, which they heard published everywher
and conceived a great wish to see him. A
break of day the house of Zaccarelli was di
turbed by a number of persons, who, wishing
see "the saint," asked to be allowed to ente
This being granted to some, others followe
and there was a continual crowd of visitors t
the evening, when it was time to carry him t
the church. All unanimously pronounced hi
a saint: they thought the family of Zaccarel
happy, in having been worthy to possess in the
house "so great a treasure, a true saint," an
in testimony of their devotion they knelt dow
before the corpse; some touched him with the
rosaries, others kissed his feet and hands devoutl
others wept through emotion, and no one wa
satiated with seeing him. These were not merel
persons of the lower ranks, who usually blindl
follow the stream, but for the most part the
were polished and educated people, nobles, priest
and also titled ladies. There were some, wh
notwithstanding Zaccarelli's care to prevent an
pious theft, contrived to carry away a little b
of the covering under which Benedict had lai

The crowd, when the news was spread over Rome, increased so much that the servants could not keep them in order, and Zaccarelli was obliged in the afternoon to place soldiers at the door of his house and of the room, if not to prevent, at least to lessen the crowd of devout people who flocked to the entrance.

In the midst of this glorious confusion Zaccarelli resolved to have the body taken to the church of Santa Maria dei Monti, for which purpose he went to the parish priest, del Santissimo Salvatore a' Monti, to request his permission, which was, however, refused, greatly to the pious Zaccarelli's sorrow. He was comforted, however, in hearing from Father Palma, rector of the church of Santa Maria dei Monti, that the deceased belonged to the parish of St. Martino ai Monti, in which was Signor Mancini's Ospizio. At this news he hastened to ask leave of the parish priest, who willingly acceded to his earnest entreaties, giving his permission in a note addressed to Father Gaetano Palma; this we may very reasonably consider a mark of Divine Providence, and a favour granted by our Blessed Lady, in wishing to have buried near to her the body of this her loving servant, who for so many years had daily honoured and venerated her here with so much fervour and so great edification.

In the evening of Maunday Thursday, the body being taken from the house of Zaccarelli, in which it had been up to this time, was placed upon the bier, but this could not be done without much difficulty, and a greater number of soldiers were required to keep the people back while they were so occupied. It was joined by the society della Madonna Santissima della Neve, who decorated one of their white robes, and clothed his corpse with it; in which we see another dispensation of Divine Providence, as he had so carefully preserved the white robe of his baptismal innocence during the whole course of his life, as we have elsewhere mentioned; and also by the religious of San Martino, by priests, and an immense number of people. This procession appeared more like a triumph than a funeral. Wherever it passed, praises of his sanctity and encomiums on his virtues resounded. One called to mind his continual prayers in the churches, another his extreme poverty, some his hidden life in the midst of Rome, many remembered his love and devotion towards the Adorable Sacrament and the Blessed Virgin. They all vied with one another in pronouncing him blessed. From time to time the voices of innocent children were heard repeating, "The saint is dead! the saint is dead!"

Amidst these applauses and honours the church was reached at last with great difficulty, but on account of the sacred functions of the day the body could not remain exposed here; it was, therefore, carried into the sacristy. Scarcely had they entered, than it became necessary to shut the doors, to keep back the immense crowd. The accustomed funeral services were performed over the body, with the doors shut, and when they were ended there was so extraordinary a press of people that the soldiers were obliged to return to prevent disorder and pious thefts. Notwithstanding this precaution, one person through devotion had the boldness to cut off a small piece of his beard with a pair of scissors. It is attested that some person in approaching to kiss the hands or feet of the corpse, or to touch it with a rosary, succeeded in secretly cutting off a small piece of the white garment which covered it: it was, therefore, necessary to increase the number of soldiers, and to watch continually till the body was interred.

But the inundation of people did not allow the burial to take place so soon. It was necessary to keep the body above ground till the Sunday evening. During these four days the concourse of persons was extraordinary, inexpressible, and continual. Almighty God increased it by the wonders which He worked by the touch of His faithful servant's body. It was a moving spectacle to see the church, the corridors, the sacristy, the piazza of the church, and all the streets which adjoin it, full of people. The number of carriages was very great; there were persons of every rank, ecclesiastics, seculars, nobles, prelates, princesses, ambassadors, cardinals, waiting and suffering inconvenience to see—whom? Not one of the great ones of this world, not a learned man, not a rich merchant; but to see and venerate him, who a few days before, went through the streets as a poor man, a beggar, ragged, shunned, and not even honoured with a look by those who did not know him on account of his dirty and wretched appearance. O God! how true it is—"Thy friends, O God, are made exceedingly honourable." (Ps. cxxxviii. 17.) Let me be allowed here to pour forth a few words in honour of virtue, and in contempt of human glory. What will it avail to be favoured with talents, nobility, riches, and the most brilliant qualities, that make a man distinguished in the world—what will it avail if he is not Thy friend, O my God? if he is not in Thy grace? His glory ends with his life, and he is soon forgotten: "God hath abolished the memory of the proud." (Eccles. x. 21.) The sight of such a man dead upon the bier, causes horror, and we feel the same for the things he has used. On the contrary, Benedict, without any of these advantages, died a saint, a friend of God. This is enough; sanctity supplies for everything else. This dead body instead of causing horror gives consolation, as it has been attested of him; it excites the desire to see him again repeatedly; those who look upon him are never satisfied; his rags are precions treasures, those who can obtain a small piece of them, or anything which he used, think themselves happy. Persons of high rank sought eagerly to obtain these things.

The room in which he died, instead of causing fear, inspired a feeling of veneration and joy. Zaccarelli deposes, that for seven or eight days after Benedict's death his house was filled in the morning and during the day with people,

"hath abolished the memory of the proud," so He "hath preserved the memory of them that are humble in mind," (Ecclus. x. 21;) and ir the memory of a sinner, whoever he be, perishes as soon as the funeral ceremony is ended, "Their memory hath perished with a noise," (Ps. ix. 8:) the memory of a servant of God will last for ever, "The just shall be in everlasting remembrance." (Ps. cxi. 7.)

But it is now time to return to the narration of what took place during those four days. When the funeral service in the sacristy was completed, and the corpse had been taken from the bier and wrapped in a sheet, it was carried into the adjoining oratory, which, through the narrowness of the entrance, would not admit the bier. The person who wrapped it up perceived in doing so a copious sweat on the forehead and face, and even the hair and beard were so wet that it was necessary to dry them, as if he had been alive; and not this person only, but others also noticed it with astonishment.

On Good Friday morning as soon as the church

bier, and this not being sufficient, soldiers was required to prevent hinder the people from pressing o The number increased so much afte it was impossible after mid-day to church. The people could not hel] look at him, and they did not hear menaces of those who wished to away. The father-rector then orde1 body should be taken from the bier, to a little room behind the high a moving it many persons strove with and thought it an honour to suppo1 the hands, and the feet, concealing tion under the appearance of assis moval, which being accomplished, was shut up with much difficulty. set a prince and a prelate of disti1 to ask the favour of being allowed saint in this room. They were 1mn tisfied. On this occasion two tumou1 a small loaf were noticed on the k servant of God. A person who to

his sanctity in enduring that great and continual pain.

On Holy Saturday morning, when the body was exposed, the crowd was beyond comparison greater than before. The subject of discourse in Rome, in company, in the shops, and every where, turned upon the heroic virtues and the sanctity of Benedict. There was no one that did not wish to see him, all believing him to be a second St. Alexis. An officer of the Segreteria of the Sacra Consulta, who approached the coffin, testifies that he, along with others, smelt a sweet odour which the body of our saint exhaled, without any sort of flower being near the coffin, though it only lasted a short time.

To obviate the confusion and tumult of the great crowd on Holy Saturday, it was necessary to remove the body from the church, and place a greater number of soldiers in the adjoining corridor. But to what purpose? A great number even of persons of distinction followed it wherever it was, and all sought to kiss the feet, to touch it with rosaries, and to cut away secretly pieces of the clothes. The church could not be shut during the whole day on account of the crowd, and not even at night till a late hour with much difficulty and with the help of soldiers.

On Easter Sunday morning the crowd was so excessive, that the indiscreet devotion of many could not be restrained even by blows, to which the soldiers were obliged to have recourse to keep order. The people knew that this was the last day, which made them very eager to see him again. Amongst those who came to visit him were two cardinals, many prelates, priests, religious of different orders, and gentlemen. The church was so full, and there was so great a confusion, that it was impossible to sing mass that morning or vespers in the afternoon, for the crowd was there continually, even in the solitary hours of the afternoon. That a painter might take his portrait, the body was carried into the sacristy. Scarcely was this done, than, as they were returning to the corridor, a cry arose from the church, in which all joined, "Here is the saint! here he is! we wish to see him!" They were obliged to yield, for it was impossible even for the soldiers to resist so impetuous a torrent. The body was, therefore, left in the middle of the church for some time, to be retaken to the sacristy for the juridical recognitien of the body. We may imagine in this duty what would be the effect of the devotion of those who surrounded the servant of God; tears of tenderness, praises of his virtures, eagerness to touch him with rosaries and handkerchiefs, and to kiss his hands and feet, all pronouncing him another St. Alexis.

When the body was carried back to the sacristy for this recognition, it could not be conveniently accomplished, on account of the number of persons who entered, with devout, though troublesome violence; it was again, therefore, taken to the oratory, and soldiers were placed to prevent the ingress of any person. The juridical recognition was then made in presence of the "Promotor Fiscale" of the Vicariato of Rome, of the notary, and several witnesses. The surgeon was also present to make some experiments on the body. After having minutely examined it, he declared it incorrupt, without any sign of putrefaction, though Benedict had been dead four days; his limbs were all flexible, and the tumours on his knees were still soft. Then taking off the garment which covered him, and the clothes which had been cut in many parts, through the devotion of the people, he was clothed again, wrapped in a sheet, and placed in a wooden coffin that had been prepared with a leaden pipe inside, containing an inscription on parchment, which was a well-composed eulogium, in which the name, surname, and country of the servant of God were mentioned, and a short account given of the very austere life he led,

commendations which each one made of his soul to his intercession with Almighty God, for they believed, and all cried out, that he was blessed. Their desire being satisfied for the last time, and the body replaced in the coffin, it was well covered, bound in several places with ribbons, and sealed in different parts with the seal of his Eminence the Cardinal Vicar, Marco Antonio Colonna; this being afterwards put inside another wooden case, similarly closed, it was interred on the 20th of April, Easter Sunday, by the permission of the same cardinal, in a place apart which had been prepared, and which is on the Epistle side of the high altar, at the foot of the picture of the Blessed Virgin, which he had so much venerated during his life.

CHAPTER XXIV.

CONTINUAL AND SURPRISING CONCOURSE OF PEOPLE, WHICH OBLIGES THE PRIESTS TO REMOVE THE BLESSED SACRAMENT FROM THE CHURCH. THE FAME OF HIS SANCTITY, WHICH QUICKLY SPREAD OVER THE WORLD.

As soon as the servant of God was buried, the concourse of people commenced that same Easter Sunday evening, a concourse which the witnesses in the Processes cannot find terms to express. Some call it incredible, others, suprising, excessive, and wonderful. It might be compared to a river, which, breaking all bounds, precipitates itself towards the sea, waves upon waves following one another. The fame of his sanctity was like the light, which in a moment extends from one pole to the other; it soon extended not only through Rome, but the whole of the Pontifical States, through the kingdoms of Italy, and even through the whole of Europe. It even penetrated into China. From Pekin, the capital of that country, an alms was sent with a letter addressed to the Padre Postulatore. Almighty God caused to be verified in His servant that promise made by our Blessed Redeemer: "If any man minister to Me, him will My Father honour." (John, xiii. 26.) To this reputation of sanctity was added the universal opinion, that Benedict was a powerful intercessor with Almighty God, to obtain graces for the benefit of those who had recourse to him; and, in fact, many were made known, which God had already granted to those who invoked his mediation.

A great concourse of people in the churches is generally accompanied by disorder and irreverence. It happened so in the church of Santa Maria dei Monti when the crowd came to visit Benedict's sepulchre, and recourse was necessarily had to unusual means for preventing these abuses. Soldiers at the church doors, a wooden palisade round the sepulchre, with guards at the entrance to keep the people from crowding in, and soldiers dispersed here and there about the church. This did not suffice; the irreverence and the confusion were so great, that it was judged expedient to take away the Blessed Sacrament from the tabernacle, and carry It to the domestic chapel. This had been made known by our Lord to His servant some months before, though the precise day was not revealed to him, and it was by him manifested to his confessor, Signor Marconi, with extreme repugnance and confusion, as we have before related.* Our Lord caused it to be verified, and instead of being offended by it, I imagine that He was pleased with it, and glorified in the honour given to His servant; as, on another occasion, He declared to His beloved St. Gertrude, who feeling some scruple and great regret, because she had been one day completely occupied in venerating a picture of the Blessed Virgin, without offering any mark of respect to the picture of Jesus which was by its side, our Lord removed her regret and scruple by saying to her, that the honour shown to the mother all redounded to His glory, as St. Jerome said, "All honour given to the mother redounds to the glory of the Son." "Endeavour for the future to honour still more and more devoutly the picture of My mother, even though you leave My own picture without marks of honour." The crowd increased so much that mass could not be celebrated on those days, nor could the usual functions of the church take place.

This is yet but little. On the 25th of April the Blessed Sacrament was to be exposed for the Forty Hours' Prayer, according to the list which prescribes to each church its days. It

* See Part III. Chap. XX.

was hoped that the concourse would cease, that this exposition might take place quietly. But what was the case? Instead of diminishing it increased to such a degree that they were obliged to transfer the exposition for those days to the church of SS. Quirico and Giulitta. It was necessary also to shut up the church, and put soldiers to guard the door for fear the tumultuous and crowding people should force it, breaking it down, as they threatened to do, in the transport of their devotion. The church being reopened after a few days, and soldiers placed inside and out, the irreverence and noise greatly diminished, but not the crowd, which continued still to come, though in better order and in moderation, regulated by the soldiers. For two whole months the military were on duty here; at the end of June, however, they were dismissed, and the palisades removed from the supulchre. It was a very surprising thing, that the soldiers, who generally think these sort of duties annoying and troublesome, watched during the whole of the time, not only without any complaint, but even with much pleasure, as their commander knew and declared.

Things being now tranquil, every one had the opportunity of showing by various external marks of respect the devotion they entertained towards the servant of God. It was a beautiful and affecting sight, to see persons devoutly kneeling and forming a glorious crown round his sepulchre, others prostrate on the ground, many pouring forth tears abundantly, some asking for favours, others returning thanks for those they had received, and all recommending themselves to his intercession. These were not merely poor and ignorant persons, who are easily carried away by feeling and fanaticism; there were priests and religious of every rank, persons who were very considerable for their dignity and learning. Their reverence and devotion, therefore, towards the sepulchre, increased these feelings in others. A bishop, after celebrating mass at our Blessed Lady's Altar, went, clothed in his pontificals, to the sepulchre, and after praying there, uncovered his head, and reverently and devoutly prostrated himself with his face on the pavement, imprinting thereon devout kisses. A lady of high rank, before entering the church, left her shoes outside with the servants, and went barefooted in a devout manner to the sepulchre; she remained there a considerable time, returned as she went, and did not put on her shoes till she was outside the church again. Another princess followed her example. One lady entering the church, went on her knees from the door to the sepulchre. Many came from foreign and distant countries, in the dress of pilgrims, attracted by the fame of his sanctity and of the graces which were said to have been granted by God to his intercession. Many came even from the eastern countries, and presented themselves reverently before Benedict's sepulchre, which became, as it were, a new sanctuary. A foreign confraternity came to venerate him in so numerous a body, that it took up a great part of the church.

Though, in the course of time, this great concourse was no longer seen, yet, no day passed without some visitors to the sepulchre of the servant of God, to pray to him, or to thank him. But Father Palma, the rector, who, from the first undertook, with the greatest diligence as postulatore, the care of seconding the Divine dispensations, affirms, that in the course of twenty-five years, not a day passed in which there were not seen at the sepulchre persons of every sex, age, and condition to venerate it.

The honours with which Almighty God would have His humble servant distinguished on earth did not end here. Besides the renown of his sanctity which soon spread everywhere; besides the great crowd at his sepulchre, which could not proceed from any cause, but the internal impulse and dispensation of Almighty God; our Lord also willed that those miserable rags which covered him in life, and rendered him an object of horror to those who did not know him, should be honoured; and by working wonders through their means, He caused them to be so highly esteemed, that he was thought happy who obtained a small portion of them, as if he had gained a treasure; and great endeavours were used to obtain them. The Signor Avvocato D. Gio. Battista Orlegiani, who was chosen to patronise the cause of his beatification, in the valuable Abridgment of our Saint's Life, (which, to satisfy in some degree the universal wish of so many cities and kingdoms, he printed and published in the very year of Benedict's death,) asserts, that during the course of four months from the day of Benedict's death, more than eighty thousand portions of them were distributed. This is also confirmed by Father Palma, who was appointed postulatore, to make the requisite solicitations for the beatification, and to whom exclusively belonged the duty of distributing relics of the servant of God. To these may be added many others given at the entreaty of cardinals, prelates, princes, ambassadors, priests, religious and seculars of every rank and sex, as it is testified in the Processes. Even up to our time the requests have not ceased, from different states and kingdoms of Europe, Asia, and America, as the postulatore gives testimeny.

Almighty God willed also that the picture of Benedict should be honoured in an extraordinary manner, and in astonishing numbers. One hundred and thirty-five thousand impressions were printed in a few months, and dispersed over many and even distant kingdoms. The city of Capua, not satisfied with those received from Rome, printed thirty thousand. Hence, we meet him everywhere, represented in various devout attitudes. We see his picture on canvass, sculptured in brass, cedar, and marble, impressed on wax, paper, and chalk. The brasses alone which were cut in the year of his death amounted to eighty-five thousand, and their number increased from year to year. These pictures, which were in great request, were circulated by thousands in the Pontifical States, in many cities and kingdoms, through the whole of Europe and other parts of the Catholic world. If, according to the assertion of Severus Sulpicius and other grave authors, the crowding of a whole population to venerate the corpse of a servant of God, is a proof that he possessed singular sanctity; ought we not to conclude that Benedict's was wonderful, when we reflect, that not merely the people of Rome, or of the surrounding provinces, but a great number professing the Catholic faith from every country and kingdom of the world, on arriving in Rome flocked in crowds to venerate his corpse in the sepulchre? What should we not infer also from the respect universally shown to his relics and pictures by all the nations of the world, which we have witnessed?

It seems also, that by so universal an opinion of Benedict's sanctity, and by spreading it so quickly, even to the most distant parts of the world, and of the East and West, Almighty God deigned to confound those modern sceptics, ill-affected towards sanctity itself, if not quite unbelievers, who wish the honour in which Benedict was held to be thought fanaticism. But, besides the common consent of so many nations, and the veneration of so many pious and learned persons, Almighty God, who is Infallible Truth, cannot authenticate by prodigies a false sanctity as if it were true. This is an incontrovertible truth in sacred theology, and we see that instead of diminishing with time, this honourable reputation has rather gone on increasing, and God has continued to authenticate it by new wonders, which will be related in the last chap-

to have him quickly inscribed in the num- of the blessed.

ifty bishops, as soon as his undoubted sanc- was made known with his death, and the ıeles which took place, offered their ardent ›lications for his beatification to Pius VI. ıappy memory; thirteen archbishops, seven linal bishops, several chapters of cathe- s, with their dignitaries, thirty-nine entire 'ents of religious, and a great number of 'istrates, made the same request. And many hese persons, so considerable for rank and ity, not content with the first most effica- s request, repeated it, some twice, some three ›s. They all adduced three reasons for their .est entreaties: the first was, the heroic :tity of the servant of God, which was known ome from his residence in their towns, as inhabitants of Amettes, Boulogne, Erin, ›tto, Fabriano, and Rome, and to others by ›ct report. The second was, the wonderful ıcles wrought by Almighty God through his 'cession after his death. The third was, the ssity of procuring his beatification, in order ppose to the libertinism which prevails in › degenerate times, the example of Bene- s heroic virtues; and to have a powerful 'cessor with Almighty God, who should ob- by the overcoming of errors, a restraint on to our holy Church, and should solicit the graces of which each one stands in need. Thirty solicitations, or, "Lettere Postulatorie," may be read at length in the Summary, where they are faithfully copied, and they are all a compendium, as it were, of Benedict's virtues, and an encomium on his sanctity, which was more sublime in proportion as it was more hidden. All the others, to the number of one hundred and seventy-four, are placed together with merely the names of the authors mentioned. Any one, who desires to read them, may find them in the Summary, from page 504 to page 533.

It will be a great consolation, and also a subject of admiration to the devout, to read at the termination of this chapter the surprising request made in these latter times to the reigning Sovereign Pontiff Pius VII., by the present most zealous Bishop of Arras, under whose jurisdiction the birth-place of our saint is at present.* After explaining to the holy father, that the flock committed to his care gloried in the fact, that Benedict had derived his origin from amongst them, and venerated him as a powerful intercessor with Almighty God, he adds, "That he is held in so great esteem for his sanctity, that the parish church in which he received baptism and worshipped God in his early years, is frequented on a fixed day every week by a numerous concourse of people, who come thither with piety and devotion." He goes on to state, that all the inhabitants of his vast diocese, and

* 5th of March, 1804.

all those to whose knowledge the name of Benedict Joseph had come, earnestly desire that he may be soon inscribed by the Holy See in the catalogue of the saints. Finally, he makes this request to the Sovereign Pontiff, "That since he has not yet declared Benedict Joseph to be amongst the blessed, he would do him the favour to send him some portion of his relics, that he might keep them ready, and place them in the chapel which would be dedicated to Almighty God under his invocation." From what we have said, the reader will admire more and more the Divine goodness towards His beloved servant, Benedict Joseph, in maintaining firm, uninterrupted, and universal, the devotion and veneration of the people.

CHAPTER XXV.

WONDERFUL MIRACLES WROUGHT BY ALMIGHTY GOD THROUGH BENEDICT'S INTERCESSION, AFTER HIS DEATH. APPARITIONS FROM HEAVEN.

It would be impossible to enumerate all the miracles wrought by Almighty God at the intercession of this His servant; another volume would be required for it, and it would also be tedious to readers. We will mention a few of the most astonishing, passing the others lightly over. Let me be allowed, however, before I relate them, to say two words to those who will not believe in miracles, and will not even

ing, blind, and firm faith, through the infallible authority of that God who has revealed them. And why should we refuse belief in those things which are not of faith, when they have been examined, sifted, juridically proved, and confirmed by the oath, not of one person only, but of many? Is it a sign of wisdom to believe that so many persons, who know well what an oath is, have perjured themselves? Is it a proof of wisdom to treat as fools, ignorant persons, and fanatics, those persons of consideration, those ecclesiastics, possessed of piety, learning, and discernment, who have examined them with the greatest rigour? To those things, therefore, which are not of faith, we should give, not a divine, but a human faith. By this we shall praise and admire the omnipotence of God in those works which are above the strength of nature; it will assist us to know the great reward which the saints possess with Almighty

advantages, for which the followers of E
care nothing.

The second is, that true miracles are w
by God, to authenticate either the truths
are preached, or the true sanctity of H
vants. This is asserted by St. Thomas:
raculum quandoque fit in testimonium v
predicatæ; quandoque in testimonium p
facientis." Miracles are "the true vo
God," as sound theology declares. Hen
it is contrary to the sanctity and truth o
to authenticate false doctrine by miracles
is equally opposite to them to authentic
false sanctity by miracles. Therefore, as A
ty God has wrought many miracles, true
cles, juridically proved, authenticated, and
to, by means of Benedict after his dea
would neither be wise nor prudent to deny
I will relate here merely those which I f
have been examined and juridically prove
authentic documents, and also with pr
directed to the P. Postulatore Palma, I
over the very great number which are t
the people without the juridical and aut
proof.

In the first place, I will mention one

Maria Melchiora Crocifissa Testasecca, lay at the point of death, despaired of by the physicians, in the monastery of St. Paul, in the city of Bivona, in the diocese of Girgonti. A complication of diseases had brought her very near to death :—Pains in her chest, constant obstruction, a continual cough, vomiting of blood, great difficulty of breathing, swelling of the legs, total loss of appetite, and sleeplessness. Her recovery appeared to be hopeless, for the remedies of art, employed during six months by three most skilful physicians, had been of no effect, and it was finally proposed by them as a last resource, that she should be taken home. Seeing her firm in the resolution not to quit the cloister and inclosure, they said to her, "Either go or die." "I prefer," piously answered Sister Melchiora, "to lose my life in the house of God, rather than to enjoy health at home." In this deplorable state she was visited for the last time by the physicians, who quite gave her up. In the meantime another nun, Sister Maria Giacinta Reitano, much grieved at the approaching death of her dear companion, who was the chief support of the chant in choir, went to the church, and addressing herself with great confidence to the adorable Heart of Jesus, earnestly begged of Him that by the merits of Benedict Joseph He would restore the health and voice of Sister Melchiora, who was very necessary to the choir. Almighty God heard her. He sent from heaven Benedict Joseph to cure her sister. During a short slumber, into which

Sister Melchiora fell the following night, she seemed to see, as it were, at a distance in the dormitory, a pilgrim, who appeared so resplendent and beautiful, that his rays lighted up everything like a sun; coming towards her he said in a joyful and amiable manner, "Dost thou know who I am? I am Benedict Joseph Labrè, who died in Rome. Know that I am sent by Almighty God to give thee health. God gives it to thee for that generous action, so pleasing to Him, which thou hast performed, in preferring to die in His house rather than be cured at home. In recompense, God grants thee health, through my means, to assist at choir and sing His praises." He then dipped his finger into a little vessel which he held, containing a most fragrant liquor, and signed her with the sign of the cross, saying to her, "In the name of God and of the Most Blessed Trinity, arise, thou art cured. To-morrow thou shalt be present with the others to chant the Divine Office in choir at the exposition of the Most Blessed Sacrament; and thou shalt sing with the other nuns the Eucharistic Hymn, Te Deum laudamus, in thanksgiving for the favour granted thee." While he was thus speaking, Sister Melchiora,

lively affections of astonishment, joy, and gratitude, she heard him say these words: "This ornament, which thou admirest on my breast, has been given to me in recompense of the devotion which I had to the Most Holy Trinity, adoring and profoundly reverencing It, and causing It to be saluted and blessed by boys in the streets of Rome." Having said this, he disappeared, and with him vanished every pain instantaneously; so that, perfectly cured, she dressed herself without assistance, and went to the choir before the others, shedding copious tears of joy and tenderness. The nuns soon beginning to come in, and seeing her in the choir cured, were filled with inexpressible astonishment, doubting whether it was really Sister Melchiora, or a phantom or ghost;—to see in the choir in perfect health her whom they expected in grief to see dead upon the bier. But their wondering doubts were removed when they heard her relate with tears what had taken place with the servant of God, Benedict Joseph, the previous night. Then entoning with joyful and unanimous voice the Te Deum, they continued with her their usual exercises of piety. The joyful sound of the bells having spread the news of this cure, all ranks of people speedily flocked to the monastery, and hearing the wonderful fact, made every place resound with the praises of God, who is wonderful in His saints, and of the name and the power of the poor man of Rome, Benedict Joseph, who had exchanged his rags for eternal greatness; who had passed from earth to heaven, and from the obscurity in which he chose to live, to become one of the favourites of the most Blessed Trinity, and of the great ones of the kingdom of heaven. This wonderful cure was examined and authenticated by the court of Cardinal Brancinforti, then bishop of Girgenti, by several theologians, by the oaths of the abbess and her nuns, of the physicians, and the happy Sister Melchiora, who was so completely cured, that no sign or vestige remained of the very serious diseases with whlch she had been afflicted.

Giuseppe Bonamano Marmaro, of Civitavecchia, having been seized in 1778 with a violent disorder in his right eye, had not received the least benefit from the many remedies applied by the medical men. Having at last lost the sight of this eye, a fistula, pronounced to be incurable, formed in it, which prevented him from following his usual employments, and gave him continually very severe pain. Hearing in 1783 of the extraordinary cures by which Almighty God honoured Benedict Joseph, who died in this year at Rome, he felt so much confidence, that he resolved to go to his sepulchre to solicit the cure of his eye. He undertook the journey on foot, with his head bandaged, on account of the eye. But his confidence was raised to the highest pitch while he was on his way, for he met Giuseppe Castardi, whom he had known in Civitavecchia, quite lame and incapable of motion, and saw him, to his astonishment, returning perfectly cured to Civitavecchia, and able to walk quickly and well, thanks to the favour he had received at the tomb of Benedict Joseph. This gave a new impulse to his confidence and to his steps, to pursue his way more quickly. When he reached the sepulchre, he prostrated himself, and fervently prayed that he might receive some sign of the favour which he hoped to obtain. He had it immediately; the bandages fell from his head of themselves, and at the same moment he found his eye perfectly cured, and the tumour and fistula gone. Filled with joy, he gave most fervent thanks to Benedict Joseph, and returned happy and well to Civitavecchia, giving glory to God, and promulgating the power and credit of Benedict Joseph with Almighty God.

The apparition of the servant of God to a devout virgin merits to be distinctly related, and it may serve as an instruction to those who will not be guided by their confessor. It happened to a pious woman in Rome, named Angela Regali. She had long suffered from chronic diseases, and had a very severe attack from them on the very day of Benedict's death, April 16th, 1783. She was attacked by violent pains in the side, difficulty of breathing, palpitation of the heart, and total loss of sleep, so that she passed whole nights in painful watching, and she had also frequently symptoms of other diseases. Hearing the wonders which Almighty God wrought at the intercession of Benedict, she had recourse to him with lively confidence and fervent prayers. Benedict appeared to her, and clearly told her that her cure depended upon herself, and that she need not seek it elsewhere. He mildly reproved her for her disobedience to her confessor, Doctor D. Giuseppe del Pino, a missionary full of apostolical zeal, saying, that if she wished to be cured she must speedily obey him; an instruction which Benedict had practised during his whole life, and now inculcated from heaven. He then disappeared. Feeling the correction, she resolved to obey, and received the promised cure. She began to sleep soundly at night, and all the other pains disappeared which had afflicted her.

But what followed? Having twice relapsed into disobedience, she was again attacked by much worse diseases, which in 1786 brought her very near death. Being incapable of receiving the Holy Viaticum, on account of her continual fainting fits, Extreme Unction was administered to her. In this state, repenting interiorly, she had recourse to Benedict's intercession; he again appeared to her, and after reprimanding her, inculcated with greater vehemence speedy obedienee to her confessor, and when she put it in practice all her pains vanished.

Wonderful was the instantaneous cure of Signora Palma Sagripanti, aged twenty-one, in the town of Fermo. A crowd of dreadful diseases had so greatly afflicted her for the space of five years, that she was thought to be certainly near the end of her life: a cancer in her breast, tumours in her body, horrible convulsions, with a disgust for food, and vomitings so frequent and violent, that three days before her cure she could not take a little bit of bread or a draught of water. All the remedies which were applied seemed to make her worse, instead of better. At last on the 6th of May, 1783, seeing herself nearly at the last extremity, from the increased violence of these diseases, she recommended herself fervently to Benedict Joseph, placing on her breast his picture, stamped on paper, which her confessor had given her; she fell into a tranquil sleep, and saw in a dream Benedict, who said to her, "Arise and eat." Awaking, she asked for food. Surprised and pleased, the servants prepared some for her; she ate with a relish, and again fell asleep. Benedict appearing again to her said, "Arise, thou art cured," and she found that she was perfectly cured, to the wonder of her friends and of Rome itself, when after coming on purpose from Fermo she was seen by many prostrate at the sepulchre of the servant of God, rendering thanks to her deliverer, after the cure had been made known.

Angela Pipino of Aree, in the diocese of Aquino, aged twenty, having been greatly tormented for nine years by an enormous scirrhus, and obliged to remain in bed, without the power of even moving a finger, invoked the intercession of Benedict, whose sanctity and miracles had been made known to her, and his picture was placed under her head. She fell into a quiet sleep, and Benedict appeared to her in a dream, saying, "Arise, thou art cured." She awoke and found herself perfectly cured, and the hard tumour, which according to the surgeon was like a loaf of nearly four pounds' weight, had disappeared. The excess of her joy almost transported her out of herself, and made her shed tears: and she, who for nine years had been incapable of moving, went alone joyfully at break of day to the church, to thank Almighty God for the great and extraordinary favour which had been granted to her through Benedict's merits. Her long and obstinate illness had been well known in the city. Great then was the surprise of all the people, when they saw her in perfect health; but when they heard of the apparition of Benedict, and the favour he had obtained, his name and his power with Almighty God were proclaimed in all the houses and public streets.

Wonderful indeed was the instantaneous cure of Gaetano and Maria Micheli, in Borgo St. Pietro. They had been both seized with a violent and putrid fever, and from their symptoms their death was regarded as inevitable by the physicians. Their innocent little boy, aged three years and four months, was standing by their bed, and he suddenly uttered these words, "Benedetto Giuseppe fa passar la bua a Tata, e Mamma." The grace and innocence of the child drew the attention of those present, and they heard repeatedly addressed to him after the words we have mentioned, "Yes, yes." They asked him who said "Yes, yes." He pointed with his little hand to a picture of Benedict Joseph hanging on the wall, repeating "Yes, yes." At that moment the fever entirely left them, the fatal symptoms ceased, and returning to themselves they were found to be perfectly cured, to the astonishment of the bystanders, who were never tired of praising God and His faithful servant. The medical men were yet more surprised, when on their arrival they found them to have passed from death to life, and they unanimously gave testimony of this supernatural change. The husband and wife immediately made a vow to go to the sepulchre of the servant of God in Rome to return him thanks, which they faithfully performed.

The widow Cecilia Girardi, in Mondolfo, had been troubled for four years by severe nephritic pains, frequent vomitings, and violent convulsions; and had used without effect many remedies ordered by the physicians. One day being more severely afflicted than usual, moved by the fame of Benedict's miracles, she applied one of his relics to her left side. While in a fainting fit she heard these words clearly pronounced by an internal voice, "Thou art cured." She repeated these words, so that those who were present thought she was delirious, but they soon perceived her miraculous eure, for she was at that moment freed from her symptoms, and from all her pains.

Domenica di Pietro, a young girl aged twelve, having entirely lost the use of her right arm by a violent contraction of the nerves, which had disabled it for four months, was taken by her father to Rome to Benedict's tomb, from the country called "le Sante Marie," in the dioceses of Marsi and Piscina, to obtain her cure, as he had heard others speak of the effects of Benedict's powerful intercession with Almighty God. Having invoked his intercession, he tied a picture of the servant of God to his child's right arm when she went to bed. During her sleep she seemed to see Benedict clearly, who, touching her arm with his hand, suddenly restored feeling and movement to it; he then disappeared. On awaking she moved and shook it, and perceived that she was perfectly cured, to her great delight no less than to that of her father, with whom she joyfully went into Rome to return thanks to Benedict.

A pernicious army of locusts horribly laid waste in 1783 the fields of Montefiascone and Viterbo, devouring everywhere the wheat which was just budding. Pompeo Renzi of Montefiascone was in great fear for the safety of his wheat, but he found out the proper weapons against the devouring enemy. Full of faith he fastened Benedict's picture to a reed, and placed it in the midst of his field; he prayed to him with that fervour with which the necessities of his family inspired him, for they would have been deprived of their sustenance during that year if the wheat had been destroyed, as he feared. Wonderful fact! Visiting his wheat frequently during six weeks, he always found it flourishing and green, not a single locust entered into his field; and from three prodigies he was made sensible of Benedict's power. The first was, that he found these devouring animals dead in heaps near his property. The second, the desolation and ruin of the fields which lay near his own. The third, that the paper picture of Benedict remained untouched, unhurt, and dry, notwithstanding the copious rains and strong winds which in so long a time would naturally have destroyed it.

Giovanni Pezzini, the carrier, went barefoot from Tolentino to the sepulchre of Benedict in Rome, on account of the wonderful and instantaneous cure which he had received by means of Benedict's picture. He had been confined to his bed for three years with severe pains in the side and continual fever. To these symptoms was added so violent a vomiting, that he became unable to take any food, and the malady being declared incurable, the Holy Viaticum and Ex-

touch of the medal which he left with a person named Catarina Gentili, who first refused it; but when it was brought to her after Benedict's death, by an unknown pilgrim, in May, 1783, she made use of it as a universal remedy against all kinds of diseases, even of a fatal kind, and those which had become obstinate by the lapse of many years. So extraordinary were these cures, that the reverend chapter, the dignitaries and canons of Tolentino, in offering their solicitations for the beatification to Pope Pius VI. of happy memory, cite them as one of the great motives of their petition.

Signora Clementina Cicconetti, a young lady, aged twenty-five, had been for eight whole years confined to her bed, with an accumulation of different painful and complicated disorders, which had rendered her incapable of moving, and reduced her to a skeleton. At the news of the miracles wrought by Benedict Joseph, it was judged expedient to take her to his sepulchre. Being removed from bed with very great difficulty and pain by the help of others, she was placed in a chair to be carried to a conveyance, in which, also with much difficulty, she was taken to the tomb of the servant of God, where, after a short prayer, all her pains vanished in an instant; she felt herself strengthened in an extraordinary manner, insomuch that she immediately rose up of herself, and with the quick step of a person in health, she refused every assistance and support, and returned home without the convenience of a carriago; being soon arrived there, she mounted the stairs, ate with appetite and relish that same evening, and remained perfectly free from all she had previously suffered. Being afterwards called by our Lord to the religious state, she was admitted into the venerable monastery of the Infant Jesus in Rome, and in memory of this favour, and out of gratitude to her deliverer, she assumed, on taking the holy habit, the name of Maria Benedetta. She there discharged without any inconvenience all the offices assigned to her, even the most laborious. At the time we write she is in good and robust health, exercising the office of superioress in that worthy community.

Similar to this wonderful cure is one which Benedict wrought in behalf of the widow, Angela Zanchi, of the parish of S. Marco, who had had two severe strokes of apoplexy, and had been long confined to bed. She was at last placed in a chair and carried by several persons to his sepulchre; and scarcely had she made a prayer there, than she received feeling, motion, and strength; leaving the chair there, in remembrance of the favour received and as a mark of gratitude, she walked home with ease, accompanied by a great multitude of people, in joy and astonishment, who had seen her and been present at the cure. Other cures, equally surprising, are related in the Processes; but that we may not exceed in length, we will let those suffice which have been mentioned, for they are a sufficient proof of Benedict's sanctity, which Almighty God has authenticated by them. There are also a great number of less important miracles, the narration of which would be tedious and superfluous. He who enters a beautiful garden adorned with valuable plants, merely bestows a passing glance on those which are of a common sort. I will, therefore, put them all before the reader together; it will suffice to look at them in this manner to know the power with which Almighty God has vouchsafed to honour Benedict Joseph.

We also read of instantaneous cures of malignant, obstinate, and even hectic fevers, apoplexies, ulcers, cancers, sciatica, dropsy, and many other kinds of diseases, one of which had existed for eighteen, and another for thirty years. It seems as if our Lord had constituted Benedict a second probatic well, like that of Jerusalem, where the sick found a remedy "for whatsoever infirmity he lay under." (John, v. 4.) In that, however, one sick person only was cured, when the angel agitated the waters; and it was necessary to wait for this movement, and to enter the first. In Benedict, however, there was no restriction of time, person, or place. At all times, in behalf of any person, and even many together, and in all places, Almighty God works wonderful cures through Benedict's merits.

They are performed on the mere approach of the sick to his sepulchre; those are worthy of special notice which are related in the Summary, in the Catalogue of Miracles, Nos. 1, 2, 7, 27, and 33, and in other places, but particularly No. 76.

With the Rosary which touched the bier on which his body was laid, page 488, No. 50.

By lying on the bed whereon he died, No. 6, page 480.

By the use of his picture, kissing and touching it, Nos. 8, 10, 14, 16, 19, 29, 31, 35, 47, 49.

By placing on the breast the book of his Life, No. 26, page 484.

By merely invoking his intercession, Nos. 5, 12, 23, 24.

By swallowing some particle of his relics, Nos. 4, 9, 13, 32, pages 479, 480, 481, 486.

By drinking a little water out of the basin which Benedict used, which had a wonderful effect on women in danger from childbirth, No. 15, page 481.

Also by confidence only, No. 18, page 482.

Finally, in the Apostolical Process of Loretto, made in 1794, we find juridically approved the wonderful miracle wrought in favour of Teresa Tartufoli, of Civita Nova, in the diocese of Fermo, in 1783. At the age of thirteen a small tumour appeared under her chin near the trachea, as large as a nut; it grew by degrees, and caused great pain with difficulty of swallowing. Suppuration being attempted without effect, recourse was had to a surgical operation, in order to extract the gland, which had already become scirrhous. This was performed by an eminent surgeon from Loretto, Signor Zannoni, but no good effect followed, for the severe pain and other very bad symptoms continued. The surgeon of Montegranaro, Signor Antonacci, also a person of great reputation, was then consulted, and after a close and repeated examination he judged a second surgical operation necessary to eradicate the root of the gland. This second operation being useless, and a fistulous ulcer having formed, Signor Cremonini, Antonacci's successor, tried with equally bad success to widen the wound and destroy the hardness, by means of the most active and powerful caustic; and at last, unanimously with other skilful men, he declared the case incurable. The seventh year of Teresa's pain and affliction had already begun, when, in the spring of 1783, Captain Giuseppe Natinguerra, her guardian, went with his invalid and family to enjoy the country at a small house he possessed near the sea; and feeling compassion for Teresa, he was induced by the reputation of sanctity which he heard everywhere given to the Ven. Benedict Joseph, to give her one of his pictures, telling her to have recourse with lively faith to his intercession. Having implored the protection of the servant of God, more by tears than words, and having applied the picture to the ulcer, she went to bed, and, contrary to her custom, immediately fell into a quiet sleep, which continued the whole night. She awoke about day-break, and found in the bed the picture stained with the purulent matter which the wound had discharged. It was now perfectly closed, free from pain, and the hard flesh which had formed itself inside and around the orifice had disappeared. We may imagine to ourselves what would be the admiration, delight, and astonishment, not only of the girl who was cured, and of the servants, but of the whole vast province of La Marca, in which this severe illness was known. She was freed from her pains, not only without the help of human remedies, which she had long discontinued, but her cure was so complete, that she never afterwards felt the least inconvenience in any way, in that part, up to the time at which we write.

In order to show how dear Benedict is to Almighty God, He has wrought miracles, and still works them, not merely in Rome, but in many cities and countries, not of one kingdom only, but in many, even very far from Rome, and distant from one another. He has wrought that greatest of miracles, which is, according to St. Thomas, the conversion of sinners, "It is a greater work to justify a sinner, than to create heaven and earth;" and St. Gregory says, "It is a greater miracle to convert a sinner, than to raise the dead to life." Many are mentioned in the Processes, who, leaving the slippery ways of vice, have entered the right path to God and to heaven, from witnessing Benedict's example, from standing by his bier when it was exposed, and from using some portion of his relics.

What we have written will be a sufficient proof of the delight of Almighty God in Benedict Joseph's great soul; and will be a strong stimulus to induce us to have recourse to his powerful protection, and especially to procure it for ourselves, by imitating his glorious actions, in proportion to our state and to the graces of Almighty God.

CHAPTER XXVI.

THIRTY USEFUL SENTIMENTS OF THE SERVANT OF GOD BENEDICT JOSEPH LABRÈ, DRAWN FROM THE HISTORY OF HIS LIFE.

"1. By the grace of God we can do everything. We can remain unhurt in the midst of the fire, like the three holy youths in the furnace of Babylon.

2. Everything may be done by the help of God, provided we have a sincere good-will.

3. To communicate through obedience is better and more pleasing to God, than to abstain from it through humility.

4. It is never allowable to use or keep anything when we know it has been stolen.

5. It is never lawful to tell a lie; we ought always to speak the truth, whatever it may cost us.

6. We offend God, because we do not know His greatness.

7. He who knows what God is, studies to avoid sin.

8. The want of proper examination, true contrition, and a firm purpose of amendment, is the cause of bad confessions, and of the ruin of souls.

9. In this world we are all in a valley of tears. Our consolation is not here; we shall have it eternally in Paradise, if we suffer tribulations on earth.

10. God afflicts us because He loves us; and it is very pleasing to Him, when in our afflictions He sees us abandon ourselves to His paternal care.

11. Where fraternal charity is concerned, everything should be sacrificed.

12. Those only are to be called poor and unhappy, who are in hell, who have lost God for eternity, not those who are poor on earth.

13. However much we suffer for the love of Jesus Crucified, it is but little.

14. Let him who seeks true humility, employ two means: mental prayer, meditating on the greatness of God, and his own nothingness; vocal prayer, asking it of God, through the merits of Jesus and Mary.

15. By talking and irreverence in churches, we show disrespect to Almighty God in His own house.

16. Acts of irreverence in churches are sins which greatly displease God; they horrify the angels, and do great harm to the soul.

17. If there were only one person to be condemned, each should fear to be that one.

18. We should often meditate on the pains of hell, in order to abhor mortal sin, which casts us into it for all eternity; and think of the small number of the elect, that we may live in fear.

19. The Providence of God is never wanting to him who confides in God as he ought.

20. With regard to corporal provision, we should not think of a future day, according to

the advice of our blessed Redeemer; "Be not solicitous for the morrow." God who provides for to-day, will also provide for to-morrow.

PARTICULAR SENTIMENTS CONCERNING TRUE POVERTY, WHICH THE SERVANT OF GOD WONDERFULLY LOVED AND PRACTISED.

22. The poor should live by alms.

23. A little suffices for the support of the body; what is superfluous, will only serve to furnish the worms with a greater feast.

24. A poor man does not seek a bed in order to sleep, he throws himself down anywhere.

25. Conveniences are not for the poor.

26. Poor people should not use a loaf, they should be content with fragments.

27. The poor should not carry money in their travels.

28. The poor should not eat dainties.

29. The poor should not be well clad.

30. The poor should not drink wine: it is not necessary; water suffices to appease thirst."

AD MAJOREM DEI GLORIAM.

RICHARDSON AND SON, DERBY.

SD - #0056 - 270223 - C0 - 229/152/20 - PB - 9781528060134 - Gloss Lamination